John Hodiak

John Hodiak brushes up on his dialogue between scenes on MGM's *Malaya* (1949).

John Hodiak
The Life and Career on Film, Stage and Radio

DAVID C. TUCKER

McFarland & Company, Inc., Publishers
Jefferson, North Carolina

ALSO BY DAVID C. TUCKER
AND FROM MCFARLAND

Rochelle Hudson: A Biography and Career Record (2023)

*S. Sylvan Simon, Moviemaker: Adventures with Lucy, Red Skelton
and Harry Cohn in the Golden Age of Hollywood* (2021)

Pine-Thomas Productions: A History and Filmography (2019)

Gale Storm: A Biography and Career Record (2018)

Martha Raye: Film and Television Clown (2016)

Joan Davis: America's Queen of Film, Radio and Television Comedy (2014)

*Eve Arden: A Chronicle of All Film, Television, Radio
and Stage Performances* (2012)

*Lost Laughs of '50s and '60s Television:
Thirty Sitcoms That Faded Off Screen* (2010)

Shirley Booth: A Biography and Career Record (2008)

*The Women Who Made Television Funny:
Ten Stars of 1950s Sitcoms* (2007)

Unless otherwise noted, all photos are from the author's collection.

ISBN (print) 978-1-4766-9473-3
ISBN (ebook) 978-1-4766-5329-7

LIBRARY OF CONGRESS AND BRITISH LIBRARY
CATALOGUING DATA ARE AVAILABLE

Library of Congress Control Number 2024037547

© 2024 David C. Tucker. All rights reserved

*No part of this book may be reproduced or transmitted in any form
or by any means, electronic or mechanical, including photocopying
or recording, or by any information storage and retrieval system,
without permission in writing from the publisher.*

Front cover image: John Hodiak in *The Sellout*, 1952 (MGM/Photofest)

Printed in the United States of America

*McFarland & Company, Inc., Publishers
Box 611, Jefferson, North Carolina 28640
www.mcfarlandpub.com*

To Lucy Eowyn Sassone,
with love from her proud great-uncle.

Acknowledgments

I'm grateful to Katrina Hodiak Lunore, John's daughter, who was only a toddler when he passed away, for sharing her memories of him and being supportive of this project. Likewise, Michael Galay, of a similar age, talked to me about his mother Mary, who was by birth John Hodiak's cousin, but adopted by his parents after the death of her own mother. My thanks to Mr. Galay's niece Kimberly for putting me into contact with him.

Author/historian Greg Kowalski kindly made available materials from the archives of the Hamtramck Historical Museum, including articles about John Hodiak from a local newspaper, the *Hamtramck Citizen*. Barbara Bogart Allen, researcher *extraordinaire*, once again plumbed the collections of the American Heritage Center at the University of Wyoming on my behalf. Others who offered valuable help include Melissa Galt, who answered a question about her mother, Anne Baxter, film historian Michael F. Blake, whose actor father Larry J. Blake worked with Hodiak, and Richard Shavinski, who described to me the friendship between his late father and Hodiak, who grew up together. I appreciate the kindness of Jaleelah Ahmed and Joanne McBryar of Hamtramck Public Schools, who shared a photo of Holbrook Elementary, which a young Johnny Hodiak attended. Whitney Manning applied her technical skills to cleaning up a key photo to make it usable, and I thank her. Martin Grams, Jr., who has written extensively about *The Lone Ranger* on radio, provided information about John Hodiak's work on that series. Margaret O'Brien, always a class act, never actually met Mr. Hodiak, though she admired his work—and was kind enough to call me in the midst of Hurricane Hilary to tell me so.

I always value my writer colleagues, among them Susan Kimmel Wright, Dan Van Neste, Derek Sculthorpe, David Meuel, Jacqueline T. Lynch, John T. Soister, Hans J. Wollstein, and last but never least, my longtime friend and mentor, James Robert Parish. For the caffeine-fueled inspiration, and the encouraging smiles, I thank Kohta, Penn, and the other nice folks at the Corner Cup.

Much love to my nephew, Tim Sassone, his wife Kim, and two sisters from another mother, Stefanie McCullers and Betsy Reedy. Most of all, to my husband, Ken McCullers, for more than 25 years of peerless love and support.

Table of Contents

Acknowledgments	vi
Preface	1
Biography	5
Filmography	59
Selected Radio Performances	181
Television Performances	195
Broadway Performances	198
Chapter Notes	201
Bibliography	207
Index	211

Preface

John Hodiak is probably best-known today for his lead role as sexy, surly, often shirtless John Kovac in Alfred Hitchcock's classic wartime drama *Lifeboat* (1944). The success of that picture made him almost overnight a rising movie star and sex symbol, though in fact he'd been acting, initially in radio, for several years. As the late Robert Osborne said in 2014, introducing a TCM telecast of the film, "The impact of him in this movie was not unlike Brando in 'Streetcar.' Hodiak was somebody like you'd never quite seen on screen before at that point," while his guest Drew Barrymore described Hodiak as "incredibly smoldering and commanding."[1]

Born into a blue-collar immigrant family of Polish-Ukrainian heritage, Hodiak was proud of his roots. As a Hollywood newcomer, he flatly refused to let studio executives change his name, unwilling to accept a screen identity that would disguise his ethnicity. Getting his first professional gigs as a radio actor in the 1930s, he soon had his eye on the movies. His chance came during World War II, when he was recruited as an MGM contract player.

John Hodiak was rejected by the armed services due to hypertension. He readily admitted that his 4-F status, though he took no pleasure in it, provided a career break in the mid-1940s. Indeed, columnist Inga Arvad reported (November 25, 1943), "At MGM pictures are being held up because they haven't got sufficient of that rare species," the leading man.

The dearth of available talent, even at a studio renowned for having "More Stars Than There Are in Heaven," meant that over the next several years, he enjoyed lead roles in several important films, including *A Bell for Adano* (1945) and *The Harvey Girls* (1946). For director Joseph L. Mankiewicz, he starred in a moody, well-received *film noir*, *Somewhere in the Night* (1946). He was believable in a variety of roles, and capably played both heroes and villains. It was ironic, given his disqualification for military service, that few actors of his era would spend more time in war movies than John Hodiak. He was in Hollywood for only about fifteen years, but during that time both World War II and the Korean War enveloped America, and became the background of numerous films.

While many of his pictures were aimed at male viewers who liked action films, John Hodiak also had more than his share of female fans. Scholar M.B.B. Biskupski wrote, "John Hodiak, born in Pittsburgh of a Ukrainian father and a Polish mother ... was one of the very few actors of Polish origin to play romantic leads. He may be the best-known Polish actor of the war era, and he was certainly the only star whose ethnicity was obvious because of his Slavic name."[2] Though it was the actor's own talent, and tenacity, that ultimately made him a success, he appreciated the help he received along the way. As John later commented, "A lot of people claim to have discovered me and a lot of people have helped me. Frankly, every one of them is right, and I'm one actor who is plenty grateful."[3]

From a personal standpoint, one of his most meaningful on-screen assignments was as the title character in *Sunday Dinner for a Soldier* (1944). He and his leading lady Anne Baxter (1923–1985) carried the scripted romance off-screen, and married two years later. The granddaughter of famed architect Frank Lloyd Wright, Miss Baxter came from a patrician background and upbringing that stood in stark contrast to Hodiak's. Both insisted that this was not important to them, but after a six-year marriage, which included the birth of their daughter, Katrina, Hodiak was sued for divorce.

By 1948, with actors such as Clark Gable, James Stewart, and Robert Taylor back stateside and working in the industry again, Hodiak was effectively demoted by his studio. Though he played an occasional lead, as when he was the male star opposite Hedy Lamarr in *A Lady Without Passport* (1950), he would never again be top-billed in a Metro picture. Increasingly he was assigned to second-fiddle parts, supporting some of these bigger names. Indeed, his part in *The Miniver Story* (1950), as the old expression goes, he could have phoned in. The films were still prestigious, and the roles sometimes interesting, but by 1952, when Miss Baxter filed for divorce, he was increasingly disillusioned about Hollywood, and knew his chance at top stardom was slipping away.

Newly single, Hodiak made changes in his life. His lengthy stint as an MGM contract player came to an end that same year. As a free-lancer, he was able to land lead movie roles again, but they were generally in second-tier films, mostly war movies and Westerns.

While still in demand for movie work, and making frequent radio and television appearances, John Hodiak set his sights on a new arena to conquer. He made his Broadway debut in 1952. That first show, *The Chase*, opened and closed quickly, but the experience gave him a new enthusiasm for acting, and the following year, he joined the company of a New York-bound production of Herman Wouk's *The Caine Mutiny Court-Martial*.[4]

As it happens, this is the second book I've written about a Hollywood figure who died at the age of 41, cutting short an impressive career. Though John and producer/director S. Sylvan Simon (1910–1951) never crossed paths, they were surely aware of each other as industry colleagues. But their deaths were oddly similar—both collapsed in their bathrooms at home while preparing to go to work, and both were said to have heart ailments. At the time of his death, Simon was Vice-President in Charge of Production at Columbia Pictures; it was only a couple of years after his demise that Hodiak began starring in action films for that studio.

This is the first full-length study of John Hodiak's life and career, though he was the subject of a chapter in Dan Van Neste's *They Coulda Been Contenders: Twelve Actors Who Should Have Become Cinematic Superstars* (BearManor Media, 2019). He also appeared in more than one book by veteran Hollywood historian James Robert Parish.

Part One is biographical, starting with his life growing up in Hamtramck, Michigan, and his success against the odds at breaking into network radio in the late 1930s. It was written with the support and assistance of his daughter Katrina, among others. Following that is an extensively annotated filmography of John Hodiak's 34 motion picture appearances, from *A Stranger in Town* (1943) to the posthumously-released *On the Threshold of Space* (1956). The third section documents an impressive radio career, both before and during his Hollywood heyday, with roles in *The Lone Ranger*, *Li'l Abner* (as the title character), the aviation drama *Wings of Destiny*, and multiple visits to popular anthology shows of the day, including *Cavalcade of America*, *Lux Radio Theatre*, and *Suspense*. The book concludes with a look at his stage and television work.

During the year-and-a-half that I researched and wrote this book, the Ukraine was on people's minds worldwide nearly every day. John was proud of his connection to that country, participating in fundraisers and other charity events for its people. He would no doubt be both saddened by the context in which it has been the subject of headlines in the 21st century, and admiring of her people's bravery.

Biography

The Boy from Hamtramck

"Where I come from?" John Hodiak was once asked by a reporter. "Well, mother is Polish and father is Ukrainian. But I am American."[1] He was born on April 16, 1914, in Pittsburgh, Pennsylvania, to Walter (born Wazyl) and Anna Porgorzeliec Hodiak. "They met in Poland," he said of his parents to columnist Ed Sullivan (October 21, 1956). "They were migrant harvesters of wheat, part of the thousands who traveled in caravans along the Ukraine-Polish border at harvest time."

Walter, born November 24, 1888, in the Republic of Poland but of Ukrainian descent, emigrated to the U.S. at the age of 23, traveling on the S.S. *President Lincoln,* which embarked from Hamburg, Germany, on November 1, 1912, destined for New York City. He applied to become a naturalized American citizen in 1922.

Years later, the elder Mr. Hodiak remembered, "On Nov. 27, 1912, mama and I arrived from the Ukraine. We had met a couple of years before in Bohemia and eight months after we landed in New York we were married. We went to Pittsburgh to live, and ... Johnny was born. He wasn't a big child. In fact, he was quite skinny until he was about 13. Then he suddenly started to grow and become broad-shouldered and heavy-limbed."[2] The couple had three children, of which John was the eldest. The family grew to include a brother, Walter Jr. (July 6, 1917–December 15, 1994) and sister Anne (March 10, 1919–October 7, 2007).

Of his early years in Pennsylvania, one memory stayed with John into adulthood: "the stump of a tree in Beaver Falls, Pennsylvania, on my way to school. It looked like a crouching bear. I was six and I believed it was a bear, waiting to spring out and tear me to pieces. I was terrified of it and used to walk blocks out of my way so as to avoid it."[3]

After a few years in Pittsburgh, Walter and Anna took their family to Michigan, where they joined a large number of immigrants who settled into a community in the city of Hamtramck, a Detroit suburb. Most

The S.S. *President Lincoln* brought numerous immigrants to American shores, including John Hodiak's parents.

had been drawn there by the possibility of employment in the blossoming automobile industry, causing the local population to swell during the 1910s and 1920s.

John was eight years old when they relocated. "We were all of us second-generation kids," he later recalled. "We were Americans, but our roots were in a people who'd had it tough for a thousand years. We were poorer than mice. But looking at the stars and dreaming of climbing out of the mud was why our people had to come to the New World, and what we wanted to do was as real to us as bread without butter and we could talk of it without shame or self-consciousness."[4]

Initially, they rented (with option to buy) a house at 2235 Grayling Avenue in Hamtramck, Michigan, and Johnny was enrolled at Holbrook Elementary School (which still stands today, on Alice Street). One writer later described it as a neighborhood of "dingy, drafty houses jammed up against one another [and] loaded with mortgages, so that nine times out of ten the landlords got them right back."[5] The white frame house which the Hodiaks occupied was modest, at best, but it offered a chance for the one-time migrant farmers to become homeowners. As John commented in a *Photoplay* interview (June 1944), "It wasn't much of a house when we got it, but eventually Pop and I rebuilt it into a nice place. And we were proud about one thing. Of five buyers we were the only ones who kept up the payments and finally got title."

With only a handful of exceptions, their neighbors up and down Grayling Avenue were of Polish or Ukrainian origin. Employed as factory workers, laborers, and machinists, they formed a tightly bonded community. The family spoke Ukrainian at home. Just a few doors down the street was the Immaculate Conception Ukrainian Catholic Church.

His mother Anna was said to have never attended school, but to be able to read and write. John later remembered Anna "singing in her kitchen. She usually sang Polish songs—she came from Poland—or the Ukrainian airs my father had taught her. Remembering that, I can smell her freshly baked bread, the soup that always simmered on her stove, the odd spices she used, and the wonderful aroma of whatever fruit she was preserving."[6]

Fascinated with performers and performers, "John always wanted to go to the movies," his father later recalled. "He used to beg mama for dimes and nickels to go to shows, and then when he came back, he would act the

Holbrook Elementary School included among its students in the 1920s young Johnny Hodiak. The school still occupies the same building in the 21st century, minus a third floor damaged in a fire. (Courtesy Hamtramck Public Schools)

whole thing out on the sidewalk."⁷ "My dad gave me 20 cents a week," he recalled years later. "But that wasn't enough for my movie needs. So I collected junk metal, melted it for the lead, and sold that."⁸ His favorite star was Douglas Fairbanks, whose movies he went to see multiple times. He also loved Westerns and serials.

John's father Walter, in his hours away from work, was a talented amateur actor who frequently appeared in church and community shows. Following in his father's footsteps, John began acting in amateur plays at the age of eleven. "The vehicle," as one reporter put it, "was a Ukrainian drama staged in the local church, with John portraying a tremulous orphan and Father Hodiak the villain."⁹ "It wasn't a large stage," John recalled, "but it seemed enormous to me when I was given child roles. I would stand in the wings, waiting to go on, stiff with stage fright, my hands icy … until my cue came."¹⁰

Acting and moviegoing provided a glimpse into lives quite different from what young Johnny and his neighbors were living. He explained, "In Hamtramck, the suburb of Detroit where we lived, the Ukrainian quarter was a world apart. Wherever there is the foreign element, the laboring class predominates. Unless you have a college education, it is taken for granted that you will be a laborer all your life like those before you. You not only respect your parents, but you follow in their footsteps. And for a Ukrainian boy to break the pattern is as unprecedented as if a genii should appear on a magic carpet."¹¹

The 1930 federal census found them still occupying that home, valued at $5500, in Wayne County, Michigan, with a monthly payment of $25. Sixteen-year-old John, still in school, was not yet shown as employed; dad

A passionate young movie fan named Hodiak saw *The Thief of Baghdad* (1924), starring his favorite actor, Douglas Fairbanks, multiple times.

Walter was a truck driver. But change was afoot. "Life really began," John said, "in the 9th grade at Hamtramck High." That's when he began to study dramatics in school. He also began skipping school, in one year missing 85 days. "I was concentrating on two seemingly unrelated projects ... dramatics and hooky!"[12]

Not long afterwards, there was an addition to the Hodiak family when John's parents adopted his cousin Mary. Born in 1917, Mary was the daughter of Anna's sister Frances and her husband John Voloshyn. The little girl was only a year old when her mother died in the influenza epidemic of 1918. Soon afterwards, Mary took up residence at the St. Basil's Orphanage in Philadelphia, though her father was still alive. "The reasoning we got," said her son Michael, "was that he couldn't take care of her."[13] He recalled that she said little about her childhood later in life, but he inferred that her time at the orphanage was somewhat unhappy. "They made her work a lot," Michael noted, though he added, "I never heard any bitterness."

She was still an "inmate" at the orphanage per the 1930 census, but her life took a turn for the better when she was offered a home by Walter and Anna Hodiak. Mary lived with the Hodiaks through her teen years and into her twenties, and developed a bond with John, becoming his second sister. As an adult, Mary sometimes told her son, "You remind me of John."

During his adolescence, one of John's best friends and classmates was Paul Shavinski, one year younger, whose family lived in the same community. "Everybody knew everybody there," Paul's son, Richard, recalled. He noted that his parents' living room proudly displayed an inscribed photo of Hodiak: "That picture stayed on the end table for years." Paul's wife, Olga, was a fan. "My mom had a crush for John," Richard recalled, noting that she was kidded about her fondness for Paul's buddy.[14]

Paul grew up with four sisters. In later years, Richard recalled his Aunt Marie telling a story about how young John Hodiak had turned up at their front door late one evening, asking, "Could I stay overnight?" Marie told him, "Mother wouldn't approve of that," and he was sent on his way.

If he had gotten himself in the doghouse at home, it wasn't because John's parents were overly strict for that era. "We never beat any of [our children], except once," said the elder Mr. Hodiak years later, "and that was John. It happened on a Saturday morning when John's report card arrived and mama read that he hadn't been to school for nearly two months. She knew that meant that he was getting into the wrong sort of company. And if there's one thing we wanted the children to get, which we never had the opportunity of getting, it was a good education. So mama took the razor strap, which was about seven inches wide and 24 inches long, and went into the boy's room and gave him a terrible licking."[15] "Yes, it's quite true," John admitted. "That is the only time any of us were punished, but I'm glad it happened because it made me pull myself together. The next year I was top in class."[16]

At Hamtramck High School, John was third baseman on the school baseball team, playing well enough to be eyed momentarily by a scout for the St. Louis Cardinals. In later years, it was sometimes said that he had spurned a surefire shot at an athletic career, rather than give up his dream of being an actor. In fact, he had been scouted for a possible opening to play on one of the St. Louis Cardinals' farm teams. But, modest as ever, John said to columnist Ed Sullivan (August 7, 1954), that his prospects had been exaggerated. "That's for the birds," he said of his alleged near miss at athletic stardom. "I was one of some 200 Hamtramck school baseball players surveyed by scouts. Steve Gromek [1920–2002, a pitcher who played for the Cleveland Indians and Detroit Tigers] was the one who made the big league grade from our area." John was a member of the school basketball team, "The Olympics," as well as playing for another formed by the Immaculate Conception Church.

Paul Shavinski (pictured) was a friend and classmate of the young John Hodiak. The two talked about moving to New York together to pursue their acting dreams, but Paul changed his mind. (Courtesy Richard Shavinski)

John's friend Paul Shavinski shared his interest in performing, according to his son Richard. "John and my dad wanted to go to New York," Richard noted. "My dad got cold feet." Paul ultimately chose to stay home, get a steady job, and marry his sweetheart. But John persisted in following his dream.

Though Hodiak hadn't forgotten his aspirations, opportunity wasn't yet knocking on his door. In the meantime, the recent high school graduate applied for a job as a caddy at the Hawthorne Valley Golf Club, hoping the boss would not notice a hole in his shoe. The gentleman in question did in fact notice, but hired him anyway. John said, "He probably thought I was in need of a new pair of shoes, but was too poor to buy them. And, to tell the truth, he was absolutely right."[17]

One golfer for whom he caddied was C.A. Kleist, a budget director for the Chevrolet division of General Motors. He took a liking to the young man, and suggested he interview for a job with the company. He started on the ground floor, working in the plant's stockroom, but soon was given opportunities to do office work, handling invoices. Coming from his background, it was a prestigious job. Friends and family members told his mother, "You have a great boy there, Anna. A boy who can work at a desk, without having gone to college!"[18]

When gubernatorial candidate Wilber M. Brucker campaigned in Detroit during John's teenage years, the boy stood and made an off-the-cuff speech on his behalf. "Like every place else, the platform was a stage to me," Hodiak noted later. After Brucker emerged victorious, he sent for the teenager, feeling he owed him a favor. The family was, at that moment, struggling financially. "Get me a job," John suggested. "'I'll do better than that. I'll get your father a job,' said the Governor. And he did. And up and down the street went excited talk in English and Ukrainian that 'Little' Johnny Hodiak, just as everybody had predicted, was turning out 'good,' for the Governor of the State was his friend."[19]

But Brucker didn't stop at that. He pulled strings to get John his first-ever audition for radio, at Detroit station WXYZ, but the results were disappointing. "Take some good advice, kid," said program director James Jewell after hearing the neophyte actor read. "Go home, get a job in a factory, marry a nice girl, and forget this radio stuff."[20] Or, as John recalled it in an interview, "The program director told me my diction was so bad, I'd better try to earn my living at anything that didn't involve talking."[21] In this instance, his longtime movie fandom hadn't helped. "I'd spent every extra dime I could earn going to the movies," he said. "But they were silents in those days, so I didn't have the faintest idea of how to use my voice. I was great on the arm-waving, though."[22]

Head bloodied but unbowed, he retreated momentarily, but wrote Jewell a cheeky letter saying, "This is to advise you, sir, that I will not stay out of radio. I will be back!"[23] After his initial resentment, John treated the comments he'd received as constructive criticism, and began to observe others in action. Gradually, he managed to polish his speech and tone. Unexpectedly, his day job handling invoices proved helpful. "My job was to read figures aloud all day to double-check expense and production sheets," he explained to Ed Sullivan (December 27, 1944). "You have to talk fast on a job like that and you have to talk so somebody can understand you."

Eventually, in the mid–1930s, John was able to get his foot in the door at WXYZ. After initially going home empty-handed, John persisted in applying for radio work, and was eventually allowed to observe others at work in the studio, and even play a few bit parts, initially in the evenings after work for no pay.

For a local radio station, WXYZ produced an astonishing amount of influential programming. It began during the Depression. Station co-owners George W. Trendle and John H. King had amassed considerable sums during the 1920s with their ownership of a chain of theaters, and plumped a goodly amount into acquiring WXYZ, where, according to an obituary of Trendle, they "proceeded to lose their shirts.... To stave off bankruptcy, they dropped CBS affiliation and plunged into local programming exclusively."[24]

To oversee the new initiative, they appointed James Jewell, who'd joined the staff in 1930. Acting as Jewell's assistant was Charles Livingstone, a station employee since 1933. Livingstone explained that, early on, the facilities at WXYZ were rudimentary: "The studio was a room about as large as a living room. A mike was hanging in the corner on a thing that they would now call a boom. There was a windowed booth where the technical man who operated the recordings was located. That was the whole place. No air conditioning."[25]

Under Trendle and Jewell's guidance, writer Fran Striker developed the concept for a show called *The Lone Ranger,* which had originated at the station in 1933, and concerned the heroics of a former Texas Ranger and his loyal sidekick Tonto. (Later book tie-ins were attributed to Striker's authorship, "based on the famous ... characters created by Geo W. Trendle.") As programming costs escalated, WXYZ's owners successfully shared some of their shows with a small network of other stations. *The Lone Ranger,* in particular, caught on like wildfire, and it was joined in 1936 by another drama, *The Green Hornet.* Striker, according to published reports, "hunts through the newspapers for stories suitable for radio presentation and then whips into shape for the 'Hornet.' He says it takes him 10 hours of thinking and two hours of typing to prepare a 'Green Hornet' script of 28 pages, and because he also writes the 'Lone Ranger' shows, he has to sit up all night nearly every night."[26]

The two kid-friendly shows alternated nightly broadcasts on WXYZ, and would quickly be heard in additional outlets. In the fall of 1936, the *Detroit Free Press* reported, "A Detroit dramatic show which has been arousing much interest is WXYZ's 'Green Hornet,' written by Fran Striker and produced by James Jewell. We understand that the show has captured the favor of the Detroit Creamery officials and that it is to be sponsored by them over eight stations of the Michigan Radio Network beginning at

8 p.m. Tuesday [November 10]. The show will be heard at that hour every Tuesday and Thursday."[27]

Though he still found the domineering Jewell intimidating, as many actors did, John's breakthrough came when a minor player in *The Long Ranger* fell ill a few minutes before airtime one night. Though still skeptical of Hodiak's abilities, Jewell spotted him in the sound booth, and gestured to him. Coming out into the studio, the startled Hodiak was handed

The Maccabees Building housed the studio facilities of Detroit radio station WXYZ, where John Hodiak won his first professional assignments.

a script, and told, "You are now one of the Lone Ranger actors." Undergoing trial by fire, he acquitted himself well enough to be allowed a few other bit parts. But it was after Jewell's departure for a rival station in 1938 that Hodiak's talent truly blossomed.

As WXYZ's programming flourished, the station built an ensemble company of actors who played multiple roles in various programs. *Variety* (June 1, 1938) noted that Jewell "took over (at WXYZ) ... with a total acting company of three and a weekly budget of $30; leaving with 45 players on payroll at weekly budget of well over $2,500." *The Lone Ranger* was being heard on 40 stations around the country, with the cast giving three performances to catch outlets in different time zones. Its company was attracting attention in national trade journals like *Variety*, which awarded WXYZ a showmanship award in 1937 for its original programs.

Radio columnist Frank P. Gill attended a Friday broadcast in late December, and reported, "The production, which carried 30 players apart from the production crew, was a stiff undertaking for any studio, since it had to be performed in three rooms simultaneously. In one studio they had the players, rehearsed and letter-perfect after some seven hours of grueling rehearsal. In the second studio the sound technicians looked after bells, footsteps in the snow and all the rest of the sound trappings. In the third Russell Wood, Jr., handled his choir of 16 voices who sang with the organ accompaniment."[28] A movie serial version was a hit at the box office with 1938 audiences.

The promotion of Jewell's former assistant, Charles Livingstone, to the job of program director, gave John a new confidence, and an important career break. The WXYZ actress Gillie Shea recalled that John's reading for Livingstone showed how far he had come since his first unsuccessful effort for Jewell. "He came in from some job in a motor plant wearing a sweater and work clothes," she remembered, "wanted to be an actor. So Chuck (Charles Livingstone, the director) gave him something to read. We were amazed. He was a natural." She recalled that her family later played host to Hodiak for weekly dinners of "Polish sausage and sauerkraut—even though his ulcers rebelled every time."[29]

Livingstone later recalled, "I got John Hodiak his first [full-time] job in radio; he was getting $120.00 a month at General Motors.... I think I got him for $130.00 a month. In order to hold this excellent company of radio actors together it was necessary to use them continuously. An actor might play a leading role on one program and a bit part on another, but he would get the same base pay."[30]

John's career progress came to a turning point when the station expressed interest in using him in more shows, such as its daytime soap opera, *Ann Worth, Housewife*. Reporting for duty after his nine-to-five job at Chevrolet was no longer enough. That assignment required Hodiak to go full-time at the station, for which he would be paid $35 a week. "When I told the folks about it, there was a slight row," he recalled. "Mom said, 'That's $10 less than at Chevrolet—and in such a fly-by-night business.' Mom always thought radio was a passing novelty. But Pop said, 'It's new. It's an adventure. Go ahead.' So I stopped reading invoices and started reading scripts."[31]

According to actor Dick Osgood, John worked more comfortably with Livingstone than he had his predecessor, and "developed into one of the best villains on the station."[32] As was commonplace in radio drama, though, he might find himself playing either a good guy or a bad guy, depending on that day's script. On *The Lone Ranger*, he frequently played one of the young ranchers whose interests the daring John Reid protected. Its success, and that of *The Green Hornet*, created additional exposure for the young actor, as both shows were quite popular. Heard on Saturday nights was *Ned Jordan, Secret Agent*, to which John also lent his voice.

As John grew more comfortable with the work, and at ease with his fellow actors, he loosened up. Though one of his movie leading ladies, future first lady Nancy Reagan, remembered him as a fairly somber fellow, others saw a different side of him. His radio colleague Dick Osgood, appreciated Hodiak's humor, even while playing a succession of bad guys. "The remarkable talent he had for clowning was never used by Hollywood. I'm sure he convulsed co-workers on the movie sets between takes, as he did between rehearsals here. It was his nature. But no director put it to use. Perhaps it was a magic too intangible to write into a script."[33]

Though he'd enjoyed a certain level of success at WXYZ, John felt ready for a change, and to take the next step forward in his career. Colleagues encouraged him to aim for radio work in the bigger market of Chicago, where many nationally heard series were produced.

His decision to move on was amplified by a sense that the Detroit station managers took him for granted, and didn't place a high value on his services. Fellow actor Jay Michael recalled, "John Hodiak's and my contract came up for renewal at the same time. John said, 'You go first.'" With difficulty, Michael said, he negotiated a small increase in pay, while being warned by the boss that there were plenty of hungry actors out there. He added, "John Hodiak went up and they wouldn't give him a cent more, and he went to Chicago and from there became a movie star."[34]

Chicago, Chicago

In Chicago, John was chosen for a steady part on a soap opera at $175 per week, but the role wasn't slated to begin for some time, and he was short on funds. He returned to WXYZ, where he was belatedly offered a pay raise. Hodiak was reluctant to let the Windy City gig slip away, but, according to Dick Osgood, "didn't have money enough to tide himself over. When the time came to go back to Chicago, he didn't even have train fare. So the actors at WXYZ took up a collection and staked Hodiak to his future. [Actor-writer] Tom Dougall staged a rip-roaring stag farewell party for him."[35]

At that time, a significant amount of network programming originated in Chicago, making it an important job market for actors. John took an apartment with roommates, and for a time he worked steadily. But he soon found himself written out of the soap opera that was his main source of income (which Osgood recalled erroneously was *Love of Life*, a show that premiered on television without a radio precursor). As the months of 1939 passed, his career momentum slowed, and he began to wonder if he'd made a mistake. He let his family think things were still going well, too proud to admit he was struggling. A discouraged Hodiak considered going back to Detroit.

"And then came the break of my life," as he later told an interviewer about the pivotal event, which occurred shortly before Thanksgiving in 1939. "I heard about a call for auditions for an important radio job. The role of Li'l Abner—you know, from the comic strip. I spent hours trying to create a voice—a sort of portrait of that naïve, gangling hunk of hillbilly muscle."[36] What he improvised for the character was described by one observer as "a dialect of his own—a weird mixture of Dogpatch, hillbilly, Ukrainian, Russian and Polish accents he remembered hearing during his childhood."[37] "Well... I was lucky," he concluded. "There must have been 50 or 60 actors after the job. I got it."[38]

Based on the popular newspaper strip by Al Capp (1909–1979), which was then in its fifth year, the comedy show was heard at 6:45 p.m. (EST) nightly. A network press release stated, "'Oh, the Scraggses and the Yokums, they was reckless mountain folkums' doesn't make good verse maybe but it adds up to some right peart [*sic*] entertainment, Mondays through Fridays, with Li'l Abner on the NBC-Red Network.... Li'l Abner, fuzzy-minded but irresistible hero, is played by John Hodiak, a newcomer to Chicago radio. He's been heard from Detroit in 'heavy' roles in the Green Hornet and other shows."[39] His leading lady, Daisy Mae, was enacted by actress Laurette Fillbrandt. Stories on the radio show aired independently of the day-to-day action in Capp's strip.

In those days, radio actors were by no means confined to one show—some appeared in half a dozen, or more, and John quickly began to plump up his resume. In 1940, he joined the cast of the daily serial *Thunder Over Paradise* (NBC Blue, 1939–1941), heard at 11:45 a.m. But there was more to come.

"Chicago radio," wrote Arch Oboler, "became the focal point of a new breed of actors-for-radio; the mushrooming soap opera needed a large supply of voices. They came from all areas and sectors of show business; from stock company character veterans to morning-glory-eyed college play hopefuls, they were attracted to this honey-pot of actors needed daily, all week, pickup-your-experience-as-you-go along, short rehearsal hours, no make-up, bring along your facile tongue, an equal facility for quick characterizations, and the ability to hold a script and read on sight with never a flub, a fluff, or a fumble."[40]

In December 1940, John took the leading role in NBC's radio aviation drama *Wings of Destiny*, supplanting actor Carlton KaDell. The series co-starred Betty Arnold and Henry Hunter. As noted in publicity for the program, "In winning the role of Steve Benton, the aviator, on KSD's Friday night *Wings of Destiny* program, John Hodiak was cast for his second major radio part and now plays in six series. Hardly known in network radio a year ago, Hodiak went to Chicago from Detroit for a chance at the title role in the Li'l Abner serial. After getting that assignment, he was given important roles in *Thunder over Paradise, Arnold Grimm's Daughter, Girl Alone* and *The Guiding Light*, in the latter an exceptionally good part.... Born in Pittsburgh in 1914, Hodiak made his start as an actor at the age of 11 in parish plays at Hamtramck, Mich. His start in radio dates from 1936 when he was assigned a role in the Green Hornet in Detroit."[41]

Wings of Destiny, under the sponsorship of Wings Cigarettes, offered "an aviation mystery story revolving about the adventures of a transport pilot, a daredevil girl photographer, and the pilot's 'grease-monkey' or mechanic." It attempted to build a following with an unusual gimmick: each episode offered listeners a chance to win their own Piper Club airplane, valued at $1,750: "After the dramatic portion of the program, the name of the week's airplane winner is announced. The winner is the person who has most successfully completed an advertising slogan in 25 words or less, and a different slogan is announced every week."[42] The sponsor plugged the show with newspaper ads that promised, "There's action, drama, suspense ... in that show that's as modern as tomorrow, *Wings of Destiny*, starring John Hodiak."

A radio columnist noted of John and his *Wings* castmates: "Odd increment of playing a radio role is that it often forces an actor to take on characterizations of the part for the benefit of fan letter writers.... Betty Arnold is having to answer plenty of fan questions about photography (on the show she's a lady press photog), and John Hodiak is having to relay information about how to fly a plane or how to become an airplane hostess. As Steven Benton he's supposed to know all these things."[43] Another source reported that both he and Miss Arnold were taking flying lessons in the hopes of adding verisimilitude to their performances.

John also made frequent guest appearances on shows like *Knickerbocker Playhouse*, despite the "audition jitters" that were stressful for actors. "In trying to explain the feeling," reported one scribe, "John Hodiak, title role player on one of the recent Knickerbocker vehicles, said that its [sic] exactly like the sensation any man gets when he goes in to apply for a job."[44] Nonetheless, he impressed the showrunners sufficiently to be cast in multiple episodes.

The following year, John was added to the cast of CBS' *Bachelor's Children*, described by its announcer as "radio's most beloved serial," where he would ultimately play at least three characters in 1941 and 1942. His stint as Davey Lane lasted into the summer of 1942. On at least one occasion, he also stepped into the lead role of Wolfe Bennett, when the usual performer, Henry Hunter, was ill.

In October 1940, while still in Chicago, John registered for the draft at the age of 26. He reported that his primary employer was the National Broadcasting Company, and his usual place of employment the Merchandise Mart. He was said to be six feet tall, and weighed 178 pounds, with brown hair and gray eyes. His contact person was his mother, Anna, still in Detroit.

A happy occasion for the Hodiak family came when John's sister Anne wed at a ceremony held in Detroit in May 1941. Her new spouse was Nicholas Sliva, a truck driver. Mr. and Mrs. Sliva subsequently raised two children, Richard and Jacqueline. For the time being, John himself was still making his way in the world, focusing primarily on his career, and not yet giving serious thought to marriage.

Metro Man

Inevitably, John's Chicago success meant that Hollywood talent scouts would hear his name, and the studios soon came calling. "For some time I had been trying to crash into the movies but it was only when radio was thoroughly combed for actors, and being 4-F, I got my chance," he admitted. Added reporter Inga Arvad, "You can discern in John's voice that he would give anything in the world to change that classification to 1-A."[45] For a time, it seemed as if he might, after all, join up—two radio columnists reported that his forthcoming enlistment was the cause of his being written out of *Bachelor's Children.*

Some radio actors didn't have faces or bodies that lived up to their voices, but Hodiak did. As one reporter put it, "an M-G-M talent scout looked him up and found him a husky-handsome six-footer."[46] *Variety* noted (September 23, 1942), "John Hodiak, Chicago legit-radio, was signed by Metro last week for a picture and left immediately for the Coast." It was, seemingly, the culmination of a young man's dream.

As John recalled, however, it wasn't quite that straightforward. He later explained to Ed Sullivan (August 7, 1954), "A nice guy named Shapiro signed me, but nothing happened until [MGM talent scout] Marvin Schenck and L.B. Mayer came to Chicago to see one of Mr. Mayer's horses run. Marvin rushed me to New York for a screen test and that's how I got to Hollywood." That screen test consisted of two parts, he explained. "I did a scene by myself and then Metro had me do a scene with Canada Lee." According to Hedda Hopper (September 30, 1943), the footage he shot with Lee, an up-and-coming African American actor who first attracted widespread notice in the Broadway production of *Native Son,* was from a forthcoming MGM merchant marine drama known as "Liberty Ship." Modest John later told another scribe that he'd only served as a "stooge" for Lee in the test. Little did he know that it would lead unexpectedly to one of the most important roles of his career—without another audition.

Known as Hollywood's glamorous and most prestigious studio, MGM was an interesting placement for a rough-hewn actor who might have been thought better suited to an action-oriented workplace like Warner Bros. The first thing executives wanted to do to polish up Hodiak's image was give him a new screen name. He rebelled out of family pride, saying, "No. When my mother and father take their friends to the movies to see their son, I don't want them to have to explain that their boy has changed his name."[47] He also felt that he had at least some name recognition from his network radio jobs, and that being known as John Hodiak hadn't caused any problems in that arena. By some accounts, MGM initially punished him for refusing to allow his name to be changed by giving him only the most minor roles. His first two films, *A Stranger in Town* (1943) and *Swing Shift Maisie* (1943), afforded him one line of dialogue each.

That year, however, also saw the release of his third film, the Red Skelton comedy *I Dood It.* After playing two previous parts that were little more than bits, John was anxious for something he could sink his teeth into, but the experience on the Skelton set initially proved frustrating. He showed up on the set with his lines carefully memorized, only to be told, "We've rewritten your part. Here's five more pages." He duly committed those to memory, only to be handed yet another rewrite, and another. Wardrobe changes followed. As the hours passed, his temper was in danger of boiling over. Not until the next day was he finally allowed to step in front of the camera, whereupon he shot the scene in one take.[48]

I Dood It, while casting John as a bad guy, at least offered a substantial featured role, one that showed anyone paying attention that he had leading-man potential. Next up was *Song of Russia,* for which Hodiak was aged to play a character role as a guerrilla fighter. Although John shot his scenes in 1943, the film didn't make it to theaters until early the following year.

MGM might have kept him confined to relatively unimportant parts for a while longer had a big break not come from an unexpected source. It wasn't his home studio, but rather 20th Century–Fox, that gave him his biggest career break up to that point. The first he heard of it was when MGM's Fred Datig one day told him, "Go over to Fox. Hitchcock wants you for a picture." He assumed that he was being considered for another minor role, especially after the star director "lumbered into Producer Kenneth MacGowan's office, barely looked at John as he handed him the script, and said, 'You're playing Kovac. Want to take this home and read it?'"[49]

Alfred Hitchcock wasn't yet the internationally recognizable celebrity that his weekly television series, and films like *Strangers on a Train* (1951) and *Rear Window* (1954), would make him. But having made a name for himself in his native England, Hitchcock had gone on to create quite a stir in Hollywood, after being signed to a contract by producer David O. Selznick in 1939. His first American film, *Rebecca* (1940), had won an Academy Award as Best Picture.

The script that the acclaimed director nonchalantly handed to MGM's 30-year-old contract player was for the suspenseful wartime drama *Lifeboat* (1944). His casting in *Lifeboat* introduced what would become a recurring motif in John's Hollywood career: being cast in stronger roles away from MGM than his home studio typically offered him. He was shocked not only to see that the character in question was an important and substantive one, but to learn that the job was being dropped into his lap without further ado. John wasn't being asked to test; Hitchcock had simply chosen him to play Kovac. As Hodiak later told it, Hitchcock saw him in the screen test he had done with Canada Lee, and said, "We can probably use that other guy to play that hard-boiled sailor opposite [Tallulah] Bankhead."[50] Luckily for their friendship, both men were hired, and John would prove to be a supportive colleague to Lee when the latter encountered racial prejudice on the set.

Hitchcock enjoyed giving himself a creative challenge, and with *Lifeboat* he'd not only envisioned a film that could be shot completely in the studio, but used only nine actors. It kept its action confined to the small titular sea craft in which the hapless refugees huddled, struggling for survival after their ship is attacked by a German U-boat. John's leading lady was Tallulah Bankhead; aside from a brief appearance as herself in *Stage Door Canteen* (1943), the 40-year-old stage star hadn't made a film in more than ten years. A strong character off-screen and on, Miss Bankhead needed a virile, powerful leading man who could hold his own with her, and John fit the bill.

Lifeboat went into production in August 1943. Hodiak was in heady company, and he knew it. Sensing the young actor's jitters on the set, Hitchcock cheerily told him, "After all, there is no need to be nervous, this is only a picture—on which your whole future depends."[51]

The players in *Lifeboat* endured some physical discomfort in the search for verisimilitude. For one scene, as a columnist described it, "Tallulah and John stepped into the boat. They stretched out side by side in the water at the bottom of the boat. Hitchcock gave the signal for the hurricane. Rain fell, wind blew. And the boat pitched and tossed." As the couple embraced, "Crash! They were buried under gallons of water from the right. Crash! They were buried under more gallons from the left."[52]

Actor Hume Cronyn, who sustained two cracked ribs during production, later recalled that the performers were "frequently wet, cold, and covered in diesel oil.... There was a large demand for anti-seasickness pills among the actors."[53] Miss Bankhead contracted pneumonia, with a 104-degree temperature, as a consequence of the frequent soakings and chills. Nor did the scenes, shot at close range, allow for the use of stunt doubles. Hitchcock said nonchalantly, "This has been something of a shock to some of the actors, but ... anybody who makes $1000 a week and up oughtn't to mind getting a little wet."[54] The film's final shot was made in December 1943.

Lifeboat attracted some controversy upon its release in early 1944, as some critics and viewers felt that it portrayed the villainous Willi, played by Walter Slezak, in too positive a light; Hitchcock argued that the film showed how a disparate group of Allied supporters, ordinary people from various walks of life, banded together under fire to fight a common cause. But if the film's themes and characterizations were much discussed, so was the handsome, little-known actor who received fifth billing for the star-making role of John Kovac.

As one scribe later wrote, "Shortly after the film began to unreel, a tall, brown young man with a big mouth, a wide grin and a terrific torso became noticeably present in the story. By the time the picture was half over, the feminine half of the audience was obviously gasping every time he appeared on the screen. And by the time the picture was finished, a new male star had been born."[55] Columnist Hedda Hopper (January 14, 1944) said Hitchcock "reached his peak" with *Lifeboat*, and noted, "John Hodiak has an unsheathed animalism about him that will have the girls standing in line." His work on the film also impressed his leading lady. Miss Bankhead expressed an interest in using him in one of her stage shows, telling him, "A good play would shorten your climb to the movie top by five years."[56]

His success in *Lifeboat* inevitably had him being labeled an overnight success. According to Hopper (November 18, 1943), he had until recently been "just another name on M.-G.-M.'s long and oft-neglected contract list." Nobody knew him on the lot.... When Hodiak went back for costume fittings the other day [on *Marriage Is a Private Affair*], even Louis B. Mayer recognized him. However, Hodiak noted, "The facts might include that, before I worked in *Lifeboat*, I did quickie-style appearances in 'Song of Russia,' 'I Dooed [sic] It,' and 'A Stranger in Town.'"[57]

Busy as his days were quickly becoming, John always took time to stay in touch with his family back home in Detroit. In the fall of 1943, John's brother, Walter Jr. wrote, "We have the pictures of yourself that you sent home. What we have gone through! Pa took them to the shop. I took them to my shop. Ma took them to her neighbors. Pa took them to bed with him that night. He cried like a baby; and Ma cried. Earlier in the evening we all went to a restaurant. Pa showed everybody your pictures.... Oh, Johnnie, we're so proud of you."[58]

His MGM paycheck allowed John to make Christmas especially merry for his family that year. "I sent them a washing machine, a phonograph and a refrigerator," John noted, "but mostly I sent them money. That meant something special to me." His father wrote to him in Hollywood: "My Dearest Son, This is Christmas Eve. We appreciate your Christmas gifts but you shouldn't have done it. Ma says you should go to good restaurants for your meals. She says not to cook for yourself and go hungry. We sent you 20 eggs from our own chickens and wanted to send you some butter but thought it would be too warm in California. Love, Pop."[59]

According to a 1944 studio biography of him, "Hodiak lives a typical bachelor's life and likes it. He has a small Beverly Hills apartment, does his own shopping and cooks his own meals. He has no romantic entanglements, but has made numerous friends among the people with whom he has worked. Athletic in school, he now lists bowling, swimming, golf, tennis and badminton as his favorite forms of recreation." He was still driving "the Plymouth coupe he bought on time payments in Chicago."[60]

With his career growing by leaps and bounds, John was content to put his social life on the back burner. He told *Photoplay*'s Kay Proctor (June 1944), "Apparently it strikes people as odd that I stay away from night clubs and big parties out here. The truth is, I haven't been asked to many big parties and, as for night clubs, I got my fill of them in Chicago when I first began to earn the kind of money that made it possible to go." Early on, he checked out West Coast hot spots like Ciro's and the Mocambo. "But once my curiosity was satisfied I had no particular desire to see them again."

John's interests were of a different sort. "His tastes," said one profile, "are definitely masculine, running to poker, basketball, baseball and, when California weather permits, driving his car in the rain."⁶¹

That same year, the Hodiaks' hometown newspaper reported that the family would be putting up for sale their current home in Detroit, in preparation for their anticipated move out West. While they stayed in touch by weekly long distance telephone, John missed his family, and wanted them close by. He promised his parents he would buy a house for them if they relocated, and they agreed to do so as soon as they could wind up their affairs in Michigan.

With *Lifeboat* a solid success, the only question remaining was what would come next for its rising male star. One who definitely had sat up and taken notice during Hodiak's scenes as Kovac was MGM star Lana Turner, who crusaded to have him for her leading man in *Marriage Is a Private Affair* (1944). One columnist claimed that MGM executives concurred, and called Fox about borrowing their player Hodiak, only to be told after inquiries were made, "We borrowed him from you."⁶² Once that was straightened out, John was soon on a soundstage at his home studio, playing Lana's husband in a well-written script about a hasty wartime marriage that hit the skids.

Hedda Hopper, visiting the set (March 7, 1944), was told by Lana, "He's a great actor. When he's through playing a scene, workers on the set clap and say, 'Gee, wasn't he great!'" She wasn't his only admirer. Hopper's chief rival Louella O. Parsons noted (October 12, 1943), "They will have to put nets under the administration buildings if the little secretaries don't stop leaning out the windows every time Mr. H looms up. He's the tall, dark and handsome who has reversed the 'whistle' procedure. The gals let him have it when he passes by." Studio executives were pleased with the finished product; Parsons (January 3, 1945) reported that MGM considered re-teaming the Turner-Hodiak duo in *The Postman Always Rings Twice*, which was then embroiled in a lengthy battle over "getting this James Cain story past the Hays office—it's that hot."

From an early stage in his career, Hodiak's talent and charisma invited comparison to one of MGM's biggest stars, one who was currently otherwise engaged. The *Los Angeles Times*' Edwin Schallert (July 24, 1943), commented, "Need for an actor to 'carry on' the duties of Clark Gable has existed ever since this top-notch box-office star has left the screen [for military service], and there is a rumor current that the best qualified at present is John Hodiak." Another observer, however, gushed that Hodiak "reminds you of no one but Hodiak. He neither looks nor acts like any other star.... He throws down a challenge that is For Women Only, a challenge that Miss America has lost no time in picking up. Yet he is such a fine actor, so much the rugged he-man, that Mr. America, too, is watching him with envious admiration."[63]

John unwittingly became part of a real-life triangle when his leading lady in *Marriage Is a Private Affair*, invoked his name to explain to her husband Steve Crane that she wanted a divorce. Louella O. Parsons mentioned "the Lana Turner–John Hodiak romance" in *Modern Screen* (September 1944), saying, "Everybody was sure 'Hi' Hodiak was Lana's secret heartbeat right after she and Steve Crane broke up." She noted, however, that the "romance dimmed before it even got started." Miss Turner later told her daughter that "she felt bad that she had used him as a reason to give to my father for why the marriage was over."[64] Another source noted that, while they were seen out and about for publicity purposes, "Insiders at the studio remember, however, that Hodiak was one of the few stars at MGM who wouldn't give in to Lana's charms, and this infuriated her."[65]

After directing him in *Marriage Is a Private Affair*, Robert Z. Leonard said, "When girls and women say 'Ah' and 'Oooh' of an actor, you know he is all set. This now holds good with John Hodiak. He has a whole bag of appeals—and each appeal will develop as he gains experience."[66] Flattering as it was to be labeled a sex symbol, though, that wasn't what provided John the most satisfaction as his career blossomed. "I've always been a dreamer," John said, "and when I was a kid 20 years ago I began dreaming about being a movie actor. I've never lost that dream."[67]

Mrs. Hodiak

Though John had quickly learned the club scene wasn't for him, he did go out occasionally. In early 1944, he told a journalist he had never been on a date with an actress, but soon was reported to be escorting June Allyson around town. She told columnist Sheilah Graham (August 15, 1944) that she had been taken to dinner by Dick Powell (whom she later married), and had been linked with Van Johnson, which she denied, but "I do like John Hodiak better than all the others. He's a gentleman. HE DOESN'T TALK ABOUT HIMSELF." Louella O. Parsons (June 22, 1944) noted that John was Miss Allyson's escort to the premiere of MGM's *The White Cliffs of Dover* (1944).

But a more important meeting was when he crossed paths with 21-year-old film star Anne Baxter, nine years his junior. After making her Broadway debut at the age of 13, the delicately beautiful actress had come to Hollywood in 1940, signing with 20th Century–Fox, and quickly became an important name.

He later told a fan magazine reporter that he had formed his first impression of his future wife in the makeup department at the studio, where he was filming *Lifeboat* and she *The Sullivans* (1944). Not a morning person, he was suitably impressed by her ready charm despite early work calls. "That girl has the most wonderful disposition of anyone I've ever seen. Imagine being bright and gay at this hour!"[68] At that point, however, they were merely formally polite to each other. As Miss Baxter later told the story, "I was just leaving Alfred Hitchcock's house and John was just coming in. He was about to star in Hitch's *Lifeboat*. I took one look at him and that was the end of me. Then we made a picture together and fell in love."[69]

The picture in question was *Sunday Dinner for a Soldier* (1944), a charming bit of Americana that cast him as the titular military man, and Miss Baxter as the young woman whose family gives him a much-needed respite from his wartime service. Once again, while his home studio kept him busy with bread-and-butter assignments like the insubstantial B movie *Maisie Goes to Reno* (1944), John was being handed better roles at Fox.

Variety's (August 16, 1944) review of *Maisie Goes to Reno* considered John "not a little miscast" as Ann Sothern's love interest, adding, "He portrays his role as if he is angry at someone, possibly his agent for getting him the part." Though he had less screen time in *Sunday Dinner*, not appearing until nearly an hour into the story, he made the most of it, creating a strong characterization and once again making moviegoers' hearts flutter. Both films had the advantage of giving him second billing, higher placement than he'd previously received. Fox's Darryl F. Zanuck considered casting him in other important roles, like the one that ultimately went to Dana Andrews in *Laura* (1944).

Anne Baxter and John Hodiak fell in love both off- and on-camera while making *Sunday Dinner for a Soldier* (1944).

Production on *Sunday Dinner*, which included a location trip to Florida, began in the summer of 1944. As their characters fell in love onscreen, between takes John and Anne were growing closer as well. Even before their first film as co-stars was in the can, Louella O. Parsons (August 21, 1944) wrote, "You may take my word for it that the next engagement announced in Hollywood will be that of Anne Baxter and John Hodiak. Everybody on the set of *Sunday Dinner for a Soldier* talks about how crazy John is about Anne." The columnist noted that Miss Baxter had denied any wedding plans, saying tactfully, "I wish it were true he likes me as much as everyone says."

Although some studio executives preferred their romantic leads to stay single, the love affair between two attractive movie stars made irresistibly good copy for gossip columnists and fan magazines. Some of what was reported about John and Anne carried more than a whiff of apocrypha, such as the story of their "strange first date," which found John arriving on Anne's doorstep several hours late with a friend in tow, both tipsy from a cocktail party. "Not only had John ignored his date with Anne, he hadn't bothered to telephone."[70] Supposedly, she was a good sport about it, and the following morning found them "still snoozing away on her living room divans."

Some observers considered Hodiak and Miss Baxter mismatched. The granddaughter of famed architect Frank Lloyd Wright, she came from a much more socially prominent background than he. Columnist Sheilah Graham (June 8, 1952) reported that the romance between Hodiak and Baxter blossomed over the objections of her mother Catherine, saying, "Mamma did not care for John. I could never understand her opposition, because Johnny was handsome and working steadily. Other suitors had been scared off, but Johnny didn't scare easily." Mrs. Baxter, said Graham, objected to Hodiak's working-class upbringing, and did not think him worthy of courting her daughter. Nor was that their only difference. In *Photoplay* (October 1945), Sidney Skolsky wrote, "I am always amused when I see John Hodiak and Anne Baxter together, for, although they are very lovey-dovey, I am aware that before the love session is over, they will have a stiff argument about politics."

When he and Miss Baxter met, John was living modestly in Hollywood, renting a two-room apartment that included a fold-down Murphy bed. He was always forthcoming about his family background when the subject came up; commented columnist Louella O. Parsons (February 29, 1944), "Let it be said to the boy's credit that when anyone asks him he says his parents were peasants in the old world before they became Americans." Both he and Miss Baxter downplayed the importance of their differences; he told one interviewer, "I come from the wrong side of the tracks and

Anne comes from the right side—but we're very happy walking down the middle."⁷¹

His open devotion to his family was made even plainer when the senior Hodiaks arrived in Hollywood to live, as he had urged them to do. John moved out of his bachelor pad to share the West Los Angeles apartment where he initially installed them. But he knew his parents weren't cut out to be apartment dwellers for long. "One of the first things I'm going to do," he said, "is put my mother and father back where they belong. On a piece of land of their own. They are people of the soil. That's what they were born to be. That's what they want to be. They love to dig in the earth, to grow things."⁷²

While continuing to work steadily, he began shopping around for a plot of land where his parents could settle down. He hoped to give them a more relaxed lifestyle, but leisure didn't come naturally to the elder Hodiaks. "When he heard that the Douglas plant was near our house," John said of his dad, "he instantly wanted to go there and get a job. Well, that's going to be up to him. If he feels happier working then no one is going to stop him. When mama's arthritis is better she can do a lot of gardening and feed her chickens. Somehow it never matters what she feeds them. They grow and grow, and nobody can cook like she [can]."⁷³

As Hodiak's fame grew, some moviegoers wondered why the handsome, virile Hodiak, as well as some other players, weren't fighting in the war. Columnist Harold Heffernan (September 6, 1943) noted, "The real reason why Hollywood is able to keep its head above the leading man situation is that it has been fortunate in having corralled an unexpectedly large number of suitable 4-F's." He added that, welcome as the opportunities for newcomers were, "These youngsters are taking little pride in their achievements. Most of them are embarrassed. Some have actually asked studio publicity departments to soft-pedal their names." John, the columnist wrote, was "a 4-F and not boasting about it." His deferment was attributed to hypertension, though another account had it that Hodiak was "measured on the scales and found ... wanting some surgery which the Army declined to provide."⁷⁴

John admitted that it went against his nature to push his career as aggressively as many actors did. "I've always been a firm believer in fate," he explained. "I'm the kind of a guy who sits back and waits for things to happen. I've always felt that if I were the one to do something, I'd be sought out to do it. Otherwise, I'd be far happier right where I was."⁷⁵ Still, he understood that he was something of a role model to many moviegoers, which he attributed to his openness about his ethnic background. "I want other Ukrainians to feel that they have a chance," he explained. "Maybe not in this field, but in any other. I receive a lot of mail, especially from Canada, from Ukrainians who thank me because I haven't changed my own name."[76]

As 1944 gave way to 1945, *Variety* (January 3) remarked, "John Hodiak was an unknown a year ago. Alfred Hitchcock gave him swift and solid importance in an exacting role in his Lifeboat at 20th-Fox.... Then came opportunities in which he scored in Metro's *Marriage Is a Private Affair*, 20th's *Sunday Dinner for a Soldier*, perhaps his most sympathetic role, and the current *A Bell for Adano*."[77]

It was in late 1944 that Hodiak was awarded the starring role in *A Bell for Adano*, based on John Hersey's bestseller. Once again, 20th Century–Fox was finding better

John Hodiak (left) and his dad Walter in their home workshop.

roles for him on loan-out than he was getting at MGM. His home studio had previously had him penciled in to team with Greer Garson in *The Valley of Decision*, but a trade allowed Hodiak to swap with Gregory Peck. Though Gene Tierney's greater star power earned her top billing for a relatively small role in *Adano*, it was Hodiak who carried the picture and won greater critical acclaim.

Looking back, he cited *A Bell for Adano* as one of his favorite roles. "The picture had great warmth," he noted, "because it gave us the chance to show democracy in action, under the American military government in Italy. Each of us in the cast—Bill Bendix, Gene Tierney, Richard Conte—felt a particular affinity for the picture because of what it represented. Henry King, who directed it, didn't have to give any of us a pep talk."[78] Filming was completed in mid–January 1945, and the film was being screened nationwide by late summer.

He'd barely finished *A Bell for Adano* when he was assigned to be Judy Garland's leading man in a lavish musical, *The Harvey Girls,* reporting to that MGM set in February 1945. Miss Garland was growing increasingly unreliable on a day-to-day basis, meaning that shooting progressed slowly, dragging on into early summer. He shared a musical number with his leading lady, but it was cut from the finished film, which would not see release until the following year.

With two important films awaiting release, John took a trip east that summer, visiting Chicago and New York. It was the first time he'd been

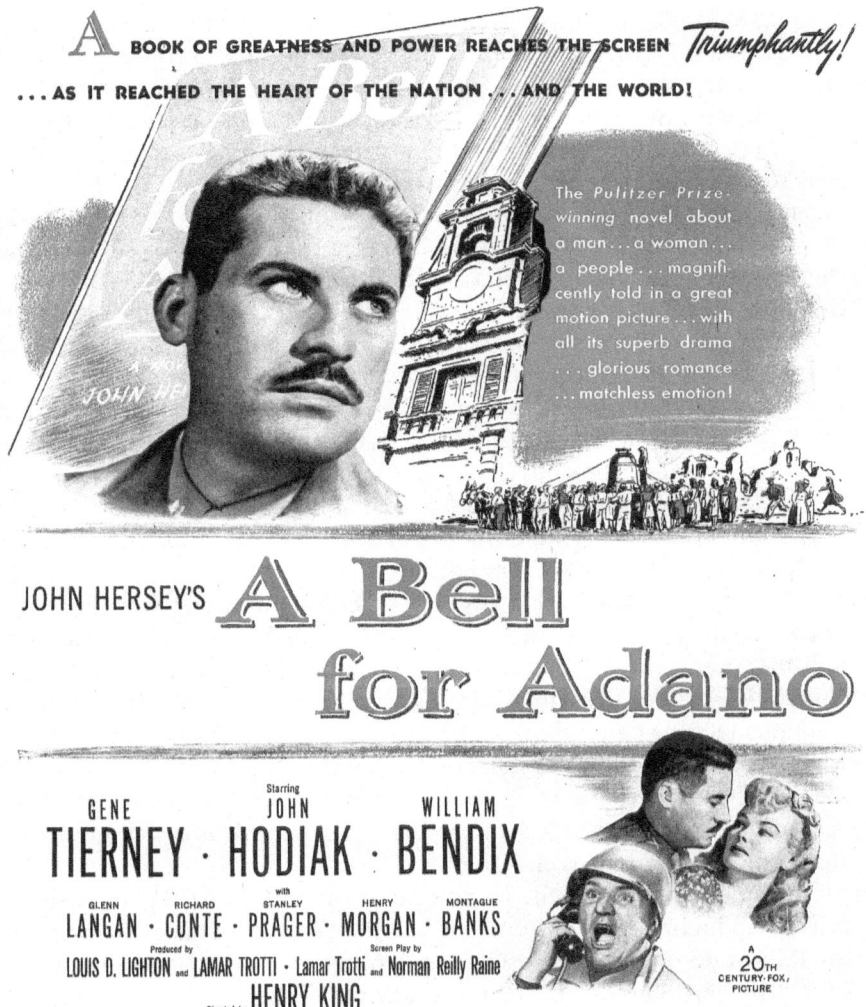

John enjoyed one of his best film assignments in Fox's *A Bell for Adano* (1945). Moviegoers and critics alike wondered why his home studio, MGM, didn't offer him more roles of this caliber.

back in the Windy City since coming to Hollywood three years earlier. He enjoyed the opportunity to catch up with old friends, especially in the Chicago radio community. A less happy summertime memory came when he was temporarily sidelined with "a most unglamorous malady ... mumps."[79]

By late 1945, it seemed to some observers that the romance between John and Anne Baxter had cooled off. Writing in *Photoplay*, Louella O. Parsons said, "Six months ago John and Anne were everywhere together. There was a glow on their faces that neither vitamins, exercise nor lots of sleep can manufacture." Then, she claimed, something had changed. "To everyone who know them," reported the gossip maven, "it seemed obvious that Anne had given John up and that whatever happens to hearts when they're supposed to be broken was happening to John's heart."[80] But more recently, she said, it was obvious they had reconciled.

With the dawn of the new year, however, the actress was still insisting there would be no wedding bells in the offing, telling Parsons, "I like John, like him a lot. But I have no intention of marrying him—now or ever."[81] Likewise, one of Parsons' rivals, Jimmie Fidler reported (March 18, 1946) that Anne was "denying published reports of her coming marriage to John Hodiak—says 'her career's the thing.'" Still, she resented suggestions that her family had rejected Hodiak as an unworthy candidate for her hand. "That's ridiculous," she said. "I have met John's family and they are charming, warm people. My parents know John and like him. Because we were born in different walks of life wouldn't make one bit of difference if I were ready to marry. But you see, I'm not."[82]

It was true, though, that any sign of looking down on working-class people could still make John bristle. Nancy Guild, a relative newcomer to films when she was chosen as John's leading lady in *Somewhere in the Night* (1946), later described him as "a very sweet man, but very cold. He had a terrible chip on his shoulder." She recalled that he took offense when, working on the scenes that took place in a church mission, she commented, "Gee, everyone really looks very poor and like a bum." Hodiak, according to the actress, "misinterpreted" her remark as disparaging and snapped, "That's what I come from."[83]

He understood that the world he had entered was still glamorous to those who hadn't grown up in it. When John's adopted sister Mary came to Hollywood on a visit, the actor took pleasure in showing her around. Escorting her to lunch at Romanoff's, he recalled, "Her knees just buckled under her when she walked in and saw Orson Welles sitting at the first table. Then she saw Joan Bennett, Gail Patrick, Linda Darnell, and some other stars, and I nearly had to carry her to our table, she was that excited. When George Jessel came over to speak to me, she couldn't eat a bite, and as we were going out and she saw Edward G. Robinson sitting at the table Welles had occupied, I thought I'd have a fainting girl on my hands." Charmed by her excitement, Hodiak admitted, "I know just how she felt. I still get a terrific kick out of seeing the stars in person myself."[84]

Somewhere in the Night (1946) was yet another instance of the Fox bigwigs providing John with an unusually good screen role. *Noir* specialist David J. Hogan wrote of it, "John Hodiak is in nearly every scene; the film is carried on his shoulders. Hodiak was up to the challenge, expressing Taylor's agitation and awful frustration. The character is tormented, angry, and confused. But he's gentle (as in a lovely, melancholy sequence with actress Josephine Hutchinson) and vulnerable, too, as in his scenes with his ally, smoky-voiced Chris."[85]

After some two years of an off-and-on relationship, news broke in the spring of 1946 that Hodiak and Baxter had applied for a marriage license. Their original plans called for a June wedding, but Walter Winchell (June 3, 1946) reported that the couple "will defer their June 14th merger date to July" in order to accommodate the shooting schedule for Anne's film *The Razor's Edge* (1946). On July 7, they became husband and wife at the Burlingame, Connecticut, home of her parents, Mr. and Mrs. Kenneth Baxter. Officiating at the 4 p.m. garden ceremony was Dr. Herbert Booth Smith of the First Presbyterian Church of Burlingame. They would spend their honeymoon in Colorado Springs. Immediately afterwards, John was set to begin shooting "Desert Town" (subsequently retitled *Desert Fury*) for producer Hal Wallis, with Lizabeth Scott as his leading lady.

Only a few weeks after they were wed, Anne was hospitalized for an emergency appendectomy. "Her telephone at Good Samaritan hospital was plugged, and she was allowed no visitors except actor John Hodiak, her husband of two months."[86] The following day brought word that John, too, was in sick bay: "Hodiak wrenched his back yesterday when he plunked into a chair at home and was taken to Hollywood Presbyterian hospital for three days' treatment of a strained sacroiliac."[87]

The newlyweds soon moved into a Beverly Hills home, despite the fact that some renovations they'd ordered were not yet complete. *Photoplay* (November 1946) reported, "There is no glass in the upstairs windows and the plumbing in the new bathroom hasn't been connected but John Hodiak and Anne Baxter are just as happy as if John had a place to put his shirts, besides the top shelf in Anne's dressing table." Though there was still speculation that Hodiak felt out of place in his wife's world, columnist Jimmie Fidler (June 19, 1946) commented, "I've met actors with plusher social backgrounds than John Hodiak, but never one with better manners."

In theaters that summer was MGM's *Two Smart People,* which found

John second-billed to fellow studio contract player Lucille Ball. Directed by Jules Dassin, the film cast Hodiak as a schemer. It didn't much impress critics, or even its own stars. Columnist Jimmie Fidler (October 31, 1946) wrote, "We're wondering if MGM bosses have heard the bitter remarks made about them by John Hodiak, who's burned because they don't give him better roles."

Increasingly, the postwar years found John playing a variety of shady characters, including a notably sleazy hood in *The Arnelo Affair* (1947). At Paramount, he was yet another man of dubious ethics in *Desert Fury*, paired romantically with Hal Wallis' protégé Lizabeth Scott. Publicly, John praised it as an interesting role that he enjoyed playing, telling columnist Harold Heffernan (October 16, 1946), "The fellow I play in this one hasn't a single redeeming trait. He's just a no-good and no one in his right mind would entertain a moment's sympathy for him. Yet it's a strong acting part—one that people should remember. That's why I took it."

Of *Love from a Stranger* (1947), adapted from an Agatha Christie story, Hedda Hopper (February 15, 1947) noted that he had been borrowed

Lucille Ball had no fondness, then or later, for *Two Smart People* (1946), in which she and John Hodiak played two "crooks in love."

from MGM by Eagle-Lion, and said, "I'm still wondering why John has to get all of his good parts on loan-outs.... MGM used to be mighty snooty about lending talent, but now it's most eager." He was playing another scoundrel, this time a potential wife-killer. On the set, Hodiak told columnist Sheilah Graham (March 29, 1947), "I'm playing my last killer on the screen. I've played four killers in a row, and even if it means waiting years for another picture, I will never again play a killer. Because it's the worst way to get typed, and I'm tired of being heavy and mean for nine hours a day." He yearned for more varied roles. Hedda Hopper reported (April 23, 1947), "John Hodiak wants to do 'The Miracle of Jeremiah Johnson' for Eagle Lion if Metro will loan him out.... The story, written by Katherine Lanier and Paul Colombo, deals with a small town school teacher who longs to become an artist. After battling the town's prejudices, he quits teaching and eventually realizes his dream by meeting success as a painter." Regrettably, that assignment didn't pan out.

Even though he was developing a reputation for embodying characters of a darker nature, that didn't keep him from being popular with movie fans. "You'd be surprised at the number of fan letters I receive," he said. "At one time I was under the impression that only the Van Johnsons, Frank Sinatras and the Peter Lawfords—the boys who play nice wholesome roles—have moviegoers writing them."[88] Lewis Allen, who directed him in *Desert Fury* (1947) pointed out that many actors—among them Bogart, Robert Montgomery, and Alan Ladd—had found bad-guy roles advanced their careers. "They became heroes later on, of course," Allen noted, "and most good heavies do. After an actor has become successful enough to pick and choose his roles, he likes a change of pace from 'good' to 'bad' characterizations. It's a healthful practice."[89] It remained to be seen, however, whether Hodiak's box office clout in the postwar era was such as to give him this kind of influence with the studio.

Away from MGM, he had other interests to pursue. A profile in his hometown newspaper stated, "He has never seen a horse race, or been interested in race tracks. He can't remember when he didn't like music—popular, classical, swing, jazz or symphony. [What] he plays is according to his mood. He and Anne are rapidly accumulating one of the finest collections of records in the movie capital."[90] Described as "an omnivorous reader, his taste runs to best sellers, history, biographies, mystery novels, and books about music." One of his goals, he told the interviewer, was to learn to play a musical instrument.[91]

His passion for books was such that he claimed he often got through a book that intrigued him in a single day. "And when I'm working, I read some more," he added. "An actor has to be on the set all day, but he probably won't be in front of the camera a total of two hours. The rest of the time he sits. While I'm sitting, I read." His primary aims in reading so much, aside from keeping himself occupied on the soundstage, were twofold. "I am constantly hunting good story material. I read a lot of non-fiction, too, trying to keep up with the world during the confinement imposed on actors while a picture is in progress."[92]

By early 1947, Anne was widely considered a strong candidate to win an Academy Award for her performance as Sophie MacDonald in *The Razor's Edge* (1946). According to one columnist, she had discouraged John from visiting the set during production: "She didn't want to take a chance on having Hodiak change his mind after getting a look at her with stringy, frowsy hair. He might have been frightened, too, at the way she could look if she took to drink."[93] According to Sheilah Graham (January 2, 1947), Miss Baxter was "upset" when she learned that her name was being submitted in the Best Supporting Actress category. "She should be," Graham huffed, "because there is nothing of that nature about her performance." Other commentators noted, however, that she probably stood a better chance of taking home an award if she didn't have to compete in the Best Actress race. Columnist Bob Thomas (January 4, 1947) predicted that the year's Oscar competition "looks as though it's going to be a knock-down, drag-out fight," as there seemed no one film that stood out in a strong field of contenders.

With their busy, two-career household, John and Anne often found that their time together was at a premium. He told Hedda Hopper (January 12, 1947) they'd recently had to postpone a trip to New York because his wife was assigned to a new film. "There's nothing for me to do now but hit the golf course," John said. "I won't go away without Anne." Though film assignments were frequent for both, he said, "We're trying to co-ordinate our schedules so we can do some summer stock together.... I'd sure like to play another part opposite Anne." They made it to New York the following month, and took full advantage of their access to Broadway, seeing eight plays in less than a week. Hopper (February 8, 1947) noted, "They liked best 'Finian's Rainbow,' Jose Ferrer in 'Cyrano de Bergerac, and Helen Hayes in 'Happy Birthday.'" A few years later, Ferrer would play a significant role in giving John his own shot at Broadway success.

In their spare time, he told an interviewer, "Anne and I love to fuss around our home in the garden. We both like gardening and do a lot of it on Sunday." Though he was sometimes obliged to make a personal appearance on Sunday, he tried to keep his schedule free that day. "I like to save Sundays for Anne," he explained. "It's our only day together when we both work—and I'll admit I don't like to have to break it up for some kind of career work."[94] Nonetheless, there were plenty of demands on his time, and one that rarely failed to win his support was any charitable activity to do with the Ukraine. In the spring of 1947, he traveled to Chicago, where he took part in a benefit concert for Ukrainian war relief, appearing before more than 3,000 people in the civic auditorium. John served as master of ceremonies for the musical program, which featured "the combined Ukrainian choruses of Chicago."[95]

John was one of several stars who took part in the Veterans' Administration's "Take Hollywood to the Hospitals" campaign. The patients reportedly appreciated what the actors did—"move among them to sit and chat about Hollywood, its people and the way they make the movies and radio programs that fill so many hours of hospital life."[96]

Seemingly, all was well in the life of John Hodiak and his wife in the late 1940s. Columnist Jimmie Fidler (September 9, 1946) opined, "I can't think of a stellar couple with a better chance for marital bliss than John Hodiak and Anne Baxter." A few months later, the same scribe (April 6, 1947) scotched rumors that Anne and John "have dated Doc Stork," stating, "Instead of buying baby clothes, they're stocking up on fishing tackle for a swordfishing jaunt in Mexico." In the summer of 1948, Anne and John were house guests of actor Zachary Scott and his parents. "Splitting up a two-week Texas visit with a three day stay at the [senior] Scott home here" in Austin, Texas, newspapers noted, "the three stars impressed with their friendly and unassuming personalities." Scott's parents hosted a party one Saturday evening. When the phone rang, "one guest got up to answer ... saying, 'That's probably my children. They want to come over and look.' Baxter, Hodiak and Scott laughed."[97]

Hedda Hopper (December 19, 1947) reported that "Anne Baxter and John Hodiak cancelled their Honolulu trip to supervise the building of a house on Anne's family estate in Burlingame, where they will spend much of their time between pictures." That was done with a definite purpose in mind. As columnist Bob Thomas (August 1, 1947) noted, the young couple "have one practice which they think will help preserve their marriage. They spend as much time away from Hollywood as possible."

Adios, MGM

For John, the end of World War II brought stiffer competition for important roles, with the actors who'd served in the military back in town and eager to work. Increasingly, MGM began using him in supporting roles to superstars like Clark Gable, James Stewart, and Spencer Tracy. The studio was undergoing upheaval, with longtime boss Louis B. Mayer's lavish production values attracting criticism amid lessening ticket sales.

John took part in the celebratory activities surrounding the studio's

25th anniversary in 1949, posing for a group photo of the contract players that found him flanked by Katharine Hepburn and juvenile actor Claude Jarman, Jr. But it was evident behind the scenes that change was inevitable. The appointment of Dore Schary, who wanted more realistic, down-to-earth storytelling in MGM features, as Vice-President in Charge of Production, might have boded well for an actor of Hodiak's type, and at times it did. But there was also a sense that the studio with "More Stars Than There Are in Heaven" had a plethora of leading men from which to choose, several of them considered stronger box office draws than he.

His 1948 releases both found him playing second (at least) fiddle to Clark Gable, the actor to whom he'd sometimes been compared a few years earlier. *Homecoming* provided another opportunity to act with his wife, but the film cast Anne as Gable's wife, with John as the star's pal. Hodiak put a positive spin on it in an interview with columnist Sidney Skolsky (October 24, 1947). "It's nice and convenient working in a picture with your wife," he explained. "She knows what you went through all day and when you get home and are tired and don't want to do anything, she understands. What's more, she is just as tired and doesn't want to do anything." *Command Decision* found him even further down the cast list, reduced to sixth billing and killed off before the final curtain fell.

As the spring of 1948 gave way to summertime, John finished his role in *Command Decision*, and went soon after into *The Bribe*, playing a character role as the hard-drinking husband of Ava Gardner. The film wouldn't hit theaters until the following year; a Jamaican vacation with Anne awaited him after it wrapped. Columnist Bob Thomas (March 1, 1949) tried to present the brighter side of the roles he was getting at MGM: "During the war years, he did picture after picture, most of them as a heavy. He has worked but 14 weeks in the past two years, but he's happier in sympathetic parts." Thomas offered Hodiak's upcoming project, "Operation Malaya" (released as *Malaya*) and the upcoming *Battleground* as examples of the new, more likable screen image. One columnist reported that Hodiak would play the role of Sitting Bull in MGM's film adaptation of the Broadway hit *Annie Get Your Gun*, but that star-making role went to Howard Keel instead.

Mrs. Hodiak was busy as ever. One early 1949 press release reported, "Her spare time, if any, will be devoted to her orchid nursery ... in Northern California," noting that she and John were planning a trip to Guatemala to buy new varieties, adding, "She now is growing 14 varieties, and she has sold 800 plants in the last few weeks."[98] Another joint project for the couple found them exploring the opportunity of making their own film. Hedda Hopper (December 3, 1948) reported, "Anne Baxter and John Hodiak have written a crime story which they hope to produce independently with young actors." John was on location in New Mexico, filming *Ambush*, when he and Anne had their third wedding anniversary in the summer of 1949. She paid him a visit on set, and took a longer commute to do the same a few months later, traveling to England, where he was filming a minor role in *The Miniver Story* (1950). Not only did the film saddle him with a minor character to play, but its failure at the box office did no favors for anyone involved.

The dwindling size and quality of his MGM roles did not go unnoticed by John's fans. A letter to the editor in *Movieland* (December 1949) complained, "I sure wish I could see John Hodiak in another film like *The Harvey Girls*, or *Marriage Is a Private Affair*. Why always the sad and tragic end kind of roles for him? In *The Bribe* he only had 3 or 4 scenes ... in *Command Decision* he didn't last long.... Here's a man—handsome, charming, likable, and healthy-looking, with a beautiful speaking voice, and what happens? Each picture he's been in lately has him gone before one gets the drift of the story. Please, producers—give Mr. Hodiak some leading roles with happy endings." Scribe Elizabeth Forrest, who'd noted some of the less-than-satisfying roles that were coming Hodiak's way, opined, "Sooner or later the man who has been patiently making good, sturdy bricks with precious little straw deserves to be recognized as a fellow capable of doing something better."[99]

John told Hedda Hopper (January 12, 1947), "Now, I don't want to be difficult. But I'm deadly interested in worth-while films. The screen is a great medium, and I don't think we're making the proper use of it. It's my belief that we can even make films along documentary and educational lines that will be entertaining as well as money-making." Studio bosses, he added, thought his paycheck should be his primary motivation as a movie actor, with the attitude, "You're getting parts, and you're getting paid, so what are you beefing about?" Describing the kind of roles he sought, Hodiak commented, "I'd like to play in simple stories that have warmth, humanity and charm about them."

The year 1950 brought signs that John's patience with his job at MGM was wearing thin. That spring, he spent one week rehearsing for his role in *Cause for Alarm* (1951), starring Loretta Young, before taking a step no one had anticipated. He notified studio executives that he would not make the film. Syndicated columnist Edith Gwynn (May 2, 1950) reported, "John alarmed everyone by refusing to show up when actual filming started, and refusing the part." His rebellion meant that MGM suspended him. Columnist Louella O. Parsons (June 17, 1950) reported that "everyone was surprised because he is an amiable, easy going soul. He waited until the day before the picture started to let his decision be known and that's why he was given one of the few suspensions ever dished out by MGM." His detention lasted until he agreed to co-star in the Western adventure *Across the Wide Missouri* (1951). It was another less-than-top-notch role, once again supporting Clark Gable, at a time when his wife was about to make one of the most important and prestigious films of her career.

Anne and John were presenters at the Academy Awards, held March 23, 1950, at the RKO Pantages Theatre in Hollywood. Introduced by emcee Paul Douglas as "a pair of people who have put together a really handsome marriage," they announced the Best Short Subject award to Warners' *For Scent-Imental Reasons,* which had introduced Pepe Le Pew to moviegoers.

In the late summer of 1950, MGM announced that John and starlet Nancy Davis would play key roles in the forthcoming film "People in Love." Information about the film was then vague, with one source terming it "a gay comedy-romance," which it was anything but. They supported Ray Milland in what eventually became *Night into Morning* (1951), playing the star's friend, with Davis as his lady friend whose attentions to another man arouse his jealousy. The future Mrs. Reagan had first crossed paths with her leading man when they both were active in the Chicago radio acting community a few years earlier. Though others who'd worked with him had spoken of his sense of humor, she later wrote, "John Hodiak was a very serious young man. You didn't think of him as suited to comedy roles, and I don't believe I ever heard him tell a joke.... Tragically, like Jean Hagen, he died young, much too young."[100] Director Fletcher Markle later described John as "quite an underrated actor, as well as a gentleman."[101] The film had many of the warm, human qualities he had described to Hedda Hopper a couple of years earlier, though it was Milland who had the most demanding and challenging role.

While John's career seemed stuck in second gear, his wife's continued to flourish. Her role as the scheming Eve Harrington netted her a Best Actress Academy Award nomination for *All about Eve* (1950), with her co-star Bette Davis also nominated. Interviewed in February 1951, Anne Baxter dismissed her chances, telling Louella O. Parsons (February 18, 1951) that the prize should go to Davis. Columnist Bob Thomas, however, who predicted Gloria Swanson would win noted, "Miss Baxter could be tabbed the dark horse, because of her adept portrait of the stage aspirant."

When Miss Parsons commented on the happy home life she seemed to share with Hodiak, Anne said, "Well, that's because the first year you're trying to get adjusted; the second year you're not sure you are adjusted, and after five years, you begin to understand each other. There's a friendship plus love that come into your lives. Johnny is really very sweet, and we have such good times together." Noting that there had been reports of in-law trouble, Parsons added, "John is such a wonderful host in his home,

A posed shot from *Night into Morning* (1951) spotlighting lead actors (left-right) John Hodiak, Nancy Davis (Reagan), and Ray Milland.

and if Anne's parents ever felt he was not right for their daughter, they are all over it now. They appreciate the fineness of his character."

As always, John refused to pretend to be other than what he was. "Why not be proud of it?" he said of his humble origins. "I think it's much better to fight your way up than to have success laid at your feet. Personally I'm glad I had to fight for what I got." When he had an early work call, he packed his own lunch. "There's no need of Anne or the maid getting up early as I have to, just to put up my lunch."[102]

Soon after, Anne Baxter notified her bosses at Fox that she and John were expecting their first child. Her pregnancy caused her to drop out of another film for Joseph L. Mankiewicz announced as "The Doctor's Diary" but released as *People Will Talk* (1951). Her friend June Haver was to accept the Academy Award should Anne emerge victorious in late March. The Oscar program was not yet being televised nationally, as it would beginning in 1953. More than 2,800 spectators were expected to attend the ceremony held at the Pantages Theater, at which time Judy Holliday was named Best Actress for her debut film, *Born Yesterday*. José Ferrer, who would figure into John's professional future, was named Best Actor for *Cyrano de Bergerac*.

Hedda Hopper (June 21, 1951) asked Anne "how she was filling in the time while waiting for her blessed event," to which she replied, "John and I have caught up on the all the pictures we missed over the years. John runs them at home." If impending motherhood had put a pause in her career, John didn't mind. He told Sheilah Graham (March 24, 1951), "It's wonderful being an expectant father. When I come home now, my wife (Anne Baxter) is waiting to greet me." The baby arrived in mid-summer. "Anne Baxter was reported doing well at Cedars of Lebanon hospital today after giving birth to a six-pound, seven-ounce daughter.... Hodiak said they had not chosen a name for the girl."[103] Ultimately, the newest member of the family was called Katrina Baxter Hodiak. Of her family heritage, Katrina later said, ""I have my mother's nose, my father's mouth, and the color of his eyes."[104]

Studio publicists noted that Katrina would occupy a crib that "held 43 other Hodiaks before [she] was born. Hodiak's great-great-grandmother was its first occupant, and each child born into the family since 1820 has started life in the old-fashioned hardwood crib."[105] John was an enthusiastic if inexperienced new dad. Left to babysit Katrina for a few hours, his wife came home to find Hodiak had used enough diapers for a week during her brief absence. According to columnist Sidney Skolsky (October 5, 1951), "Hodiak said he didn't know there was any other reason babies cry," and changed her every time she did. "He was the light of my life when I was a baby," Katrina later recalled. "He spoiled me." That fall, Anne and John took their baby to Tarzana to meet her paternal grandfather, who was not himself well enough to travel.

Katrina's arrival was followed a few months later by a milestone in John's professional life, when he brought to a close his nine-year stint as an MGM contract player, around the same time Louis B. Mayer was ousted as vice-president. In hindsight, MGM may never have been the ideal studio for him, and it didn't go unnoticed that he frequently got better roles on loan-out than he did at his home base. According to Hedda Hopper (September 11, 1951), "John Hodiak asked for and got his freedom for one reason only: He wanted greater opportunity and believes he'll find it in freelancing." He told columnist Erskine Johnson (September 27, 1951), "I'm not talking about it. It's just that I was looking for opportunities that could be found elsewhere. I'm not planning a thing. Being free is kind of exciting, though. It's a challenge."

The results of his new freedom to choose his own jobs would quickly become apparent. In December 1951, Louella O. Parsons reported that John "flies out to do a TV show Christmas night. He'll be joined New Year's Day by Anne Baxter." In January 1952, John made his television debut, on Kate Smith's nighttime NBC show. While under contract to MGM, he had been expressly forbidden to appear on TV, as most contract players were during that era. Within the same month, he made a guest appearance on *Gangbusters,* and visited *Your Show of Shows.*

But it would also be the year that he would fulfill a long-standing dream of acting on the New York stage. With what Parsons described (February 13, 1952) as "just barely time enough to pack and kiss Anne Baxter and the baby goodby, John Hodiak is off to a Broadway in a cloud of dust." He was going into rehearsals for José Ferrer's production of *The Chase,* a play by Horton Foote (best-known for *The Trip to Bountiful*). Parsons added, "John took leave of Hollywood so fast that Anne Baxter, who is in the middle of a picture, hasn't yet made up her mind what to do. But she'll probably pack up Katrina, nursery and all, and follow John to New York as soon as possible."

In the *New York Daily News* (April 17, 1952), reviewer John Chapman described Foote's play as "a psychological Western or as a Texas version of Sidney Kingsley's 'Detective Story.'" *The Chase* centered on Hawes (no first name given), a sheriff in the small Texas town of Richmond for the past eight years. Hawes, who ran wild as a kid, is now a happily married man whose wife Ruby is expecting their first child. As a police officer, Hawes is accustomed to being at the beck and call of the people he serves, saying, "A sheriff is a public servant. The public elects him, they pay his salary, an' they have a right to call on him for anything they want, day or night." But he's weary of those responsibilities, and hopes to buy a farm where his family can settle down once the baby arrives.

Hawes faces a crisis when he learns that Bubber Reeves, a killer he put behind bars, has escaped from prison not far away. Ruby is frightened for her husband's safety, and he tries to reassure her. Though his mother urges him to flee the area, and many expect him to head for the Mexican border, Bubber hides out at the nearby cabin of his pal Knub McDermont, who was involved in his jailbreak. Anna, Bubber's wife, is also at the hideout. The elder Mrs. Reeves confronts Hawes, pleading with him not to kill her son, but the local townspeople want Bubber hunted down and killed before he does any more damage.

JOSÉ FERRER
Presents

JOHN HODIAK and KIM HUNTER
in

"THE CHASE"

A new play by HORTON FOOTE

Directed by MR. FERRER

Associate Producer: MILTON BARON

Settings and Lighting by Albert Johnson. Costumes by George Bockman

with

Eugenia Rawls   Murray Hamilton   Kim Stanley
Ralph Theadore   Sam Byrd

CAST

Sheriff Hawes	John Hodiak
Rip	Richard Poston
Tarl	Lin McCarthy
Ruby Hawes	Kim Hunter
Edwin Stewart	Sam Byrd
Mr. Douglas	G. ALBERT SMITH
Anna Reeves	Kim Stanley
Mrs. Reeves	NAN MCFARLAND
Knub McDermont	Lonny Chapman
Bubber Reeves	Murray Hamilton
Hawks Damon	Ted Yaryan

The action of the play takes place in Richmond, Texas, in the present day.

ACT ONE
Scene 1: The Office of the Jail. Twilight
Scene 2: Knub's cabin. Later the same night
Scene 3: The Jail. Later the same night

ACT TWO
Scene 1: The Jail. The next evening.
Scene 2: Knub's cabin. Later the same night
Scene 3: The Jail. Later the same night

ACT THREE
Scene 1: The Jail. Later the same night
Scene 2: Knub's cabin. Later the same night
Scene 3: The Jail. Early the next morning

John made his Broadway debut in Horton Foote's *The Chase,* directed by José Ferrer.

    Though the synopsis would seem to suggest an action-oriented melodrama, Foote's script had more on its mind. As author Wilborn Hampton states, "Over nine scenes and three acts, Foote examines civic, social, and ethical questions: How much does a civil servant owe his community against the obligations he has to his family? At what moral price can peace of mind and a sense of security be bought? And to what extent should the wife, mother, and best friend of a murderer protect him, knowing he is intent on killing again?"[106] In the play's third act, Knub's cabin is the setting for a violent confrontation between Sheriff Hawes and the fugitive.

Early on, there was talk of casting Gary Cooper as Sheriff Hawes, but the veteran film actor suffered from stage fright, and passed. The playwright's agent, Lucy Kroll, had suggested Hodiak for the starring role, despite his lack of stage experience. Foote himself envisioned Franchot Tone in the part. The producer who won the right to stage Foote's play was 40-year-old José Ferrer, a whirling dervish of activity who was simultaneously playing the lead role in *The Shrike* at the Cort Theatre. Foote had reworked the play, with Ferrer's assistance, over a period of several years, while turning out television scripts.

Ferrer first crossed paths with John Hodiak on the West Coast, when both were dinner guests at the home of actors Hume Cronyn and Jessica Tandy. Ferrer "was impressed by the man's sincerity and warmth.... When Ferrer read 'The Chase,' he felt that he had discovered a play for which Hodiak's talents were eminently well fitted.... He wired Hodiak on the Coast and told him to fly East."[107] With John cast in the lead role, Ferrer signed Kim Hunter, a recent Academy Award winner for *A Streetcar Named Desire*, as his wife Ruby. Actor Murray Hamilton was chosen to play the killer, Bubber, with a young Kim Stanley as his wife Anna. Lonny Chapman took the role of Knub.

The Chase preceded its Broadway run with out-of-town previews in Philadelphia. Committed to his role in *The Shrike*, Ferrer left Foote in charge of daily rehearsals. When he did appear, Ferrer coached his players gently, with statements like, "Johnny, that gets a little dim on me. The action is too uncertain," or "Kim, sweetie, could that line be more factual, less whine?" After seeing the actors go through their paces, Ferrer had to dash back to New York, telling Hodiak and company, "Thank you very much. You were very, very good."[108]

Sounding like a Texan took a bit of work for a guy of Ukrainian-Polish ancestry who'd grown up in Michigan, but Hodiak had been adopting accents as far back as his days as a radio villain in *The Lone Ranger*. The people who surrounded him proved helpful. "Take Horton Foote," he told a reporter, "he's from Texas, and so is Kim Stanley. Kim Hunter, who plays opposite me, was born in Florida. Sam Byrd comes from North Carolina. In fact, I haven't heard a word of Yankee English since I got into this show."[109]

The Chase had its New York opening at the Playhouse on 48th Street on April 15, 1952, with John and Miss Hunter billed above the title.

Initial critical notices were mixed, but Hodiak's contribution was generally well-received. John Chapman's *New York Daily News* review (April 16, 1952) noted that John "is giving an admirable performance as the sheriff; he looks, moves, talks and thinks the way such a character should do, and I welcome him to the footlights." Of producer-director José Ferrer's efforts, the reviewer commented, "Ferrer knows how to pick actors and how to direct them after he gets them."

In the *Brooklyn Eagle* (April 16, 1952), Louis Sheaffer wrote, "*The Chase* isn't a profound play or uncommon piece of writing, doesn't raise its thriller pattern to the level of art, but there is heart in it ... and recognizable human beings." Sheaffer praised John's performance as Sheriff Hawes as "a decent, everyday sort of man who loves his wife, tries to do his job to the best of his ability, [and] hates the violence it entails frequently. He's tired of fighting, he tells his wife, wants a peaceful life on a farm and hopes to buy one before their baby arrives." As always, there were some critics who looked askance at actors from Hollywood daring to perform on the legitimate stage, as when the often-acerbic George Jean Nathan described John as "an exponent of the Ralph Bellamy histrionic school, though less theatrically experienced in it, [who] indicated a remaining fondness for those prolonged pauses and meditative stares into space which, I am apprised, pass for extremely proficient acting in the films."[110]

A confident Ferrer, journalists noted, stated that *The Chase* "will do $16,000 for its first seven performances ending tonight, that a steady line has been at the box-office since opening, and that the advance sale is encouragingly solid." If MGM had lost confidence in Hodiak's ticket-selling power, the same couldn't be said of his presence on the Great White Way. It was noted that many of the tickets were sold to women, who wanted to be assured "if Hodiak is actually playing all performances."[111] Modest as ever, John supposedly took a hatchet to the wordy *Playbill* biography that had been prepared for him, slashing it to a single paragraph.

John was interviewed in New York by Hedda Hopper (April 30, 1952), who wrote, "He says getting back on the stage is like sipping rare old wine. On the opening night of his play, John was too busy to be nervous, but now that he's had time to relax, the footlight jitters have caught up with him." For her part, Anne told Louella O. Parsons (March 19, 1952) of hurrying to New York: "I wouldn't do that to John. He'll be nervous enough without knowing that I'm out front. But I hope to go East after he's been on the stage long enough to get over the first nervousness."

The production proved to be a disappointment, closing on May 10 after only 31 performances, though his work was recognized at the Donaldson Awards (an early rival to the Tonys), where he was named for "Best Debut Performance—Actor." There was speculation that John would take the lead role played onstage by Ferrer in *The Shrike,* as a film commitment was causing the actor to bail out, but this didn't transpire. Some years later, Lillian Hellman used Foote's play as the basis for a film directed by Arthur Penn, also called *The Chase* (1966), and starring Marlon Brando.

Meanwhile, John's final film as an MGM contract player, *The Sellout,* landed in theaters. He was now looking to a future as a free-lance actor, at a time when the movie industry was in dire straits, threatened by the burgeoning popularity of television.

Returning to Hollywood that summer, John took his first post–Broadway film assignment when he signed for the lead role in an Allied Artists Korean War programmer, *Battle Zone,* co-starring Stephen McNally and Linda Christian. "It was a little tough during the first three or four months away from MGM," he admitted. "I was offered the same kind I had done at Metro—the best pal of Clark Gable, etc. But I finally got away from all that."[112] Having worked at Hollywood's top-drawer studio during the lavish reign of Louis B. Mayer, some of John's experiences making lower-budget movies for other producers would introduce him to quite a different way of moviemaking.

Anne, meanwhile, was being directed by Alfred Hitchcock in a more prestigious assignment, *I Confess* (1953). She told an interviewer that she and John kept their careers strictly apart. "Both are run separately. My public life belongs to the public but my marriage is my own business. John and I agree on that."[113] John's sojourn in New York as a stage actor inevitably led to gossip about the state of their marriage. Columnist Erskine Johnson (September 30, 1952) noted that John "spiked the rumors that all is not well between himself and Anne Baxter by flying to Quebec," where she was shooting the Hitchcock drama.

Though Eve Harrington had showcased Miss Baxter's ability to play more varied roles, Anne found herself too often being pigeonholed into "nice girl" roles, and thought it was limiting her career progress. As she later explained, studio boss Darryl F. Zanuck appreciated her intelligence, and patrician good looks, but didn't think she radiated sex appeal. "Zanuck thought all women were either broads or librarians," she noted. "He thought I was a librarian."[114] By the early 1950s, publicity that often centered on her happy home life and new motherhood only exacerbated the problem.

She longed to play more glamorous characters, such as that of Lorelei in *Gentlemen Prefer Blondes.* With her contract at Fox winding down, she opted to freelance in search of more varied opportunities. Miss Baxter became a blonde temporarily, and acquired a new, flashier wardrobe. Asked what Hodiak thought of her transformation, she said, "I didn't think he'd really noticed ... but he finds me more attractive.... You know, you can't let these husbands get too used to you. The reason there are so many divorces in Hollywood, I'm convinced, is because women, having once caught the streetcar, just relax. If you relax, you're pretty apt to lose a husband, so I've decided I'm going to hang on to my husband and put up a battle against playing dull roles."[115] "He knew I had sex appeal," she told columnist James Bacon (December 28, 1952) of her husband, "else he never would have married me." Designer Don Loper said that Hodiak picked many of his wife's outfits. "She used to dress drab and plain," wrote one reporter.

John and newly blonde wife Anne Baxter made an elegant couple at the premiere of *The Snows of Kilimanjaro* (1952).

"Marriage not only made her a smart dresser, but her figure became more alluringly feminine," according to Loper.[116] "I'm tired of posing for pictures showing me whipping up a nice meal or diapering the baby," she complained of her public image. "I've been presented as terribly nice, a good actress, wife and mother. That's wonderful—but is it interesting? ... You don't go to the movie houses to see the commonplace—or the girl next door."[117]

Primarily, the transformation Anne was undergoing was an actress' shrewd attempt to update her public image. But some observers put the blame at John's feet. Rather than his acquiring more polish and sophistication from his to-the-manor-born wife, they charged, he was instead bringing Anne down to his more plebeian level.

That summer, the family celebrated Katrina's first birthday. The Hodiaks' daughter would always prize the telegram she received from her father, which read, "My darling Katrina, Happy, happy birthday, from Daddy." Despite that happy occasion, there continued to be signs that all was not well with John and Anne's marriage.

By fall, the rumor mill was working overtime. Hedda Hopper

(September 17, 1952) asked John about claims that he and Anne were growing apart, which he denied. "We're working people," he told the columnist. "I was in New York four months doing a play while Anne worked here. Now I'm home and she's on location for a picture in Canada." For her part, Anne told Erskine Johnson (November 11, 1952), "It's untrue and infuriating. I don't understand it. It happens every time John and I are separated by our work. Believe me we're HAPPILY MARRIED." Left unsaid was that John's wife was enjoying a level of career success that somewhat overshadowed his own.

Just before the Christmas holiday, Anne "startled the film colony," per published reports, by filing for divorce. The court complaint stated that, being married to Hodiak, she experienced "great humiliation, mental anguish and embarrassment," adding that "her husband's attitude had caused her to become nervous and rundown."[118] "For the first time in my life, I've been a failure," Anne said about the impending dissolution of her marriage.[119] The couple released a joint statement for the press which said, in part, "We feel heartsick and defeated in spite of all our hopes and efforts at understanding. Basic incompatibilities have made our life together impossible.... Our decision to separate after six years is a painful one."[120] Too young to truly understand what was happening was their daughter; "I was eighteen months old at the time," Katrina noted.

Though they said little about their marital problems for public consumption, the gossip flew nonetheless. According to Sheilah Graham, "Everyone has a reason for the break-up of the Anne Baxter–John Hodiak marriage. It's her mother. It's her grandfather. He bores her. She embarrasses him. She's a snob. He's a sourpuss. She's too ambitious. He isn't ambitious enough. She's an extrovert. He's the retiring type. She loves publicity. He hates it. She's a poet, and he's a peasant. It all adds up to some fancy psychoanalysis."[121] Columnist Harrison Carroll (January 1, 1953) opined, "Friends say the breakup of the marriage ... was due to the fact that they couldn't see eye to eye on anything. Argued until their life was miserable." He was reported to have temporarily taken up residence at the Beverly Hills Hotel.

Hedda Hopper (January 1, 1953) chimed in: "Three days before Anne Baxter announced her divorce from John Hodiak, she was giving out their plans at home. Said they'd take the baby to Arrowhead to see its first snow. The news must have come as quite a shock to Hodiak. He told me he was certain it wouldn't take place." Early on, Dorothy Kilgallen (January 18, 1953) reported "Intimates think there's a good chance of John Hodiak and Anne Baxter reconciling. Too much in-law trouble was the reason for the split, they say."

Much as they tried to conduct their parting with dignity and discretion, however, obtaining a divorce in that era required Anne to be a little more forthcoming in court. Miss Baxter shed tears as she testified, according to news reports, that "Hodiak sometimes failed to acknowledge introductions to her business associates and once when an author came to their home to play dramatic records, Hodiak laid down on the couch and went to sleep."[122] Her attorney, Norman Tyre, stated that John had signed an agreement to make monthly contributions to his soon-to-be-ex-wife of $1 in alimony, $350 for child support, and $30 toward a trust fund for Katrina. The divorce was uncontested.

More than twenty years later, when writing her memoir, Anne Baxter still admitted feelings of guilt about the breakup with John, and had been hesitant to remarry, fearful that her "emotional instability" made her a dubious marital prospect.[123] "We'd eventually congealed in the longest winter in the world," she wrote. "Daily estrangement. Things unsaid. Even a fight would have warmed us. To my shame, I'd picked one at last in order to unfreeze the word 'divorce.' Slamming drawers, running around our silver-ceilinged bedroom, and avoiding his motionless eyes." Rather than shifting the blame to him, she added, "No one else came between us. Just us. And a lot of that was me."[124] She would continue to speak kindly of John Hodiak for the remainder of her life.

Early 1953 found John in front of cameras for two modestly-budgeted action features, *Conquest of Cochise* and *Mission Over Korea*. Both were shot on tight schedules that little resembled MGM's production methods, but they had the virtue of offering Hodiak star billing in leading roles. Studio publicity for *Conquest of Cochise* (1953) alleged that the actor "dislikes horses," but had "conquered his dislike of the animals."

According to syndicated columnist Louella O. Parsons (January 12, 1953), John was pointedly keeping busy after his split with Anne Baxter—"he hasn't dated anyone since he and Anne broke up and is always stag when he shows up at a night spot." *Modern Screen* reported, "Already Hollywood hostesses are vying to snare John Hodiak for their parties, and almost every glamor girl in town is pulling her charms together and rolling her eyes his way. So far he hasn't seemed too interested in a rebound romance. Neither has Anne."[125] In that same publication, columnist Lynn Bowers (April 1953) labelled him "lonesomest boy in town," adding, "Afraid most of the sympathy goes to John [rather than Anne], one of the nicest guys in or out of this town."

That summer, John was said to be escorting actress Kay Spreckels around town. Sheilah Graham (August 23, 1953) said, "John Hodiak is shown as a heartbroken guy over the breakup of his marriage with Anne Baxter. But just a few weeks ago he met a blond, blue-eyed charmer, Kay Spreckels, and it looks like he's in love again." Louella O. Parsons

Biography 49

and Ed Sullivan also reported the twosome being seen out and about in August. The following month, Dorothy Kilgallen (September 8, 1953), who noted that Mrs. Spreckels "made headlines the other day when her sugar heir ex-husband was charged with beating her," added that the lady "is responding nicely to John Hodiak's romantic therapy." In 1955, the divorcée became the wife of Clark Gable, and gave birth to his son, shortly after his death in 1960.

John's name was linked to another Broadway show, *Suddenly*, by playwright Richard Sales, with a cast of eight. However, the planned show never opened in New York, but instead became the basis of a 1954 film starring Frank Sinatra in the role that had been earmarked for Hodiak. In the meantime, he continued to keep busy in action movies, primarily westerns and war films.

In his filmography of Korean War films, Robert J. Lentz wrote, "A handsome, capable actor in regimented roles, Hodiak came to represent capable American soldiers professionally doing their jobs in his trio of Korean war movies."[126] One of those was *Dragonfly Squadron*, for which producer John C. Champion signed John in the summer of 1953. About a

Now-single Hodiak escorted glamorous Kay Spreckels to an evening out at Ciro's.

month later, trade papers reported that actress Barbara Britton, known most recently as co-star of TV's *Mr. and Mrs. North,* won the part of his leading lady. After completing *Dragonfly Squadron* together, writer/producer John C. Champion announced in trade papers that his next project would be an adaptation of Edward Everett Hale's *The Man Without a Country,* starring Hodiak. Production was anticipated for the summer of 1954.

As it happened, however, another opportunity presented itself, one that would enable John to put some distance between him and his less-than-optimal circumstances on the West Coast. And when opportunity knocked, Hodiak was ready to answer.

Hodiak's Mutiny

With good film roles at a premium, John welcomed a chance to return to the stage, in a Broadway-bound production of Herman Wouk's *The Caine Mutiny Court-Martial.* "The picture business was going stale for me and I was for it. I just wasn't cut out to play the star's brother all the time. I was getting second fiddle roles.... It began to be obvious to me that I wasn't in line to become a Gary Cooper, a John Wayne, or a Bing Crosby. Oh, I had good parts. But not top star roles." Watching television, he felt that there, too, was work likely to frustrate a good actor. "It was the same as the movies, maybe worse. Neither medium gives an actor time to develop a character fully, to let a man feel that he's given everything he has to a performance."[127]

The kind of offer he'd been seeking finally came to pass when producer Paul Gregory paid him a visit. Gregory had already collaborated with actor-director Charles Laughton on touring productions such as *Don Juan in Hell* and *John Brown's Body.* John's ex-wife Anne Baxter had taken part in Gregory's staging of the latter a year or two earlier. "We talked and talked," John recalled. "I was sure Greg had something in mind for me. Then he left without a word and I fumed. About two hours later he called to say he'd forgotten to mention that I could play Maryk if I wanted to."[128]

Oddly, Gregory's press releases sometimes presented Hodiak as a stage neophyte, leaving unmentioned his previous Broadway run in *The Chase.* One stated, "John Hodiak had accumulated a fan following of immense proportions as a rugged, he-man star of motion pictures before the opportunity came along for him to transfer his outstanding talents to the legitimate theater—the ambition of nearly every actor—but when his chance did finally arrive, it was, as he puts it, 'like finding gold.' For Hodiak has triple insurance that this, his first major venture on the stage, will bring him a resounding success." The three elements in question were said to be the production team, the vehicle itself, and the cast headed by Henry Fonda.

"It was only a short step for John Hodiak from playing virile he-man roles in films to the rugged hero Lt. Steve Maryk whom he impersonates in the Paul Gregory–Charles Laughton production of Herman Wouk's new play The Caine Mutiny Court-Martial," read another blurb. "It is a step which Hodiak has taken with distinguished success. But for him professionally it is a seven-league stride, which has catapulted him exactly where he has yearned to be, in the legitimate theater, in an outstandingly successful show, and under what is concededly the hottest management now functioning on the American stage."[129]

The two-act play was adapted by Wouk from his novel *The Caine Munity*, with assistance from the more theatrically knowledgeable Laughton. The latter told an interviewer that, despite what some might think, Wouk's writing was not intended to cast the military in a bad light. "This play expresses Wouk's respect for authority," Laughton said. "It's an affirmative play. It took a patriotic American to write 'The Caine Mutiny,' a man with deep feeling for his country."[130] Hodiak would play the pivotal role of Lt. Stephen Maryk, whose decision to take over command of his ship due to the erratic behavior of Lt. Cmdr. Philip Queeg has put his career on the line. In the starring role of Lt. Barney Greenwald, who conducts Maryk's defense, was Henry Fonda, with Hodiak's old cohort Lloyd Nolan cast in the showier part of Queeg.

Press for the play noted that it lacked the "obscene, racy dialogue" that had appeared in other contemporary dramas about military life like James Jones' novel *From Here to Eternity*. Getting underway in California, the production was under the direction of Dick Powell, better-known as an actor, but who'd won plaudits for his recent direction of a suspense film, *Split Second* (1953). As the co-author of Fonda's memoir later wrote, "It required a short time for the cast to learn that the director knew little if anything about staging a play."[131] Over lunch, Fonda, Nolan, and Hodiak agreed there was a problem.

"I had no communication with Dick Powell," Fonda commented. "We never exchanged a harsh word. I just believed I'd been doing plays long enough to know the company wasn't getting what it should from a director."[132] He told Laughton that, with opening night approaching in Santa Barbara, the show was not shaping up. Powell had what he later described was "a little beef" with leading man Henry Fonda, and withdrew from the production.[133] Laughton assumed the directorial reigns, and whipped the overlong text into shape.

Before heading for Broadway in the new year, Gregory's company opened the show in Santa Barbara in previews on October 12, 1953. Two days later, in San Diego, came "an official premiere before top Navy officials and West Coast critics."[134] Columnist Bob Thomas (October 25, 1953), who caught a performance at Pomona College, described the show as "stirring theater," adding that John Hodiak "in a less showy part, is the perfect Maryk."

Over the next several weeks it embarked on an atypical cross-country tour. Rather than concentrating on multi-night runs in a few major metropolitan areas, the tour, as *Time* magazine explained, took place "mostly in one- or two-night stands through 60 cities, playing any kind of hall where its busload of simple courtroom props can be set up." Audiences saw "a play [that] has almost no action but makes up for it by an eloquent script, suspense and good acting."[135] Critic Ralph Green commented, "As the man being tried, Hodiak gave a genuine and finely-shaded performance as a man who won an empty victory at the expense of another."[136] Also to be numbered among those who admired John's work was ex-wife Anne Baxter, who saw a preview in New Haven shortly before the Broadway opening and, according to Hedda Hopper (February 6, 1954), was "singing his praises."

John came to his co-star's defense when Louella O. Parsons (December 11, 1953) reported that Henry Fonda "stays aloof from everyone in 'The Caine Mutiny Court Martial' company," adding that, while Hodiak and Lloyd Nolan palled around, "Hank is never with them, nor does he fraternize with the other members of the company." A few days later (December 14, 1953), Parsons wrote, "All the way from Cincinnati John Hodiak telephoned to tell me I had done Henry Fonda wrong." Though she claimed to have several sources for what she'd reported, the columnist quoted Hodiak as saying, "We've had no trouble. Just one happy family, and except for a few minor misunderstandings we are all very congenial." She walked back her earlier claim that Fonda intended to leave the show before it opened in New York.

More backstage controversy erupted when Dick Powell, who'd left his post as director back in California, sought an injunction to prevent opening night, after learning that Gregory would not be giving him billing as the play's director. "Gregory asked me to direct the play and I have a written contract that I receive a percentage of the gross and be given billing as director of the production at all times, even though I quit," Powell told a columnist. Paul Gregory responded by stating that Powell had been "removed" from his job as director, and that credit in that capacity would go to Charles Laughton.[137]

On January 20, 1954, the curtain rose on *Caine* at Broadway's Plymouth Theatre. "We had 18 weeks on the road before coming to the Plymouth," Hodiak noted. "It was the most wonderful experience of my life.

And now being in a hit with the prestige of this one gives me a whole new lease on life."[138]

Act One, "The Prosecution," takes place in the Court-Martial Room of the Twelfth Naval District, in San Francisco, as Lt. Stephen Maryk prepares to go on trial. As Maryk, Hodiak spoke the play's opening to lines to his attorney, played by Henry Fonda: "What are they doing out there? This is a hell of a long recess. This is the longest recess yet."[139] Act One mostly calls for Hodiak to listen as his shipmates testify, and grow concerned that his lawyer Barney Greenwald's tactics have him headed for "fifteen years in the brig."[140] Act Two, "The Defense," returns to the courtroom. Maryk is called to the witness stand, explaining to the jury why he believed Captain Queeg "might be mentally ill,"[141] and felt compelled to assume command of the ship during bad weather. Hodiak had several lengthy speeches to deliver as part of his testimony. In the closing moments, there's a brief climactic scene set in a hotel banquet room.

The show's playbill carried a disclaimer from the playwright: "The Caine Mutiny Court Martial" is purely imaginary. No ship named U.S.S. *Caine* ever existed. The records show no instance of a U.S. Navy captain relieved at sea under Articles 184–186. The fictitious figure of the deposed captain was derived from a study of psychoneurotic case histories, and is not a portrait of a real military person or type.... "The author served under two captains of the regular Navy aboard destroyer-minesweepers, both of whom were decorated for valor." The pertinent passages from Navy regulations were also reproduced.

Publicly Hodiak was full of praise for star Henry Fonda and his other castmates. Talking with columnist Earl Wilson (April 5, 1954), John mentioned "fly-catching," the practice of some actors to do something distracting onstage to divert attention away from another player. "This guy," he said of Fonda, "wouldn't raise a finger or brush a fly off his nose if somebody else had the scene." When he came down with a cold, Hodiak warned the star that he was carrying a handkerchief, which he would use during a scene only if necessary. Fonda replied, "That's all right ... just as long as you don't take it out and wave it."

Columnist Leonard Lyons (April 13, 1954) reported one indication that Hodiak and Lloyd Nolan were settling into their roles: "They've had their wardrobes and golf clubs sent East from Hollywood, and are joining country clubs here." In his dressing room backstage, John prominently displayed photos of his young daughter Katrina, proudly telling Ed Sullivan, "She's a nice little girl."

Among the company members was a neophyte actor named James Bumgarner, who would later find success with the truncated surname Garner. He earned $100 a week playing the mostly silent role of a judge at the court-martial, and also served as Hodiak's understudy. "I used to go around with the three of them—Fonda, Hodiak, and Nolan—as a sort of bodyguard-gofer-mascot. On my first night in New York, they got me a date with a gorgeous model ... and they took us to the '21' Club. I miss those guys."[142]

With little to do onstage but adopt a sober expression and not distract attention from the stars, the future television star recalled, "I learned from them in the theater, by sitting there on the bench night after night after night with nothing to do except watch them work. I learned about phrasing, and I learned about concentration. I began to be able to dissect their performances."[143] He recalled some welcome career advice he was given. "John Hodiak urged me to get into the movies where my lack of acting training wouldn't matter so much," he told columnist Bettelou Peterson (January 5, 1958). "I did a couple of movie tests and flopped, mostly because I was scared stiff." But eventually he was signed by Warner Brothers, where his television role in *Maverick* led to a long and impressive career.

Hodiak was surely disappointed that he wasn't invited to reprise his stage role in the 1954 film, which was an adaptation unconnected to the Broadway show, but played it down in his interview with Wilson, saying with a smile, "All I know is what Stanley Kramer told me about myself. He told, not that I wasn't the type... I was too much the type. I don't know what anybody can do about that."

His Broadway commitment forced him to decline an invitation to take part in a civic event taking place in his old stomping grounds of Hamtramck, Michigan. "But I do want to extend my best wishes for a grand success of your Hamtramck Dodge City Week celebration," he told organizers by phone.[144]

When Henry Fonda left the company in May 1954, producer Paul Gregory signed Barry Sullivan to step into the role of Barney Greenwald. Sullivan praised the ensemble of players with whom he was working, saying, "The teamwork in the company is wonderful. I think we've got the same kind of esprit that a smartly trained crew of a Navy vessel would have."[145]

The Caine Mutiny Court-Martial closed its Broadway run in January 1955, after a one-year stint. Louella O. Parsons (March 10, 1955) reported, "John Hodiak hadn't been back in town two days before [producer] Charlie Schnee invited him out to MGM to put his John Hancock on a deal to play the district attorney in 'Trial.'" Having spent the past year in a stage courtroom, "He laughed when he told me, 'and now I'm back in a courtroom again.'" He supported Glenn Ford in the return to MGM soundstages.

In April, John and other Broadway cast members brought the play to

Los Angeles. Lloyd Nolan and Barry Sullivan also reprised roles they had played in New York. As always, John took his work as an actor seriously, and gave it his best efforts, but didn't overanalyze it. He said, "It's my belief that acting is essentially a quality within a person and not a mere bag of tricks and mannerisms to be exhibited externally."[146]

After his divorce, John lived with his parents in the house he'd had built for them at 5732 Donna Avenue in the city of Tarzana. Also in residence were his sister Anne and brother, Walter Jr. For John, who prized his family ties, it was a satisfying arrangement. Though his social life was limited after the divorce, columnists did link his name with several beautiful actresses, among them Eva Gabor, Betsy von Furstenberg and Janis Paige. Hal Eaton (June 23, 1954) even reported that the "Janis Paige–John Hodiak romance [was] reaching marital stage." However, a friend later commented, "We felt he was not interested in marrying again—he had been hurt once. There was no bitterness when he and Anne divorced, but he was upset. He always was terribly fond of their child."[147]

That fall, John was signed to a co-starring role in Fox's "Threshold of Space" (released as *On the Threshold of Space*). Little did he or anyone else realize that he was embarking upon his final film project. As was common practice in the industry, John had undergone a physical examination for insurance purposes prior to beginning work, as some of his scenes would be strenuous. He was given a clean bill of health. His film *Trial* had opened only a couple of weeks previously to good notices.

On October 19, 1955, John, having returned home a few days earlier from location work for the new film, was due at Fox studio that morning to shoot some additional footage. He felt slightly ill, but intended to report for work regardless: "He had been up an hour, complaining of gas."[148] Getting ready to leave, he collapsed in his bathroom a few minutes before 7 a.m. His sister Anne heard him fall and summoned help.

First responders tried without success to revive him; Dr. Sydney Spies, when he arrived on the scene, pronounced Hodiak dead. Dr. Spies told reporters that he was unaware of his patient having heart trouble previously, and that Hodiak had not been ill in recent days. Katrina remembered her mother gently breaking the news, telling her, "Darling, your daddy's gone to heaven."

At the time of his death, John was already booked for an upcoming television adaptation of *The Caine Mutiny Court-Martial*, and was due to depart for New York later that week to begin rehearsals. Louella O. Parsons (October 25, 1955) reported that Hodiak had also signed an agreement with producer Art Cohn for a television series to be called "Storm Carlson," and "expressed himself as delighted because he would play a sports writer and each one of the series would highlight some big sports event."

Paul Gregory, who had hired Hodiak for *The Caine Mutiny Court-Martial*, identified one stressful circumstance in the star's life, telling columnist Leonard Lyons (October 25, 1955) that he had spoken with the actor the night before his death, and "Hodiak said he was troubled—because of his father's serious illness."

Anne Baxter issued a statement that read, "He was one of the most sensitive persons I've known. He was hurt inside by many, many things. I feel dreadful. He was a magnificent husband, a tender and loving father and a far more brilliant and sensitive actor than anybody knew. I have the deepest respect and love for him."[149] To another reporter, she added, "He never wanted to hurt anybody and he never did."[150]

This handsome portrait shot of John Hodiak was frequently used to illustrate newspaper stories reporting his untimely death at the age of 41.

Some friends and co-workers thought that sensitivity, and his emotional nature, might have contributed to his heart ailment. "Being Slavic, he had moods," Lloyd Nolan recalled of his stage and film co-star. "He had ultra-sensitiveness. He was very sincere about acting, and very serious about it. He also was terribly nervous at times. Even at parties in New York he'd get butterflies in his stomach, like a child. He was also terribly loyal to his friends, and sentimental."[151] Hodiak had occasionally told interviewers over the years that he never suffered from nerves, but few who knew him well would have agreed with this self-assessment. Nolan told Hedda Hopper (October 27, 1955), "Johnny and I did 614 performances of the 'Caine Mutiny' and never missed one. He was a fine man, an exceptional actor, and a very good friend indeed."

Richard Shavinski recalled that he came home from work one day and found his parents both in tears, having learned of their friend's death. His father, Paul, who'd known John as a kid in Hamtramck, flew out to the East Coast, where he served as a pallbearer. Similarly, Michael Galay, still a young boy, found his mother Mary crying over the news of her brother's death. "You're going to California with me," she told him, though he didn't understand everything that was happening. At the mortuary, he was allowed to view John's remains in his casket. "That was the first dead person that I'd ever seen," Galay noted.

A brief memorial service was held on Saturday, October 22, in the chapel of the J.T. Oswald Mortuary of North Hollywood. As described in newspaper reports, "Hodiak's body, clothed in a dark blue suit, lay in a bronze, pink-lined casket.... Resting in his left hand was a rosary. A crucifix was mounted in the casket above his head."[152]

Among the mourners was John's ex-wife, Anne Baxter, who sat with her former in-laws. Hollywood friends and colleagues in attendance included Lloyd Nolan, Fred MacMurray, Robert Wagner, Cesar Romero and his *Night into Morning* co-star Nancy Davis. As reported in the *Los Angeles Times*, "The actor's mother, sobbing and on the verge of collapse, left the chapel on the arm of a private nurse. His father, leaning heavily on a cane, was aided by mortuary attendants."[153] His brother Walter Jr. and sisters were attendance as well; his young daughter was not. More than once, according to her son, Hodiak's sister Mary said, "John was good to me."

In a letter to a friend, author John Steinbeck wrote, "This has been a bad year in the loss of friends. About seven in the last few months.... I guess it is a symptom of the ages. But it seems to me a lot of what I think of as the young ones of my friends toppled over—like John Hodiak and Lemuel Ayers."[154]

Actor Frank Lovejoy stepped into the role of Maryk in the television production of *The Caine Mutiny Court-Martial*. As was an old theatrical custom, his paycheck was sent to Hodiak's wife. Barry Sullivan, cast as Barney Greenwald, told Louella O. Parsons (February 10, 1956) that he and Lloyd Nolan had tried to bow out of the television performance after Hodiak's death. "We had our pictures taken with John the day before he died," Sullivan noted, "and Lloyd Nolan and I were so shocked by his death that we didn't see how we could go on without John.... The three of us were very close.... Frankly, we couldn't get out of our contract with TV, and it was like a nightmare doing the show." The show as broadcast concluded with what *TV Guide*'s Harold V. Cohen described as "Charles Laughton's short but touching tribute" to Hodiak.

Surely not expecting to pass away at such an early age, Hodiak had failed to leave a will behind, dying intestate. His sister, Anne Sliva, filed court paperwork reporting that he had as assets "cash not exceeding $10,000, stocks of less than $5000 and other personal property not exceeding $10,000."[155] The house he had bought for his parents became a source of contention, when Anne Baxter tried to claim it on her young daughter's behalf, putting her at odds with her former in-laws. John had neglected to put the house in the elder Hodiaks' name, but John's mother told the court, according to a wire service story, that "the late actor bought the home in 1945 to induce his parents to come here from Detroit. She said she and her husband Walter, 69, spent $10,000 of their own money to improve the home, but left title in their son's name."[156] Judge Burnett Wolfson sided with the parents, and awarded title to them.

His final film, *On the Threshold of Space,* opened in New York City in late March 1956, and nationwide shortly afterwards, to mostly positive notices. Though he hadn't quite finished the film, he was present in enough of it to single out mention by several reviewers. As friends, colleagues, and family continued to mourn his loss, columnist Louella O. Parsons wrote in *Modern Screen* (January 1956), "I never heard anyone say he didn't like John Hodiak. What greater epitaph can be written for any man?"

John's father Walter survived him by seven years, passing away in Tarzana in 1962; his mother Anna died in 1971. Five years after Hodiak's death, his ex-wife Anne Baxter married a second time, to a cattle rancher in Australia, Randolph Galt. That marriage also ended in divorce, after nine years, but not before Katrina's mother gave her two half-sisters. Miss Baxter's final marriage, to stockbroker David Klee in 1977, was cut short by his unexpected death less than one year later.

Some twenty years after divorcing Hodiak, Miss Baxter wrote respectfully of him in her memoirs. John's ex-wife stated of Katrina, "She'd barely known her own father. John Hodiak and I were divorced when she was only fifteen months old; he died tragically a little over a year later. Her memories of him were few but of the purest pleasure."[157]

Publicly, Anne never bad-mouthed him. In a 1980 interview, John's onetime wife spoke, "with sparkling eyes," about him. "He was one of the most handsome men I've ever met. He had eyes like a lion, the color of yellow chartreuse. He just stunned me at 21."[158] Her daughter Melissa Galt could not remember his name ever being mentioned, but commented, "She only had nice things to say about everyone. She wasn't a gossip, kept secrets, and looked for the best in everyone."[159]

"I wish I'd known him more as a father," Katrina said in later years. As she grew into adulthood, she continued to watch his films whenever possible, saying, "It's my way of knowing him." She sometimes asked her mother about events that had taken place when she was a child, and was often told about her father, "He was there." As an adult, Katrina became an actress, primarily on stage. Though she grew up without her father as a steady presence in her life, she kept him in her thoughts nonetheless. "I still have dreams about him," she said.

Filmography

Minor Film Roles

Like most newcomers to motion pictures, John Hodiak launched his career playing small speaking roles and bit parts. Newly under contract to MGM, the studio let him get his feet wet by appearing briefly in these films.

A Stranger in Town (MGM, 1943)

Director: Roy Rowland. *Cast*: Frank Morgan, Richard Carlson, Jean Rogers, Porter Hall. Beloved character actor Morgan stars as a Supreme Court justice who gets involved in small-town politics while trying to enjoy an incognito hunting vacation, with Carlson and Rogers as the ingénues. This unremarkable but pleasant B movie finds an idealistic but headstrong lawyer running for mayor against a corrupt longtime power player.

Billed fourteenth in the opening titles, John has virtually nothing to do as Hart Ridges, a local businessman who's the landlord to Carlson's character, and a crooked crony of his opponent. It's surprising that Hodiak is billed at all, as his sole line of dialogue is, "Who's the girl?"

Swing Shift Maisie (MGM, 1943)

Director: Norman Z. McLeod. *Cast*: Ann Sothern, James Craig, Jean Rogers, Connie Gilchrist.

As in his film debut, John is allotted one line here: "All green card holders, follow me." John will return to the series the following year, upgraded to being Miss Sothern's leading man.

Major Film Roles

I Dood It (1943)

Red Skelton (*Joseph Rivington Renolds*), Eleanor Powell (*Constance Shaw*), Richard Ainley (*Larry West*), Patricia Dane (*Suretta Brenton*), Sam Levene (*Ed Jackson*), Thurston Hall (*Kenneth Lawlor*), Lena Horne, Hazel Scott, Jimmy Dorsey and His Orchestra, Helen O'Connell, Bob Eberly (*Themselves*), John Hodiak (*Roy Hartwood*), Butterfly McQueen (*Annette*), Marjorie Gateson (*Mrs. Spelvin*), Andrew Tombes (*Mr. Spelvin*), Morris Ankrum (*Banker*), Charles Judels (*Stage Manager*)

Director: Vincente Minnelli. *Producer*: Jack Cummings. *Screenplay*: Sig Herzig, Fred Saidy. *Musical Director*: Georgie Stoll. *Dance Direction*: Bobby Connolly. *Director of Photography*: Ray June. *Recording Director*: Douglas Shearer. *Art Director*: Cedric Gibbons. *Associate*: Jack Martin Smith. *Set Decorations*: Edwin B. Willis. *Associate*: Helen Conway. *Musical Presentation*: Merrill Pye. *Costume Supervision*: Irene. *Associate*: Sharaff. *Men's Costumes*: Gile Steele. *Film Editor*: Robert J. Kern.

Songs: "Star Eyes" (Don Raye, Gene DePaul), "So Long Sarah Jane" (Lew Brown, Ralph Freed, Sammy Fain), "One O'Clock Jump" (Count Basie), "Swingin' the Jinx Away" (Cole Porter), "Taking a Chance on Love" (music, Vernon Duke; lyric, John La Touche, Ted Fetter), "Jericho" (words, Leo Robin; music, Richard Myers; arrangement, Kay Thompson)

MGM; released September 1943. 102 minutes. B&W.

Bumbling but likable Joe Renolds [sic] is employed as a pants presser in the valet shop of the Park Savoy Hotel, where to his boss Ed Jackson's displeasure, he borrows the male customers' evening wear to enhance his own wardrobe. Infatuated with Broadway performer Constance Shaw, star of a romantic Civil War melodrama, "Dixie Lou," Joe is one of many men who buys a kiss from her at a USO benefit. Connie is engaged to her on-stage leading man, Larry West, but his attentions are also being sought by her rival Suretta Brenton. Unbeknownst to his fellow company members, Roy Hartwood, who plays a villain in "Dixie Lou," is a real-life saboteur who's using his access to the theater and its cellar to dig a tunnel to the munitions warehouse next door.

On the night when Joe attends Connie's show for the 65th time, she flies into a rage backstage when Suretta shows off a ruby bracelet Larry gave her. Storming out of her dressing room, Connie is presented with flowers by a smitten Joe, and decides in a fit of pique to give him a chance to make Larry jealous. When she's approached by her producer, Kenneth Lawlor, Connie introduces Joe as her new husband. In the bridal suite of the hotel, Connie tries to administer sleeping pills to Joe, but gets a strong dose herself, and doesn't awaken until morning.

The next morning, Connie is visited by Kenneth, Suretta, and Larry. Suretta, aware of Joe's lowly occupation and borrowed wardrobe, makes sure Connie finds out as well. A dejected Joe leaves—after punching out the two-timing Larry.

After a failed suicide attempt, Joe tries to see Connie backstage at the theater. Going in through the cellar, he encounters Larry. When Larry is told by his cohorts that the bombing must take place that evening, he presses Joe into service to play his part in the stage show, while he tries to put the finishing touches on his nefarious plans.

I Dood It is one of the lesser films of the Academy Award–winning director Vincente Minnelli (1903–1986), filmed a year prior to his classic *Meet Me in St. Louis*. It is a loose remake of the Buster Keaton comedy *Spite Marriage*. Minnelli was assigned to the project as a replacement for director Roy Del Ruth. Though warmly received at the time, its reputation has diminished in recent years. Still, the finished film worked both as escapist entertainment for wartime audiences, and as an appropriate film to be spotlighted at military fundraisers, with Skelton's character triumphing over an attempted act of enemy sabotage

Red Skelton (1913–1997), signed to an MGM player contract in 1940, was moving up fast, augmenting his popular radio program with increasingly important movie assignments. His trio of "Whistling" comedies for director S. Sylvan Simon (1910–1951) demonstrated that Skelton could carry a film on his own. The film's title adopts a catchphrase popularized by the star's radio show, in which one of his recurring characters, bratty little Junior, was regularly threatened with a whipping if he did whatever misdeed his mother suspected him of. After triumphing in well-made B comedies, here Skelton is elevated to a higher plane, which doesn't always work in his favor. MGM executives seemed always to believe that comedians should be accompanied by song and dance routines, placing musical numbers even into the likes of the Marx Brothers films. At least in the case of this film, the quality of the specialty acts is high, especially the lengthy segment in which Lena Horne (1917–2010) leads a troupe performing "Jericho," accompanied by Hazel Scott's flying fingers on the piano.

The grace and athleticism of Eleanor Powell (1912–1982) serve her well as Skelton's leading lady, not only in her skillfully executed dance sequences but in the lengthy pantomime that finds her zonked out on sleeping pills in their hotel room, while Joe struggles to put her to bed.

Patricia Dane (1919–1995) shows her gift for menace, playing another sharp-tongued denizen of the Broadway world as she had the previous year in *Grand Central Murder* (1942), though she doesn't meet such a grim fate here. Richard Ainley (1910–1967), billed at the top of the supporting cast, has a thankless role as Connie's unworthy fiancé, which he plays drably. The always-welcome Butterfly McQueen (1911–1995), as Connie's maid, is too little seen, but is charming in a scene with Skelton where she consoles him on the loss of his lady, saying sympathetically in that inimitable voice, "I had a tragic romance in my life, too."

From his first scenes, it's apparent that John's character Roy is not on the side of the angels, as he almost misses his stage entrance while he digs in the cellar. We see him as Captain Allen, enacting a dramatic scene with Connie, then John disappears from the film for nearly an hour. He resurfaces to play a significant role in the final reel, as Joe is called upon for heroics when he realizes Hartwood's treachery. Though his screen time is limited, John looks fine in military regalia, something he will adopt with regularity in coming roles. He's effective as the strong Captain Allen in the show-within-a-show (a sequence Skelton later burlesques), and shows off his brawn in the fisticuffs with Joe. Amidst the ample comedy, Hodiak is also shown to be an actor who has leading-man chops, which his later film roles will amply exploit.

Reviews: "The studio's latest Red Skelton comedy is a humdinger that looks like a million. Grosses are certain to look like that, too.... The screenplay ... and the direction of Vincente Minnelli maneuver Skelton into some extremely uproarious situations.... Miss Powell proves an excellent foil for [Skelton]. Sam Levene stands out among the others as Skelton's boss. Of the others, [Richard] Ainley, Patricia Dane, [Thurston] Hall, John Hodiak, and Andrew Tombes are the best."—*Film Daily*, July 30, 1943

"[Skelton's] no less than sensational, and not to be compared with anybody in pictures in straight stretches of pantomime without a word spoken for minutes on end.... Production by Jack Cummings and direction by Vincente Minnelli are to be remembered hereafter as the works of the gentlemen who gave Skelton's talent room in which to thrive." —*Motion Picture Herald*, July 31, 1943

Lifeboat (1944)

Tallulah Bankhead (*Connie Porter*), William Bendix (*Gus Smith*), Walter Slezak (*Willi*), Mary Anderson (*Alice MacKenzie*), John Hodiak (*John Kovac*), Henry Hull (*Charles J. Rittenhouse*), Heather Angel (*Mrs. Higley*), Hume Cronyn (*Stanley Garrett*), Canada Lee (*Joe Spencer*)

Director: Alfred Hitchcock. *Producer*: Kenneth Macgowan. *Screenplay*: Jo Swerling. *Original Story*: John Steinbeck. *Director of Photography*: Glen MacWilliams. *Art Direction*: James Basevi, Maurice Ransford. *Set Decorations*: Thomas Little. *Associate*: Frank E. Hughes. *Film Editor*:

Dorothy Spencer. *Costumes*: Rene Hubert. *Makeup Artist*: Guy Pearce. *Special Photographic Effects*: Fred Sersen. *Technical Adviser*: Thomas Fitzsimmons. *Sound*: Bernard Freericks, Roger Heman. *Music*: Hugo W. Friedhofer. *Musical Direction*: Emil Newman.

20th Century–Fox; released January 28, 1944. B&W. 97 minutes.

An American ship is attacked by a German U-boat, leaving the passengers and crew to take to the lifeboats. Among those struggling for survival are journalist Connie Porter, wealthy C.J. Rittenhouse, crew member John Kovac, Army nurse Alice MacKenzie, steward Joe Spencer, and an injured seaman, Gus Smith. Joe helps rescue Mrs. Higley, a young Englishwoman, who is suffering from shell shock after the death of her baby.

The occupants of the lifeboat are torn when Willi, a U-boat escapee, finds his way to them. Connie, able to speak German, converses with the new arrival, and the passengers argue over what should be done with him. He tells her that he was only a crew member, carrying out orders like any sailor, and for a time is believed. At sea with no compass available, they must decide whether to believe Willi, who indicates to them what he says is the correct direction to head for Bermuda.

Their plight, already serious, worsens as they face stormy weather, illness, and the loss of their supplies. Recognizing the seriousness of Gus's injury, Willi says that he is a trained doctor, and with the aid of nurse Mary, Gus' leg is amputated with only brandy to anesthetize him. Eventually, they are without food and water, except for a flask that Willi is careful to conceal from the others. With Gus near death and delirious, Willi gives him a final push overboard. Enraged when they awaken to see what he has done, the other passengers attack him.

Just as Connie's bracelet succeeds in baiting a plump fish, Joe spots a ship on the horizon. As it comes closer, the lifeboat passengers recognize that it is an enemy vessel that will not help them. The German ship begins to be fired upon by an approaching Allied vessel, and it appears that the lifeboat passengers may have a chance—if they aren't torpedoed first.

Strong stuff for the 1940s, *Lifeboat* tells a compelling story of a random group of strangers with little in common, and their efforts to pull together as they fight to survive. They bear little resemblance to the standard heroic characters of classic films: though they sometimes have noble instincts, they are also torn by the ethical questions that wartime and their dangerous situation put before them. Industry censors and studio executives expressed concern about the story elements, which included the suicide of a young woman, the death of a baby, and an emergency leg amputation. It's startling yet somehow apropos when the villainous Willi is beaten with the boot from Gus' amputated leg.

Tallulah Bankhead and John made a powerful couple in *Lifeboat* (1944). Also pictured: Canada Lee (left) and William Bendix (back to camera).

Hitchcock himself had the idea of making a film that took place entirely in such a confined setting, but he enlisted the distinguished novelist John Steinbeck (1902–1968) to concoct the story. Despite the author's impeccable credentials, the director proceeded to make multiple changes to what Steinbeck drafted, with the help of veteran screenwriter Jo Swerling (1893–1964), who penned the final script. Swerling later said, "After the first reading that I gave to the Steinbeck story, I never again referred to it, nor did anyone else working on the picture."[1]

Top-billed Tallulah Bankhead (1902–1968), playing a character not unlike the well-known writer and politician Clare Boothe Luce (1903–1987), manages to incorporate some of her own familiar persona (dropping a few "Darling"s along the way). She enlists audience sympathy, though, as she perseveres through hardship, and learns a little more about the human condition. Hodiak's career received a sizable boost when Alfred Hitchcock borrowed him from MGM for the role of her leading man. Though at least one Hitchcock biographer has implied that John was cast primarily because he could be had cheaply, he in fact delivers a strong performance as Kovac that elevates the role and the film. He gives the sometimes cynical and headstrong character an intensely masculine presence (he spends nearly half the film bare-chested), and holds his own against the powerful leading lady.

The two of them play out a curious relationship that's unlike a typical movie romance of that era, with passion matched by a veneer of hostility and mistrust. Kovac bluntly tells her the problem with her writing is that, even in her war reporting, she makes everything about herself. When she flirts with him, he's obviously tempted, yet snaps, "Quit slumming!" Completely unsympathetic to Willi, Kovac says roughly, "Throw the Nazi overboard!" Later, after it's revealed that Willi speaks perfect English, and it's clear that he intends to deliver them into the hands of his countrymen, Kovac snarls, "I'd rather take my chance with the sharks!" In one of the lighter interactions between Bankhead's character and Hodiak's, she eyes the tattoos on his chest, which commemorate various romances, and asserts that she can't understand anyone "making a billboard of one's torso." Once she's counted five instances of body ink, Kovac retorts, "Remind me to show you the rest of them sometime."

Other noteworthy performances include that of William Bendix (1906–1964) as Gus, a decent blue-collar guy who fears that losing a leg will cost him the woman he loves, as she's a passionate fan of dancing. Canada Lee (1907–1952) gives dignity and gravitas to the sometimes stereotyped role of the steward who's initially addressed by Connie as "Charcoal." Walter Slezak (1902–1983) is suitably menacing as Willi, yet allows the audience to maintain uncertainty about him in the early scenes.

Columnist Harold Heffernan (September 2, 1943), visiting the set during production, watched as Bankhead and Hodiak rehearsed the scene in which his character makes a pointed reference to Connie's mink coat. Hitchcock paused and said, "Wouldn't John say 'fur coat' instead of 'mink coat'?" He expressed doubts that a man of Kovac's background would know mink when he saw it, to which his leading lady responded, "Of course he would. He goes to the movies, doesn't he?"

Lifeboat received three Academy Awards, including a Best Director statuette for Hitchcock, and became the film that truly put Hodiak on the map in Hollywood.

Reviews: "Alfred Hitchcock has worked his magic again to make 'Lifeboat' a masterpiece of sustained suspense that impresses with its power ... easily qualified for a place among Hitchcock's finest work.... The film is very much a series of character studies—and superb ones at that.... Hodiak [plays] vividly and effectively."—*Film Daily*, January 12, 1944

"A film of unusual quality and frequent dramatic intensity.... The reactions of the individuals to their situations and each other provide the successful and often gripping dramatic interest.... Two screen newcomers, John Hodiak and Mary Anderson, show themselves to be unusually attractive and talented performers."—*Motion Picture Herald*, January 15, 1944

Song of Russia (1944)

>Robert Taylor (*John Meredith*), Susan Peters (*Nadya Stepanova*), John Hodiak (*Boris Bulganov*), Robert Benchley (*Hank Higgins*), Felix Bressart (*Petrov*), Michael Chekhov (*Stepanov*), Darryl Hickman (*Peter*), Jacqueline White (*Anna*), Patricia Prest (*Stasha Bulganov*), Joan Lorring (*Sonia*), Vladimir Sokoloff (*Meschkov*), Leo Mostovoy (*Yanovitch*), Zoia Karabanova (*Natasha*), Konstantine Shayne (*Wounded Soldier*), John E. Wengraf (*Red Army Commissar*), Barbara Bulgakov (*Truck Driver*), Tamara Shayne (*Mme. Orlova*), Walter Lawrence (*Singer*), John Nesbitt (*Commentator*)
>
>*Director*: Gregory Ratoff. *Producer*: Joseph Pasternak. *Screenplay*: Paul Jarrico, Richard Collins. *Based on a Story by* Leo Mittler, Victor Trivas, Guy Endore. *Director of Photography*: Harry Stradling. *Music*: Peter Ilyich Tschaikowsky. *Adapted for the Screen by* Herbert Stothart. *Conductor*: Albert Coates. *Song*, "Russia Is Her Name": Jerome Kern, E.Y. Harburg. *Dance Direction*: David Lichine. *Recording Director*: Douglas Shearer. *Art Director*: Cedric Gibbons. *Associate*: Leonid Vasian. *Set Decorations*: Edwin B. Willis. *Associate*: Edward G. Boyle. *Special Effects*: Arnold Gillespie. *Costume Supervision*: Irene. *Men's Costumes*: Gile Steele. *Makeup*: Jack Dawn. *Montage Sequences*: John Hoffman, Peter Ballbusch. *Film Editor*: George Hively.
>
>MGM; released February 1944. B&W; 107 minutes.

Famed American composer John Meredith is making a concert tour throughout the Soviet Union, accompanied by his agent, Hank Higgins. Among the crowd greeting him when he arrives in Moscow is a young woman who tries in vain to capture his attention, saying it's important that she speak to him, but she isn't able to get close enough.

Later, after finishing rehearsal with the Russian orchestra, John hears a piano solo being played by the same young woman, Nadya Stepanova. He praises her talent, and agrees to meet with her. Nadya tells John that her hometown, Tschaikowskoye, has a fine music school, and implores him to appear at its annual festival. Charmed by the young woman, John puts off giving her an answer for the moment, escorting her to dinner. Learning that she knows little more about Moscow than he does, he arranges for them to take a tour of the city.

Ultimately John agrees to take part in the festival, which is several months away, but doesn't want to lose contact with Nadya in the meantime. He tells her he has fallen in love with her, and believes she reciprocates his feelings, but Nadya says a relationship between them is out of the question. Describing herself as "an ordinary Russian girl from a little village," she explains that she has duties on her family's farm, and responsibilities as a citizen. At John's next concert, he is pleased that she is observing the performance from a box, but when he finishes she has disappeared.

Back in Tschaikowskoye, Nadya returns to her daily life on the farm, until word is received that John Meredith will soon arrive at the train station, much earlier than expected. When she declines to be on the platform for his arrival, her father goes instead, and arranges for John to be their guest at the family farmhouse. He meets Nadya's sister Anna and brother-in-law Boris Bulganov, as well as a young student from the music school, Peter. Hank shows up, angry that John has abandoned his concert schedule to make this unplanned side trip. Though Nadya initially rebuffs John, he wins her over and they are married.

Talking over their future plans, John wants Nadya to accompany him back to America, where she can continue her piano studies while working with him as a soloist. At his next Russian concert, Nadya is struck with stage fright, but recovers to give a performance that her family and people around the country hear on the radio.

The summer of 1941 brings the Nazi invasion of Russia, throwing the people's lives into chaos, and making Nadya return where she is needed. Boris explains that the music festival has been canceled, and that the area surrounding Nadya's village is now under martial law. John and Tanya speak by telephone, but she is unable to break the news. After his final concert, John, the musicians, and the audience members are evacuated to a shelter.

In a radio address, Stalin warns the Russian people that they are in danger of being enslaved by Nazis, and must take steps to prevent their valuables from falling into German hands. The people of Nadya's village are told they should burn their crops rather than have them taken over by the Nazis. Boris and Nadya speak to them, and she urges them to wait as long as possible before destroying their food. Worried for his wife's safety, John has difficulty securing a travel pass as the war worsens. Hank manages to obtain the necessary papers for John through the musicians' union, but it is a difficult journey. He takes the last leg on foot, and is initially denied entrance to the territory, but finally gets through with the help of a sympathetic commandant, who understands that John is desperate to check on his wife because his own has just been killed.

John arrives in the village to find it devastated by fire and destruction, with Nadya's father among the dead. The crops are burned, and after a desperate search John and Nadya are reunited. "We'll make them pay in blood," Boris vows of the Nazis, but Peter, the young boy who idolized John, is shot and killed before their eyes. Boris urges John and Nadya to return to the United States, so that they can tell the world what is happening in his beloved country.

Released at a time when the U.S. and Russia were allies, *Song of Russia* treats the people of the Soviet Union as heroes, caught in a tragic situation. It had its origins in a request made by the Office of War Information that "the studios ... do something to celebrate the American alliance with Russia."[2] The name of Russian-born composer Pyotr Ilyich Tchaikovsky (1840–1893) is invoked frequently, with Nadya's village named in his honor. Several of his best-known pieces are heard in part, including his Fifth and Sixth Symphonies, his Piano Concerto #1 and, inevitably, *The Nutcracker*.

World War II serves as a backdrop for the seemingly doomed love story between John and Nadya. Robert Taylor (1911–1969) is effective as the famed composer, conducting orchestras with some degree of believability in several scenes. Within a few years, Taylor, one of Hollywood's strongest anti–Communist activists, would disavow the film, claiming he had made *Song of Russia* under duress from his studio bosses. The winsomely beautiful Susan Peters (1921–1952) was being given a star buildup by MGM, and contributes a sensitive performance as Nadya, conveying her character's sorrow and struggles with her expressive face and gestures. Sadly, her career would be cut short within a few years, after she was paralyzed in a hunting accident. She made one last film, and did some television work, before dying at the age of 31.

Little-seen in the film's first hour, John's role as guerrilla fighter Boris is inconsequential until its final reels when he gives a stirring curtain speech that sums up the film's message. He's donned aging makeup and sports gray hair, playing a character older than himself. Hodiak is billed above humorist Robert Benchley (1889–1945), who has a substantially larger role as Hank. Benchley died of cirrhosis of the liver one year after *Song of Russia*'s release.

Director Gregory Ratoff (1893–1960) was of Russian birth, and had become a successful character actor in Hollywood before transitioning to directing. MGM borrowed him from Columbia to give *Song of Russia* his knowledge of the country's culture, as well as his experience with musical films. He plays a minor role in the film as well.

A set on MGM's Lot Three, known to insiders as "Cloudy Street," stood in for the ill-fated town of Tschaikowskoye in *Song of Russia*. The scenes in which the village was bombed took their toll on the outdoor set, which was later used mostly in Westerns.

Reviews: "M-G-M's contribution to the fostering of a better understanding of the Russians is fundamentally a grand, appealing romantic film.... It should score handsomely with the customers; it is entertainment of the better kind.... Under Gregory Ratoff's capable direction the romance is neatly fused with more somber elements."—*Motion Picture Daily*, December 29, 1943

"Entertainment with the E underscored by the box office appeal of Robert Taylor and MGM's rising youngster, Susan Peters, in a thoroughly appealing love story, boosts this contribution to the understanding of Russia into the prime bracket of box office values.... Audiences are bound to take away new appreciation of an ally. But, as with 'Mrs. Miniver,' the war and messages never overshadow entertainment story values.... Gregory Ratoff's sure direction combines drama, background and appealing humanity."—*Motion Picture Herald*, January 1, 1944

Marriage Is a Private Affair (1944)

Lana Turner (*Theo Scofield West*), James Craig (*Capt. Miles Lancing*), John Hodiak (*Lt. Tom Cochrane West*), Frances Gifford (*Sissy Mortimer*), Hugh Marlowe (*Joseph I. Murdock*), Natalie Schafer (*Mrs. Selworth*), Keenan Wynn (*Maj. Bob Wilton*), Herbert Rudley (*Ted Mortimer*), Paul Cavanagh (*Mr. Selworth*), Morris Ankrum (*Elliott Scofield*), Jane Green (*Martha*), Tom Drake (*Bill Rice*), Shirley Patterson (*Mary Saunders*), Neal Dodd (*Minister*), Nana Bryant (*Nurse Jones*), Cecilia Callejo (*Señora Guizman*), Virginia Brissac (*Mrs. Courtland West*), Byron Foulger (*Ned Bolton*), Addison Richards (*Col. Ryder*), Cecil Weston (*Flora*), Jimmy Hawkins (*Tommy West, Jr.*), Ann Codee (*Madame Cushine*), Charles Coleman (*Selworth Butler*), Sam McDaniel (*Porter*), Arthur Space (*Drunken Man*), Fred Coby (*Roger Poole*), Alexander D'Arcy (*Mr. Garby*), George Meeker (*Jonesy*), Celia Travers (*Secretary*)

Director: Robert Z. Leonard. *Producer*: Pandro S. Berman. *Screenplay*: David Hertz, Lenore Coffee. *Based on the Novel by* Judith Kelly. *Director of Photography*: Ray June. *Musical Score*: Bronislau Kaper. *Recording Director*: Douglas Shearer. *Art Direction*: Cedric Gibbons, Hubert B. Hobson. *Set Decorations*: Edwin B. Willis. *Associate*: Richard Pefforle. *Costume Supervision*: Irene. *Associate*: Marion Herwood. *Makeup*: Jack Dawn. *Film Editor*: George White.

MGM; released August 23, 1944. B&W; 116 minutes.

On her wedding day, lovely Theo Scofield finds herself at the altar thinking, "How did I get into this, anyway?" She flashes back to the day when, while playing piano at the Officers' Club, Lt. Tom West of the Air Corps implored her to marry him after three days' acquaintance, before he's shipped overseas. Theo's mother, Irene Selworth, isn't in favor of the marriage, as Tom is not well-to-do or socially prominent. She suggests that her daughter marry Capt. Miles Lancing instead. Theo isn't impressed by her mother's advice, as Irene already has three broken marriages behind her.

Miles shows up to advise Theo that, while he likes Tom, a flyer, he wouldn't make her a suitable husband, and suggests she stay single until after the war. Instead, she impulsively accepts Tom's proposal. At the wedding, Theo gets reacquainted with her father, Ed Scofield, after a 15-year separation; he doesn't really approve of the way she's been brought up. Tom introduces her to his longtime friends Ted and Sissy Mortimer, explaining that he, they, and his best man Joe Murdock grew up together in Vermont.

On their first day as husband and wife, Tom is impressed to see that Theo can cook. She quickly realizes that they grew up very differently, and is afraid that Tom married her without really knowing her. She likes his family and his values, but isn't sure she can live up to them. Tom, who assures her they'll find common ground, receives a telegram notifying him that his father died. He's expecting to be called to active duty, but is instead notified to remain in his civilian post at the West Optical Works, where his expertise with lenses can be applied to the manufacture of range finders for military use. The plant is run by Joe Murdock, who has a drinking problem. Tom is angry to have his commission made inactive, and Theo fears that this development will bring about an everyday existence she isn't ready for. "I'll be a model wife, even if it kills me," she vows to Sissy as she undergoes her first year of married life in Boston.

To her mother's dismay, Theo is soon expecting. Tom is overjoyed, but Theo finds raising a baby stressful. When Miles passes through town, his life suddenly seems quite glamorous to the young wife, whose husband works long hours and can't spend as much time with her as she would like. Meeting Miles at the Officers' Club, Theo senses the sparks that still exist between them. Tom arrives on the scene, and is none too pleased to find his wife mingling with an old beau instead of celebrating her son's first birthday. The resulting spat sends Tom to sleep in the den.

Wanting advice from Sissy, Theo is shocked to learn that her married friend is having an affair with Joe Murdock. Disillusioned to think that happy marriage has eluded even her sensible friend, Theo moves toward reconciliation with her husband, but can't bring herself to tell Tom that his idealized friends, the Mortimers, aren't as securely married as he believes. Tom takes it upon himself to help Joe solve his problems, which include his estrangement from his other lady friend.

Feeling she's destined to follow in her mother's footsteps, Theo visits Miles at his apartment. She's ready to make a move, but he steels himself to resist her. Back at home, Theo is surprised to learn from Tom, who's just returned from Vermont, that Joe married his girlfriend Mary Saunders. An awkward meeting between Joe and his former mistress at the Wests' apartment leads to the revelation of Sissy's affair, and a breach between Tom and Theo. Sure that their marriage is unsalvageable, Theo soon finds herself destined for Reno. With her mother's fourth marriage in tatters, and Tom back in the military, Theo is challenged to consider whether her way of being wedded was any better than the example with which she grew up.

Based on Judith Kelly's 1941 novel of the same name, *Marriage Is a Private Affair* is a worthy drama of marital discord as caused by the coming together of two people quite different in backgrounds. Lana Turner (1921–1995) is well-cast as the spoiled, immature young Theo, of whom her beau Miles says, "You don't belong to anybody but yourself.... You're a selfish little brat who can't make up her mind, and torments everybody while she tries." While it's a fair statement, the character doesn't lose audience sympathy thanks to the actress' portrayal. Still, reviewer Kate Cameron

Not the happiest married couple on the block: Mr. and Mrs. West (John Hodiak, Lana Turner) in *Marriage Is a Private Affair* (1944).

felt she was miscast, and noted of a recent screening, "The story of the Wests is presented with a deadly seriousness by director Robert Leonard, but there was laughter in the house when there should have been sadness and tears."[3] The actress was pregnant with daughter Cheryl at the time of the shoot, which reportedly had to be delayed while five additional male roles were cast. Columnist Inga Arvad (November 25, 1943) reported prior to the start of filming that Miss Turner disliked the movie's title, making it "almost a cinch it will be changed before long," but this prediction proved false.

Hodiak plays a character to whom he could surely relate—a fundamentally decent man from modest beginnings, who tries to make a go of marriage to a woman from a more elevated background, and promises his fidelity "until forever freezes over." If Miss Turner's character Theo took her husband somewhat for granted, female moviegoers didn't, seeing an idealized, handsome, understanding mate who represented quite a catch at a time when many husbands and boyfriends were caught up in the war. However, he later told a British journalist that "he didn't enjoy the part ... because he doesn't feel he can ever play that social type of fellow with any conviction."[4]

Natalie Schafer (1900–1991), some twenty years before she landed on *Gilligan's Island*, exudes cool sophistication as Theo's mother, who says things like, "Darling, I'm perfectly willing to admit that first marriages should be romantic." Later, as she looks askance at her daughter's married life, she tells Theo, "That, my dear, is what you get for selling your birthright for a mess of canned tomatoes." Little seen in the film's first half, second-billed James Craig (1912–1985) plays the lesser role of Miles, who tells Theo he's "worked like a fool to get you out of my blood," and assesses her character more clearly than anyone else. Frances Gifford (1920–1994) plays an unfaithful wife here, as she will again in *The Arnelo Affair* (1947), with Hodiak cast as her lover. Keenan Wynn (1916–1986) turns up in the last act, portraying a soldier who becomes the reluctant go-between as Tom and Theo pledge their love for each other.

Marriage Is a Private Affair may look better in the 21st century than it did at the time of its release, when it likely didn't represent the type of film that Miss Turner's fans most wanted to see. Instead of using its running time to build up the love affair between two people, the film takes a somewhat realistic look at what happens after the wedding vows are pronounced, to a couple that married too hastily. Easy to dismiss as soap opera, it may wear out its welcome for some at nearly two hours' running time, but it has much to offer for viewers willing to give it a serious look.

Miss Turner and Hodiak reprised their roles when "Marriage Is a Private Affair" was adapted for radio's *Screen Guild Theater* in 1946.

Reviews: "*Marriage Is a Private Affair* dramatizes the first two years of marriage of a young couple, with the selfish and adulation-loving wife in constant state of confusion over the restrictions of wedlock. Basically, it's a timely tale, but displayed in overlong footage that incorporates minor incidents for many dull minutes, thus failing to balance several sparkling sequences.... Miss Turner capably carries the lead spot, getting sterling support from Hodiak, who—despite inadequacies of the script—should increase his audience popularity."—*Variety*, August 16, 1944

"So the picture ... finds one troubled union ending in a suicide, another that was deemed extraordinarily happy climaxing in the divorce courts, and a third—in which we are most interested ... reaching toward Reno.... Production handles the varied group of characters and their viewpoints very efficiently, and the direction by Robert Z. Leonard and performances are in a class of excellence. Miss Turner has much to convey of mood change, which she does with capability. The work of Hodiak is solid."—Edwin Schallert, *Los Angeles Times*, December 8, 1944

Maisie Goes to Reno (1944)

Ann Sothern (*Maisie Ravier*), John Hodiak (*Philip Francis "Flip" Hennahan*), Tom Drake (*Bill Fullerton*), Marta Linden (*Winifred Ashbourne*), Paul Cavanagh (*Roger Pelham*), Ava Gardner (*Gloria Fullerton*), Bernard Nedell (*J.E. Clave*), Roland Dupree (*Jerry*), Chick Chandler (*Tommy Cutter*), Bunny Waters (*Elaine*), Donald Meek (*Parsons*), Larry J. Blake (*Policeman*), Anthony Caruso (*George*), Byron Foulger (*Dr. Cummings*), Leon Tyler (*Boy*), Edward Earle (*Clerk*)

Director: Harry Beaumont. *Producer*: George Haight. *Screenplay*: Mary C. McCall, Jr. *Original Story*: Harry Ruby, James O'Hanlon. *Based Upon the Characters Created by* Wilson Collison. *Director of Photography*: Robert Planck. *Musical Score*: David Snell. *Song*, "Panhandle Pete": Sammy Fain, Ralph Freed. *Recording Director*: Douglas Shearer. *Art Direction*: Cedric Gibbons, Howard Campbell. *Set Decorations*: Edwin B. Willis. *Associate*: Helen Conway. *Costume Supervision*: Irene. *Film Editor*: Frank E. Hull.

MGM; released September 28, 1944. B&W; 90 minutes.

After 16 months working as a riveter, and volunteering at a war nursery, Maisie Ravier is exhausted, having developed a nervous tic that looks more like a wink. Her doctor prescribes a two-week vacation with plenty of rest. Running into her former boss, bandleader Tommy Cutter, he invites her to spend the vacation in Reno, singing at night with his band but otherwise relaxing. The only catch is that she has to find her own way there.

Lining up to buy her ticket, she's told the trains are sold out for three weeks. At the station, she is lucky enough to meet a woman who's cashing in her ticket, and buys it. Before she can depart, however, Maisie is approached by a soldier, Bill Fullerton, who pleads with her to let him have the ticket so he can reconcile with his wife, who's in Reno seeking a divorce. The well-to-do Mrs. Fullerton separated from Bill after he

Maisie (Ann Sothern) gets an eyeful of blackjack dealer "Flip" Hennahan (John Hodiak) in *Maisie Goes to Reno*.

enlisted, when she realized he'd known of her wealth before they were wed, but he insists to Maisie that he loves his wife. Softhearted Maisie hands over the ticket, but Fullerton is called back to active duty and has to settle for entrusting his new friend with a letter to deliver to his estranged wife.

At her Reno hotel, Maisie's inconvenient wink catches the eye of handsome blackjack dealer "Flip" Hennahan, who overhears her asking for Gloria Fullerton and offers her a ride to the ranch where she's awaiting her divorce decree. Maisie delivers the letter to a woman who claims to be Gloria Fullerton, and tells Miss Ravier that Sergeant Fullerton's letter is just asking her for money. Sorry she got involved, Maisie goes back to her hotel, and when Fullerton phones, tells him off.

In the hotel nightclub with Flip, Maisie learns that the woman posing as Gloria is her secretary, Winifred Ashbourne, but Gloria's crooked business manager, Roger Pelham, who's in cahoots with Winifred, prevents Maisie from getting to Gloria. Threatened with being fired by the hotel manager, Maisie is rescued by Flip, who promises to be responsible for her. Maisie accompanies Flip to his remote cabin, where they become better acquainted, though not as well as he'd like.

Back at the hotel, Maisie's inadvertent wink attracts the attention of J.E. Clave, the forger Roger employed to write fake letters from Bill to Gloria. Infiltrating his suite, Maisie plies him with liquor while she searches for evidence of the forgery, but her flirtation with Clave is misunderstood by not only Flip, but Jerry, the young bellboy who's infatuated with her. Roger and Winifred retrieve Maisie's evidence before she can square things with Flip, and her absence from the show floor costs her her job. Undaunted, she calls Bill and tells him to arrive as soon as possible. Desperate to prevent Gloria from appearing in court the next morning to finalize her divorce, Maisie enlists Jerry's help to kidnap her. As the hour of the court appearance approaches, Maisie is taken into custody by the police, Flip thinks she's in need of psychiatric attention, and only a last-minute miracle will set things right.

Maisie Goes to Reno was the eighth of ten films starring Ann Sothern as a brassy but lovable showgirl. A typical series entry offered some light comedy, at least one musical number by Miss Sothern, and a romance that rarely lasted beyond one film. The modestly budgeted B series was popular with 1940s audiences, and often gave an early starring role to a handsome MGM contract player like Hodiak. His typical male heartthrob role couldn't have been much of a challenge after *Lifeboat*, but he works well with his leading lady, and they make a sexy couple.

Though the screenwriters have crammed the story with incidents that keep everyone busy, this film, like most of the Maisie series, thrives primarily on Miss Sothern's personable charm, energy, and beauty. She performs a lively specialty number, "Panhandle Pete," and generates sparks with Hodiak as the cynical blackjack dealer who's smitten with her from the outset.

Maisie Goes to Reno contains multiple references to American life in wartime, with travel restrictions, gasoline shortages, and a hero who has to explain to Maisie why he's not in the military (as Hodiak wasn't). "You don't look exactly like a 4-F," she points out, before Flip tells her he was wounded and discharged. Although he asserts, "I never ran after a girl like this in my life," he's more than ready to get friendly on short acquaintance, but she's hesitant: Flip: "I'm a gambler, honey." Maisie: "Well, I like a safe bet, honey."

Still a starlet being groomed for better things, Ava Gardner (1922–1990) capably handles the undemanding part of Gloria. Roland Dupree (1925–2015), whose film career mostly comprised unbilled bit parts, has a couple of nice moments here as the lovesick bellboy who thinks Maisie is an undercover FBI agent. Like Hodiak, Marta Linden (1903–1990) was a veteran of *Swing Shift Maisie*, but gets more screen time here as Gloria's duplicitous secretary. Byron Foulger (1899–1970) is unbilled for his brief role as the slightly dotty psychiatrist Flip entrusts with treating Maisie's disorder.

Busy character actor Larry J. Blake (1914–1982) is seen as a policeman in the film. His son, industry makeup artist and film historian Michael F. Blake, recalled that his dad "liked Hodiak. Said he was a great guy who left us too soon."[5]

Reviews: "The latest offering in the Maisie series sustains the entertainment average of its predecessors and has 'something added' in the person of a new leading man, John Hodiak, who looks like a strong contender for the women's vote. As regular fare, there's Ann Sothern ... with a new batch of trouble, with more laughs than drama, but a satisfactory measure of each.... George Haight and Harry Beaumont, who produced and directed, keep the pace swift and the characters to the fore."—*Motion Picture Herald*, August 12, 1944

"Followers of the Maisie pictures should find this newest of the series to their liking, for it is quite amusing.... The story itself is far-fetched and even slightly silly in spots, but the pace is fast, it has some excitement, and the comedy situations are plentiful.... Ann Sothern gives her usual good performance."—*Harrison's Reports*, August 12, 1944

Sunday Dinner for a Soldier (1944)

Anne Baxter (*Tessa Osborne*), John Hodiak (*Sgt. Eric Moore*), Charles Winninger (*Dudley Osborne*), Anne Revere (*Agatha Butterfield*),

Connie Marshall (*Mary Osborne*), Chill Wills (*Mr. York*), Robert Bailey (*Kenneth Normand*), Bobby Driscoll (*Jeep Osborne*), Jane Darwell (*Helen Dobson*), Billy Cummings (*Michael Osborne*), Marietta Canty (*Samanthy*), Barbara Sears (*WAC Lieutenant*), Alice Fleming (*Neighbor*), Bernie Sell, Larry Thompson (*M.P.s*)

Director: Lloyd Bacon. *Producer*: Walter Morosco. *Screenplay*: Wanda Tuchock, Melvin Levy. *Based on a Story by* Martha Cheavens. *Music*: Alfred Newman. *Orchestral Arrangements*: Edward Powell. *Director of Photography*: Joe MacDonald. *Art Direction*: Lyle Wheeler, Russell Spencer. *Set Decorations*: Thomas Little. *Associate*: Fred J. Rode. *Film Editor*: J. Watson Webb. *Costumes*: Kay Nelson. *Makeup Artist*: Guy Pearce. *Special Photographic Effects*: Fred Sersen. *Sound*: Alfred Bruzlin, Harry M. Leonard.

20th Century–Fox; released December 8, 1944. B&W; 82 minutes.

Tessa Osborne is a young woman bearing a heavy load of responsibility, struggling to support her sister, brothers, and grandfather on a houseboat in Florida. She has a would-be suitor in Kenneth Normand, a well-to-do young man who asks her to marry him, but whom she doesn't love. She's uncertain whether marrying him would be the best thing for her impoverished family.

Like their neighbors, the Osbornes want to show their patriotism by hosting a soldier for a dinner at their home through the USO. Tessa frets about whether they can make their home presentable, and furnish enough food. Her grandfather, known to all as "Grandfeathers," thinks they should sacrifice the family's chicken to provide a decent meal, but she puts him off.

Unbeknownst to them, their neighbor Agatha Butterfield, who's sweet on Grandfeathers, tore up their application after a quarrel, and no soldier was invited to their dinner. Meanwhile, all the Osbornes chip in to earn money for the dinner, and they wind up with four chickens. Tessa is upset when Grandfeathers refuses to explain where he got his, and it develops that Mary's pet chicken, Miss Easter, is missing. Grandfeathers confides in Mary that he traded her chicken for one of the ones raised at the Butterfield Poultry Farm, but his pique prevents him from confiding in Tessa after the dressing-down she gives him.

As preparations are underway for the Osbornes' dinner guest, Tessa confides in her grandfather that she plans to accept Kenneth's marriage proposal, thinking it best for the stability of the family. Agatha learns of the Osbornes' efforts to provide dinner, and feels guilty for destroying their application to host a serviceman. She entreats Mrs. Dobson of the USO to find another, but she's unsuccessful in doing so. On Sunday, the children eagerly await their visitor on each passing bus, but the driver is finally forced to tell them there was a mix-up, and they will have no dinner guest.

Just then, Mary spots a soldier walking down the beach. The children descend on him so eagerly he doesn't have a chance to tell them he's not the man they were expecting. The Osbornes are excited to extend their hospitality to Sergeant Eric Moore, who's on his last day of furlough. The dinner they've planned is almost spoiled by Mary's grief over her pet, until Agatha and her maid Samanthy return Miss Easter alive and well.

After dinner, Eric and Tessa get better acquainted as they wash dishes, his comments making it clear that he hasn't had the happy home life that the Osbornes have. Later, the family goes into town, where Eric and the Osbornes have a photo taken together, just before an Army truck pulls up, summoning all soldiers for immediate return to duty. Before flying out, Eric arranges to have his allotment assigned to the Osbornes in his absence. As his bomber passes over their riverboat, they see the wings flap, and Tessa wishes him a safe journey home to them.

Unabashedly sentimental, *Sunday Dinner for a Soldier* is a charming piece of Americana, a time capsule of the efforts by everyday people on the

Sgt. Eric Moore (John Hodiak) is made to feel right at home by Tessa Osborne (Anne Baxter) and family in *Sunday Dinner for a Soldier*.

home front to support the military and the war effort. Though there is no seasonal aspect to the story, its initial release during the Christmas season was appropriate for its tone and content.

John makes his first appearance nearly an hour into *Sunday Dinner for a Soldier*, playing one of his most sympathetic and endearing characters. Columnist Robbin Coons (December 28, 1944) commented that John "has the kind of 'entrance' actors dream about. For considerably more than half the picture, others are talking about him and little else." Coons added, "After the long build-up, many an actor would disappoint when he actually appeared. Hodiak has the strength and honesty to fill the bill." One viewer on whom he made an impression was his daughter, Katrina, who recalled that, upon seeing her dad's first entrance, "My jaw dropped. Man, he was good-looking."

The film marks his second time at the Fox studio, following his chores with Hitchcock. His wide grin is put to good use here, playing a character quite different than what movie audiences had seen earlier that year in *Lifeboat*. Though the screenplay doesn't give his character a great deal of depth, Hodiak's performance gives sincerity to his statement, "You don't know what a difference it makes, having someone to say goodbye to. I wouldn't trade one second of today for all the other times I've had in my life."

Anne Baxter (1923–1985) gives charm, strength, vulnerability, and radiant beauty to the role of Tessa. John and Miss Baxter have only a short amount of time in which to depict the growing attraction between Tessa and Eric, but convey it nonetheless, the two actors' own emotions doubtless helping to animate their performances.

Charles Winninger (1884–1969) has a good showcase here as the maddening, irresponsible, yet lovable Grandfeathers. Two fine character actresses, Anne Revere (1903–1990) and Jane Darwell (1879–1967), are seen in supporting roles, adding to the film's charm. A screen newcomer, child actress Connie Marshall (1933–2001), registers strongly as Mary. She and Miss Baxter share a lovely scene in which Tessa talks about death in a way that her young sister can accept.

The underrated, always-busy Lloyd Bacon (1889–1955) made a number of memorable films, in various genres, over the course of a directorial career that dated back to the silent era. Among his best-known efforts are *42nd Street* (1933) and *Marked Woman* (1937). A versatile filmmaker able to handle multiple genres with skill and taste, he's well-suited to telling the kind of story that *Sunday Dinner for a Soldier* offers. John remembered his flair for colorful outfits. "Bacon," he said, "loves wild ties, brilliantly colored shirts, anything loud and gay. He can get away with them. We used to lay bets on the set as to what he'd wear next, and he got a great kick out of being kidded. I like that, but I'm a sober-hued bird myself."[6]

Variety (October 13, 1943) reported that early plans were for Lewis Seiler to direct the film, with Monty Woolley and Mary Anderson in lead roles. First announced as leading man was young Fox contract player William Eythe. However, just before shooting was due to begin in the summer of 1944, the trade journal (June 28, 1944) informed its readers that Eythe had been assigned to another project, and John Hodiak would be borrowed from MGM to take his place. Bobby Driscoll and Billy Cummings had previously been directed by Bacon in *The Fighting Sullivans*. According to columnist Louella O. Parsons (April 29, 1944), Jennifer Jones had "been in and out of 'Sunday Dinner for a Soldier,' like a jack-in-the-box, [but] is now definitely out," with Miss Baxter finally chosen to play Tessa.

The company traveled to Sarasota, Florida, for some location shooting, which was hampered by an unexpected lack of sunshine. Later, they returned to the studio, where a set reported to cost $50,000 had to replicate the beach environment where they'd shot on location. Robbin Coons (July 28, 1944) reported that some of the seaside scenes were shot with "California sand carted from the Pacific beach to the studio stage," which was also found to include "some good old California sand fleas that had to be spray-gunned to quell an epidemic of red welts on thespian epidermises." At least the studio version of the sunny beach was air-conditioned.

In the *Motion Picture Herald*'s "What the Picture Did for Me" column (September 8, 1945), a small-town California exhibitor called *Sunday Dinner* "a picture that is right down the alley for any man's theatre. It clicks all the way. John Hodiak and Anne Baxter are tops and the audience voted it a dandy picture. Good business the first night and better the second."

Reviews: "A very appealing comedy-drama.... The story, though simple, has been told in a heart-warming manner.... All the players perform very well. The romantic interest is pleasing. It is the sort of picture that leaves one with a pleasant feeling, for all the characters are sympathetic."—*Harrison's Reports*, December 9, 1944

"Where the taste leans to the sentimental 'Sunday Dinner for a Soldier' ought to prove good film fare ... plays an extremely human tune on the heart strings, creating a sense of warmth.... The film has been well acted."—*Film Daily*, December 8, 1944

A Bell for Adano (1945)

Gene Tierney (*Tina Tomasino*), John Hodiak (*Maj. Victor Joppolo*), William Bendix (*Sgt. Borth*), Glenn Langan (*Lt. Crofts Livingstone*), Richard Conte (*Nicolo*), Stanley Prager (*Sgt. Trampani*), Henry [Harry] Morgan (*Capt. Purvis*), Montague Banks (*Giuseppe*), Reed Hadley (*Commander

Robertson), Roy Roberts (*Col. Middleton*), Hugo Haas (*Father Pensovecchio*), Marcel Dalio (*Zito*), Fortunio Bononova (*Gargano*), Henry Armetta (*Errante*), Roman Bohnen (*Erba*), Luis Alberni (*Cacopardo*), Edwardo [Eduardo] Ciannelli (*Mayor Nasta*), William Edmunds (*Tomasino*), Yvonne Vautraut (*Francesca*), John Russell (*Capt. Anderson*), Minor Watson (*Gen. McKay*), Grady Sutton (*Edward*), Anna Demetrio (*Rosa*), James Rennie (*Lt. Col. Sartorius*), Peter Cusanelli (*Craxi*), Mimi Aguglia (*Rosa Tomasino*), Minerva Urecal (*Italian Woman*), Harry Carter (*Non-Com*), Eva Puig (*Woman*), Earl Easton (*Boy Violinist*), Frank Lackteen (*Photographer*), Charles Judels (*Afronti*), Frank Jaquet (*Basile*), Ed Munday (*Emancipated Man*), Charles La Torre (*Mercurio Salvatore*), Nino Pipitone, Jr. (*Boy*), Eddie Hyans (*Military Policeman*), John Bagni (*Priest*)

Director: Henry King. *Producers*: Louis D. Lighton, Lamar Trotti. *Screenplay*: Lamar Trotti, Norman Reilly Raine. *Based on the Novel by* John Hersey. *Director of Photography*: Joseph La Shelle. *Music*: Alfred Newman. *Orchestral Arrangements*: Edward Powell. *Art Direction*: Lyle Wheeler, Mark-Lee Kirk. *Set Decorations*: Thomas Little. *Associate*: Frank E. Hughes. *Film Editor*: Barbara McLean. *Costumes*: Yvonne Wood. *Makeup Artist*: Ben Nye. *Special Photographic Effects*: Fred Sersen. *Sound*: W.D. Flick, Roger Heman. *Technical Advisers*: Capt. Morton L. Seligman, Col Wilson C. Williams, Maj. John L. Porter, Jr.

20th Century–Fox; released June 21, 1945. B&W; 143 minutes.

Major Victor Joppolo, accompanied by Sgt. Borth, both of the U.S. Army, arrives in the small Italian village of Adano near the end of World War II, to serve as an American military governor. The town has sustained heavy damages during the war, and the people who remain are hungry and frightened. Zito, who admits he was formerly a fascist, offers the military men his help, while bemoaning the loss of the town's church bell, which he says was taken by Mussolini's forces.

Giuseppe, an American living in the village, tells Joppolo that food is the local people's greatest need. But his neighbors insist the loss of their bell is even more important, because of what it symbolized to the townspeople. According to the local priest, Father Pensovecchio, the bell was the center of life in Adano, and a source of inspiration. Major Joppolo assures the priest that the incoming Americans want only to help the town in its time of need, but explains that they will need the villagers' cooperation to meet them halfway. Pensovecchio promises to lend his support, provided the major agrees to attend a mass at which he will speak about the Americans' presence. The priest urges his followers to support the Americans' taking charge, and to follow their proclamations aimed at restoring law and order.

A young blonde woman sitting in the same pew as Joppolo attracts Joppolo's notice. Giuseppe identifies her as Tina Tomasino, daughter of a local fisherman, but the major denies being personally interested in her.

Joppolo institutes inquiries into the whereabouts of the church bell, and meanwhile tackles other concerns of daily life in the village. The townspeople are favorably impressed when Joppolo tells local officials they must forego favoritism, and wait their turn in bread lines. At the dock, the major introduces himself to the elder Tomasino as the new town administrator, urging him and the other fishermen to go back to work so that the people can be properly fed. His plan is threatened by interference from Lt. Livingstone of the Navy, but Joppolo ultimately wins their cooperation. Joppolo comes to the rescue of Nasta, the town's mayor, when he comes under attack by his angry constituents, but refuses to support the corrupt politician's reinstatement in office, putting him to work in a lowly capacity instead.

Tina visits the major on her father's behalf, and invites him to their home for dinner. In response to her request, he agrees to look into the whereabouts of Italian prisoners of war from Adano. Joppolo learns that the church bell has been melted down, but will seek a replacement. He receives orders that the main streets of the town are to be reserved for American military use, but the townspeople protest the edict. After hearing the concerns of the citizens, Joppolo countermands the order issued by Colonel Middleton, and allows the local men to continue traversing the roadway with their carts. Cynical Captain Purvis of the military police refuses to lend his support to defying a general's orders, and insists that a report be sent, but Sgt. Borth manages to mislay it.

At the Tomasinos' home, Joppolo dances with Tina, and they get better acquainted. She's surprised to hear him refer to his mother-in-law, and he confirms that he has a wife back at home. The son of Italian immigrants, he understands the way of life in Adano, but believes his parents are happy to have escaped its poverty by relocating to America. Tina, who senses Joppolo's loneliness, tells him she dyed her hair blonde as an expression of individuality, saying, "I know what it is to be restless." He admits she reminds him of his wife.

Tina asks when Italian prisoners of war might be allowed to return to Adano, and tells Joppolo she does not know what became of her fiancé Giorgio, who went off to defend Italy in the war. Shortly afterwards, the women of Adano are overjoyed when their fighting men come home, but Giorgio is not among them. His friend Nicolo has the difficult task of telling Tina that Giorgio died at the hands of a drunken mob of Italian soldiers rebelling against Mussolini.

When Joppolo is unable to obtain a bell for the town through Army channels, he appeals to his Navy colleague Livingstone, who succeeds in getting one delivered to Adano. Meanwhile, despite his pal's best efforts, the report concerning cart traffic finally reaches an infuriated Col. Middleton. Back in Adano, as the townspeople joyfully celebrate the arrival of their new bell, Joppolo is soon to learn that he has been charged with insubordination, and relieved of his duties in Adano.

Episodic in its storytelling, the film version of *A Bell for Adano* was adapted from the novel of the same name by John Hersey, whose credit goes above the title here. Hersey (1914–1993) won the Pulitzer Prize for his book, a first novel, after its 1944 publication. A wartime correspondent whose work often appeared in *Time* magazine, Hersey based the novel on his experiences in Licata, where he observed the clash that arose between the American military governor and General George S. Patton, Jr. Unable to put into his reporting the resentment he felt over Patton's heavy-handed oversight in Europe, the writer turned out a work of fiction instead, completing the novel in only three weeks. The screenplay depicts an Army colonel whose decisions negatively affect the people of a small Italian town, but spends more of its running time depicting the daily lives of the working-class Sicilians who populate it, Hersey's theme of flawed American military intervention somewhat downplayed.

Hodiak is unquestionably playing the lead role in *A Bell for Adano* as Victor Joppolo, an Italian-American son of immigrants who, before the war, was leading a blue-collar existence in the Bronx. As Hersey's text describes Joppolo, "His face was round and his cheeks seemed cheerful but his eyes were intense and serious. He was about thirty-five."[7] No other actor is onscreen as much as he is, and John is quietly effective as a man who presents a stern exterior, but understands his role is to meet the people's needs. He has no patience for graft, or favoritism, and is accepted by the Italian people as a fair and honest leader.

Trying to explain the American way of life to Tina, he responds to her inquiry about the Bronx by telling her about his parents, saying, "They came from a little town over here.... In Italy, they were very poor.... In America, my father has a good job.... My mother has a washing machine, they have an automobile, enough to eat. Yes, to them, I think [the Bronx] is very beautiful." As for himself, he admits, "I always wanted a little more than we had." John admitted the role hit close to home for him. "I was born of foreign parents, just as Major Joppolo was, and I had worked at unimportant jobs before getting the chance to do the thing I most wanted to. Like him, too, I had inherited a deep sympathy for the unfortunate people left in the wake of the armies that marched across Europe."[8]

Before the role of Joppolo was awarded to Hodiak, other actors, including Gary Cooper, Gregory Peck, and Brian Aherne, were said to be under consideration, while Hedda Hopper (July 10, 1944) made a pitch in her widely syndicated column for casting studio contract player Lloyd Nolan. A few weeks later, her rival Louella O. Parsons (August 18, 1944) announced that Fredric March would take the starring role in a Broadway adaptation. The production, which co-starred Mexican-American actress Margo as Tina, opened in December, and ran for nearly a year, closing in late October 1945.

By the end of the month, Parsons was able to report that Fox executives had secured a deal to borrow John Hodiak for the film adaptation. For Hodiak, the assignment meant a return to the studio where his career had received such a substantial boost with *Lifeboat*. "I think 20th has

Looks like love for Major Victor Joppolo (John Hodiak) and Tina Tomasino (Gene Tierney) in this promotional shot with the stars of *A Bell for Adano*.

something there," she wrote (August 31, 1944). "He'll be good." The gig would reunite him with his *Lifeboat* co-star William Bendix, cast as his loyal second-in-command.

Gene Tierney, having enjoyed great popularity the previous year as the title character in *Laura,* gets top billing for her secondary role as Tina. She's been decked out in a blonde wig that isn't flattering to her, and struggles to deliver a convincing Italian accent. Of her performance, critic Eleanor Wilson noted, "Tina was not a very important or strong character in the novel, and Miss Tierney has done nothing to make her worthy of more notice in the picture."[9] The actress later recalled that she chided director Henry King, normally "one of the gentlest of people," for his "rudeness" to other actors, to which he responded, "I'm sorry I've been so tough today. But I've just learned that my son is missing in action."[10]

Hodiak found King a supportive and helpful director. "Realizing I was an emotional guy—not exactly the kind of intense, tough soldier Joppolo was supposed to be—[he] took me in hand and smoothed over rough spots where I'd be likely to mess up scenes. That's the kind of encouragement I've been getting."[11]

Among the supporting players are Harry Morgan (1915–2011), long before he became the kindly Col. Potter of TV's *M*A*S*H,* here playing quite a different Army man, one who's coolly cynical but rulebound nonetheless. Richard Conte (1910–1975) has one strong scene here as Nicolo, the military man obliged to break the news to Tina about what happened to her fiancé; he will enjoy more screen time when he and Hodiak are reunited for *Somewhere in the Night.*

A reporter was on set the day a tumultuous scene with Miss Tierney went into multiple takes: "Today, John Hodiak tumbled downstairs five times trying to remember not to break his neck and to keep an expression of fury, embarrassment, and awkwardness on his face. And that's a lot of emotion to register when thumping your hide ka-plunk o each step."[12] The need to see his facial expressions made it impossible to turn the rough-and-tumble scene over to a stuntman, so John did the honors himself, with a studio nurse on standby in case of injury. The relationship between Joppolo and Tina is unusual in that they take notice of each other romantically, but each is emotionally involved with someone else who's not currently on the scene. There's a bit of closeness and familiarity that develops between the two, and one quick kiss, but Joppolo respects his marriage vows despite his current loneliness.

Lamar Trotti (1900–1952), who penned the screenplay with Norman Reilly Raine, was a longtime Fox employee who wrote dozens of scripts for the studio, winning a Best Original Screenplay Academy Award for his film *Wilson* (1944). He incorporates a good deal of Hersey's story, dialogue and characterization in adapting *A Bell for Adano*. In addition to the Broadway adaptation, *A Bell for Adano* was also the basis for the September 12, 1948, episode of radio's *Theatre Guild on the Air*, for which Robert Montgomery assumed the role of Joppolo.

Reviews: "Despite its episodic quality and a few draggy sequences, [*A Bell for Adano*] remains an absorbing human-interest drama, as well as a meaningful document concerning the problems that face the civil affairs officers of the Allied Military Government.... Unlike most war pictures, which have become outdated owing to the Allied victory in Europe, this one, because of its subject matter, is timely.... John Hodiak, as the Major, is militarily proper but warm and sincere."—*Harrison's Reports*, June 23, 1945

"It gives a reviewer cause for sincere regret that he cannot give *A Bell for Adano* unqualified approval, for there is so much that is superlative in its presentation. But, unfortunately, there is also a great deal of footage that slows the pace, almost bringing it to a dead stop at times.... A more liberal use of the shears would have tightened *Adano* into an outstanding boxoffice attraction, as well as an artistic triumph.... John Hodiak does excellent work as Major Joppolo.... Gene Tierney, in a blonde wig, is adequate as Tina."—*Film Bulletin*, July 9, 1945

The Harvey Girls (1946)

Judy Garland (*Susan Bradley*), John Hodiak (*Ned Trent*), Ray Bolger (*Chris Maule*), Angela Lansbury (*Em*), Preston Foster (*Judge Sam Purvis*), Virginia O'Brien (*Alma*), Kenny Baker (*Terry O'Halloran*), Marjorie Main (*Sonora Cassidy*), Chill Wills (*H.H. Hartsey*), Selena Royle (*Miss Bliss*), Cyd Charisse (*Deborah*), Ruth Brady (*Ethel*), Jack Lambert (*Marty Peters*), Edward Earle (*Jed Adams*), Morris Ankrum (*Rev. Claggett*), Wm. "Bill" Phillips (*1st Cowboy*), Ben Carter (*John Henry*), Norman Leavitt (*2nd Cowboy*), Horace [Stephen] McNally (*"Goldust" McClean*), Catherine McLeod (*Louise*), William Hall (*Big Joe*), Vernon Dent (*Engineer*), Virginia Hunter (*Jane*), Paul Newlan (*Station Agent*), Ray Teal (*Conductor*), Frank Austin, Al Kunde (*Ranchers*), Jane Allen, Jean Ashton, Eleanor Bayley, Joan Carey, Lucille Casey, Ruth Clark, Virginia Davis, Meredyth Durrell, Mary Jane French, Virginia Gumm, Daphne Moore, Loulie Jean Norman, Shirley Patterson, Dorothy Raye, Joan Thorsen, Dorothy Tuttle, Jacqueline White (*Harvey Girls*), Hazel Brooks, Georgia Davis, Gwen Donovan, Virginia Engels, Kay English, Jane Hale, Jane Hall, Thelma Joel, Peggy Maley, Edith Motridge, Erin Selwyn, Elinor Troy, Dorothy Van Nuys, Tyra Vaughn, Bunny Waters, Eve Whitney, Herberta Williams, Dallas Worth, Katherine Yorke (*Alhambra Girls*)

Director: George Sidney. *Producer*: Arthur Freed. *Associate Producer*: Roger Edens. *Screenplay*: Edmund Beloin, Nathaniel Curtis, Harry Crane, James O'Hanlon, Samson Raphaelson. *Additional Dialogue*: Kay Van Riper. *Based on the Book by* Samuel Hopkins Adams. *Original Story*: Eleanore Griffin, William Rankin. *Words and Music*: Johnny Mercer, Harry Warren. *Musical Direction*: Lennie Hayton. *Orchestration*: Conrad Salinger. *Vocal Arrangements*: Kay Thompson. *Musical Numbers Staging*: Robert Alton. *Director of Photography*: George Folsey. *Technicolor Color Director*: Natalie Kalmus. *Associate*: Henri Jaffa. *Film Editor*: Albert Akst. *Recording Director*: Douglas Shearer. *Art Direction*: Cedric Gibbons, William Ferrari. *Set Decorations*: Edwin B. Willis. *Associate*: Mildred Griffiths. *Special Effects*: Warren Newcombe. *Costume Supervision*: Irene. *Costume Designer*: Helen Rose. *Men's Costumes*: Valles. *Makeup*: Jack Dawn.

MGM; released January 18, 1946. Color; 102 minutes.

In the late 19th century, young Susan Bradley travels by train from Ohio to the Old West town of Sandrock, where she will meet for the first time the husband-to-be she found through a correspondence program. Many of her fellow passengers are women on their way to the same town to staff a newly opening restaurant, the Harvey House.

Susan meets her fiancé and is taken aback that not only is he homely, and old enough to be her father, but readily confesses that the many letters they exchanged were not actually written by him. H.H. Hartsey quickly senses he and Susan are not right for each other, and lets her off the hook. The actual author of the letters is Hartsey's pal Ned Trent, the handsome proprietor of the town's bar, the Alhambra Saloon. He is intrigued with Susan when they meet, much to the annoyance of his tart-tongued barmaid Em, but she upbraids him.

Adrift, Susan joins the staff of the Harvey House, which Ned's friends and employees warn him will cut into the Alhambra's business, though he's skeptical. While Ned is not involved, the ladies of the Harvey House are unnerved by the rough-and-tumble town and its residents, and an unexpected gunshot in their quarters prompts a few of them to head back home. When Ned orders a meal at the newly opened Harvey House, and requests a steak, Susan learns that all of their meat has vanished. Feeling certain she knows what happened, she arms herself with two pistols and goes over to the Alhambra, where she manages to retrieve it in time to serve Ned the entrée that's not only rare, as he requested, but raw.

Having learned that Ned likes to spend time alone out in the open country, Susan follows him there one day, and they get better acquainted, leading to a kiss. He comes to the rescue when one of the Harvey waitresses is terrified by a rattlesnake, quickly dispatching it. Still, neither of them will acknowledge their mutual attraction, and she continues to be uncertain if he is involved in the tribulations the Harvey girls are facing.

Opposing the Harvey establishment is Ned's silent business partner, Judge Sam Purvis. After a dance at the Harvey House brings the townspeople together, Purvis decides desperate measures are called for. Before long, the Harvey House is set ablaze, and Ned dives into the conflagration to help. Afterwards, the Alhambra becomes the temporary home of the Harvey House, and Ned tells Susan he and his business are relocating to another city. Susan watches him go, with Em triumphantly in tow, but there's a twist yet to come.

John made a strong leading man for Judy Garland in *The Harvey Girls* (MGM, 1946).

The Harvey Girls is an entertaining musical that provides plenty of splash, color, dance, and song. As an opening card notes, "When Fred Harvey pushed his chain of restaurants farther and farther West along the lengthening tracks of the Santa Fe, he brought with him one of the first civilizing forces this land had known—the Harvey Girls. These winsome waitresses conquered the West as surely as the Davy Crocketts and the Kit Carsons—not with powder horn and rifle, but with a beefsteak and a cup of coffee." The first Harvey Houses opened in 1876.

MGM had disclosed plans to make the film as early as 1941, but it wasn't until late 1944 that studio publicists announced that production would get underway soon; it began in early 1945. According to author Holly Van Leuven, top-billed Judy Garland "delayed production considerably by showing up on set late, or, some days, not showing up at all."[13]

Columnist Bob Thomas (June 2, 1945), visiting the screening room with Miss Garland during production noted that she found rushes helpful. "It helps to keep in character," she explained. "Sometimes, too, I might be doing a closeup in which I say, 'John Hodiak, you're a dirty rat,' when in reality John Hodiak is miles away from MGM. It's hard to remember what you're trying to do without rushes." Her companion described what he saw after the clapper: "Hodiak is gazing abstractedly at the sky and Judy is rubbing her nose. Then a voice says 'action' and they go into an emotional love scene. After a minute or two of dialogue, a voice says, 'cut.' Judy and Hodiak break their embrace and stand with bored expressions until the screen is blank again."

Billed below the title, John offers a strong portrayal of Ned Trent, a self-sufficient and charming man who is soon taken with Susan. On the heels of finishing *A Bell for Adano*, John reported to the set of *The Harvey Girls* in February 1945. If his musical contribution to *The Harvey Girls* is slight, it's partly because his duet with Miss Garland, "My Intuition," was cut from the finished film, though it appears as an extra on the DVD. It originally was destined to come at the end of the scene in which Ned and Susan meet up in the desert. According to columnist Erskine Johnson (February 24, 1945), John's period look as a Western hero featured a wig so long he joked, "It's a wonder more of 'em weren't shot for buffalos."

Seen as Susan's fellow waitresses and friends are Virginia O'Brien (1919–2001), as unlucky-in-love Alma, and a young Cyd Charisse (1922–2008) as good-hearted Deborah. Enjoyable supporting performances are given by Angela Lansbury (1925–2022), as Susan's tough rival Em, Marjorie Main (1890–1975) as a den mother to the Harvey waitresses, and Chill Wills (1902–1978) as Susan's erstwhile spouse. Many years later, Miss Lansbury confessed to having had "a great crush" on Hodiak, though off-camera she was an inexperienced young woman quite unlike the brassy Em. "I really was a homebody," she said, "and I was afraid to go out."[14]

Though prominently billed, Judy's *Wizard of Oz* co-star Ray Bolger (1904–1987), gets relatively little screen time here as a love interest for Miss O'Brien, a newly appointed blacksmith who's afraid of horses. Early announcements had Ann Sothern announced as a cast member, but she didn't appear.

The real-life Harvey Girls were not too impressed with MGM screenwriters' version of their story. The hard work they did was downplayed, while as one noted, "And then there wasn't all that much singing and dancing!"[15] As author Don Tyler points out in his book *The Great Movie Musicals*, it suffers from having only one truly top-notch song. "It is one of the top musicals of the Forties," he writes of *The Harvey Girls*; "it is a very good musical film, but it needs more than one outstanding song to be great."[16] Indeed, the lavish production number "On the Atchison, Topeka and the Santa Fe," showcasing Johnny Mercer and Harry Warren's song, is a standout, which nothing else in the film quite lives up to. Still, it remains understandably a favorite film for many Garland fans, as well as demonstrating Hodiak's skill at essaying leading man roles.

Reviews: "Make way for *The Harvey Girls*. In the manner of latter-day M.G.M. musicals it is probably due for big-time popularity.... This production is one of clichés. However, it has atmosphere, a good old western accent, and most inviting natural scenery shown to advantage in Technicolor.... Miss Garland puts over the songs with sentiment and sincerity. Hodiak does a good-bad hero effectively. Miss Lansbury is pictorial, if pouting."—Edwin Schallert, *Los Angeles Times*, January 19, 1946

"It doesn't sound like much, but it's plenty, for this is a musical and story weight is not important. What is important are songs, comedy, striking photographic composition, in attractive Technicolor, and above all the intelligence of the production and directorial auspices.... Thus there is an engaging air about 'The Harvey Girls' which is delightful and charming.... There is Hodiak, the square-shouldered one who turns out to be square." —*Motion Picture Daily*, January 2, 1946

Somewhere in the Night (1946)

John Hodiak (*George W. Taylor*), Nancy Guild (*Christy Smith*), Lloyd Nolan (*Lt. Donald Kendall*), Richard Conte (*Mel Phillips*), Josephine Hutchinson (*Elizabeth Conroy*), Fritz Kortner (*Anzelmo*), Margo Woode (*Phyllis*), Sheldon Leonard (*Sam*), Lou Nova (*Hubert*), Houseley Stevenson (*Michael Conroy*), John Russell (*Marine Captain*), Philip Van Zandt (*Navy Doctor*), Charles Marsh (*Hotel Clerk*), John Kellogg (*Hospital Attendant*), Charles Arnt (*Man with Glasses*), Jack Davis (*Dr. Grant*), Louis Mason (*Brother William*), Maynard Holmes (*Stenographer*), Mary Currier (*Nurse Jones*), Clancy Cooper (*Tom*), Paula Reid, Polly Rose (*Nurses*)

Director: Joseph L. Mankiewicz. *Producer*: Anderson Lawler. *Screenplay*: Howard Dimsdale, Joseph L. Mankiewicz. *Adaptation*: Lee Strasberg. *Story*: Marvin Borowsky. *Director of Photography*: Norbert Brodine. *Art Direction*: James Baseri, Maurice Ransford. *Set Decorations*: Thomas Little. *Associate*: Ernest Lansing. *Editorial Supervision*: James B. Clark. *Costumes*: Kay Nelson. *Music*: David Buttolph. *Musical Direction*: Emil Newman. *Orchestral Arrangements*: Arthur Morton. *Makeup Artist*: Ben Nye. *Special Photographic Effects*: Fred Sersen. *Sound*: Eugene Grossman, Harry M. Leonard.

20th Century–Fox; released May 30, 1946. B&W; 110 minutes.

A wounded Marine awakens in a Navy hospital in Hawaii bandaged and with his jaw wired, after being injured by a grenade. Aside from his physical ailments, he's suffering from amnesia, though he learns that his name is apparently George Taylor. His only clue to his past is an unsigned letter from someone who wrote, "I despise you." He recuperates at Camp Pendleton in California, but does not confide in anyone that he has lost his memory. Discharged, he's told that his previous civilian address was the Martin Hotel in Los Angeles, but the clerk there has no record of him.

Booking a room, he uses a claim check that was in his sea bag to retrieve a briefcase from Union Station. It contains a gun and a letter to George Taylor from Larry Cravat, telling him $5000 has been deposited for his use in a nearby bank. He visits the bank, but leaves abruptly when they try to question him. The letter was written on the notepaper of the Elite Baths; the attendant there denies knowing Cravat, but refers Taylor to a nightclub down the street called The Cellar. He inquires there about Cravat, getting no information but attracting the attention of two men. Giving

Somewhere in the Night (1946): Christy Smith (Nancy Guild) may be one of the only people amnesiac George Taylor (John Hodiak) can trust.

them the slip, he finds his way into the dressing room of a singer, Christy. On her table is a photo and a note from "Mary," saying she will soon be marrying Larry Cravat. He pockets the note.

He makes it safely back to his hotel, where a woman, Phyllis, chats him up, arousing his suspicions. A telephone call from the bartender at the Cellar brings him back to the club, where an older man, Mr. Anzelmo, asks him for a talk in his car. When Taylor resists, he's forced into the man's car and warned to stop asking about Larry Cravat. Bruised and battered, Taylor is dumped at Christy's front door, since he was carrying the note with her address. Desperate to confide in someone, he tells her he wants to know about Mary and Cravat. She explains that Mary was her friend, who was stood up by Cravat on her wedding day and then run down in the street.

Christy invites Mel Phillips, owner of the Cellar and other nightclubs, to meet with George. Mel is also interested in locating Cravat, and suggests they enlist the help of his friend, police Lt. Donald Kendall. Though initially hesitant, George agrees.

Over lunch, Lt. Kendall explains that Cravat was a private investigator who dropped out of sight about three years ago, along with $2 million in Nazi money. Though George was introduced to the policeman under a false name, Lt. Kendall clearly knows about the ex–Marine's recent activities. When they leave the restaurant, a note addressed to George has been affixed to Christy's car, giving a San Pedro address for Larry Cravat.

At the San Pedro location, George finds not Larry but a brute, Sam, and Phyllis, the woman he met in the hotel corridor. Sam denies any knowledge of Larry, but Phyllis suggests he seek a fortuneteller at the Terminal Dock. There, George sees a signboard for "Dr. Oracle's Crystal Ball," but the doctor in question turns out to be Anzelmo. Sizing each other up, the two men exchange a little information. Anzelmo tells him Cravat is wanted in connection with a murder that took place on the dock three years ago, and says he can produce him for a financial consideration. He believes George was present at the murder scene.

Back at the Cellar, Mel urges Christy to steer clear of George, who may bring trouble into her life, but she admits she's falling for him. She tells him George has gone to track down a possible witness to the murder, Michael Conroy. Conroy's daughter, Elizabeth, tells George that her father was hit by a car, and has been confined to a sanatorium for the past three years.

Refused admittance to see Conroy, who he's told is insane, George breaks into the sanatorium, and finds the witness dying of a stab wound. Conroy tells him the suitcase with two million dollars was hidden at the dock. George goes back to Chris' apartment, where Lt. Kendall shows up looking for him. Kendall gives him two hours to turn himself in at police headquarters. George and Chris locate the suitcase, with the money intact, but another discovery has him suddenly believing that he has discovered his true identity at last. After entrusting the suitcase to a mission worker to deliver to Lt. Kendall, they are accosted by Anzelmo's strong-arm man, Hubert. He takes them back to the fortuneteller's lair, where a final confrontation leads to at least two surprising discoveries for the man Christy loves, and doubts as to who they can trust.

Originally titled "The Lonely Journey," *Somewhere in the Night* is a well-made *film noir* with a longish running time and a plot convoluted enough for two movies. Given the centrality of George Taylor to the film's narrative, the responsibility for engaging viewers largely rests with John Hodiak, and he's more than equal to the task, playing a man who says wearily, "I live running away." Though he's wary and on his guard much of the time, Hodiak arouses audience sympathy for his character's plight, alone in the world and in danger. He tells Christy that he considered merely starting life over because of his amnesia, "but you can't just throw away ... how many years of living?" Hodiak's expressive face conveys the emotion as George realizes at that instant, "I don't even know."

The film introduces audiences to a new leading lady, actress Nancy Guild (1925–1999) as Christy, who calls herself "the girl with the cauliflower heart," but admits on short acquaintance with George, "I'm nuts about the guy." She's effective as the woman whose faith in him gives the hero the strength to go on even when things are at their darkest. Columnist Sheilah Graham (February 11, 1946) reported that Hodiak went to bat for his leading lady when, "after the first two weeks of shooting there was a powwow on whether to put Nancy in a different type of picture." John advised, "Just tell her what to do and she'll be okay." Although Fox promoted her heavily as an up-and-coming star, her career had peaked by the end of the decade.

Columnist Virginia MacPherson (January 22, 1946) reported that Miss Guild received her first screen kiss from Hodiak, "whom she's had a crush on ever since she saw *Lifeboat*." The young actress admitted to nerves. Hodiak "asked her if she'd ever kissed a boy goodnight." She acknowledged that she had, saying, "He just kissed me. And I just let him." Her leading man grinned and said, "Well, that's all you do here. Only you might try to cooperate just a little." Another scribe, Bob Thomas (December 6, 1945) noted that John was suffering from a cold during the early stages of production, but came to work regardless, "to preserve his record of never having missed a day's work."

Lloyd Nolan (1902–1985) enters the film at around the halfway point to deliver a solid character performance as Lt. Kendall. Handed a lot of exposition to deliver in his opening scene, he uses Dimsdale and Mankiewicz's sharp dialogue to characterize the savvy cop who describes Larry Cravat as a private eye who "investigated husbands that played golf in the rain, and wives that didn't come back from the public library till midnight." Later, there's a bit of a Fox in-joke when the dedicated cop gets all the answers to the mystery, and cracks, "It'll make better reading than *Forever Amber*." Hodiak and Nolan will be re-teamed in *Two Smart People*, released only a few weeks later. Boxer Lou Nova (1913–1991) has a small featured role as hired muscle Hubert, who's mostly the strong silent type. When he makes his lengthiest speech of the film, Hodiak's character remarks, "Whaddya know? He said three whole sentences!"

This is a strong early directorial credit for Mankiewicz, who'd first gained attention as a screenwriter. He would go on to win Academy Awards two years in a row for his subsequent films as director and screenwriter, *A Letter to Three Wives* (1949) and *All about Eve* (1950).

Film historian William K. Everson wrote, "Too long by about 20 minutes, [*Somewhere in the Night*] is still a model of its kind: literate, witty, evocative of its period, well knit in its plotting, and with a fascinating array of characters.... It ranks with *Murder, My Sweet* as the best and most representative of the 'film noire' [sic] thrillers of the forties."[17]

Reviews: "Zingy melodrama, tightly-knit, earmarked for excellent b.o. [box office] returns. It's a good example of thoughtful coordination of production, direction, writing and playing into gripping meller entertainment for all.... Hodiak delivers a strong performance in the lead role, making every scene count and giving [his] character plenty of punch."
—*Variety*, May 8, 1946

"The picture is an intriguing one, notwithstanding it relies on that all too familiar loss-of-memory device.... Probabilities are strained.... You'll have to accept some situations and developments in the feature at their face value, and nothing much besides.... John Hodiak ... and others help to give considerable verity to events, the burden being especially on the Hodiak shoulders. He does a very commendable dead-pan job." Edwin Schallert—*Los Angeles Times*, June 1, 1946

Two Smart People (1946)

Lucille Ball (*Ricki Woodner*), John Hodiak (*Ace Connors*), Lloyd Nolan (*Bob Simms*), Hugo Haas (*Senor Rodriguez*), Lenore Ulric (*Senora Maria Ynez*), Elisha Cook, Jr. (*Fly Feletti*), Lloyd Corrigan (*Dwight Chandwick*), Vladimir Sokoloff (*Jacques Dufour*), David Cota (*Jose*), Clarence Muse (*Porter*), Helen Dickson (*Woman Passenger*), Gabriel Canzona (*Monkey Man*)

Director: Jules Dassin. *Producer*: Ralph Wheelwright. *Screenplay*: Ethel Hill, Leslie Charteris. *Story*: Ralph Wheelwright, Allan Kenward. *Director of Photography*: Karl Freund. *Film Editor*: Chester W. Schaeffer. *Musical Score*: George Bassman. *Song*, "Dangerous" (Peligrosa): Ralph Blane, George Bassman. *Recording Director*: Douglas Shearer. *Art Direction*: Cedric Gibbons, Wade Rubottom. *Set Decorations*: Edwin B. Willis, Keogh Gleason. *Costume Supervision*: Irene. *Men's Costumes*: Valles. *Hair Designs*: Sydney Guilaroff. *Makeup*: Jack Dawn.

MGM; released June 4, 1946. B&W; 93 minutes.

At a Los Angeles hotel, charming con man Ace Connors is about to make a deal with gullible Dwight Chandwick for an investment in "eight miles of the most beautiful swamps you ever saw, with millions of gallons of oil just begging to be taken out." At the last moment, Chandwick bails out when the other guest at his table, beautiful Ricki Woodner, convinces him that it's too risky. As it happens, Ricki has a deal of her own for Chandwick, pitching a series of paintings supposedly "smuggled in from Europe." Ace tags along to her room, and queers Ricki's pitch just as she did his, smiling all the while.

Heading back to his room, Ace soon has company. First, slimy Fly Feletti shows up to demand the money he claims he's owed from their joint venture in government bonds. When Ace refuses to pay him, Fly pulls a gun, but is persuaded to go away quietly when New York policeman Bob Simms appears. Simms intends to arrest Ace for a con involving $500,000 in government bonds, but is disappointed when Ace informs him he is accepting a plea deal that will earn him a five-year prison stretch without returning the money. Reluctantly, Simms accepts Ace's offer to accompany him on the trip east, where he's agreed to turn himself in five days hence. In the meantime, says Ace, they'll have "a whirl I can remember for five long years." Simms suspects that the fugitive con man has the bonds in his possession, and in fact Ace has hidden them in a cookbook he's carrying.

Just as their train is due to depart, Ricki appears as a last-minute passenger. Simms offers her his compartment, which will allow him to stay with Ace and keep a close watch on him. Ricki suggests to Ace that they join forces, saying, "Two minds that work as much alike as ours belong together. Instead of outsmarting each other, we should combine our talents." They agree it's strictly a business deal, but it's sealed with a lingering kiss.

When Ricki catches Simms in the act of searching Ace's luggage, he identifies himself as a policeman, and warns her that her new acquaintance is "one of the biggest operators we've ever been after," and on his way to serve a prison sentence. He recognizes that Ricki is attracted to Ace, and warns her, "He's an awfully easy guy to fall for."

(Left-right) Lloyd Nolan, Lucille Ball, and John Hodiak make an odd threesome in *Two Smart People* (1946).

Ace invites Ricki to stay at the romantic Inn of the Four Winds in El Paso, but when they arrive, with Simms still in tow, the latter is angry to realize he's been tricked into crossing the border into Mexico. He threatens to take Ace into custody immediately, but the charming swindler points out that having to have him extradited from outside the U.S. will prove embarrassing and might cost Simms his pension.

The romantic hotel, where Ace is welcomed as an old friend, is the perfect setting for the burgeoning love between Ace and Ricki, but he's dubious that, given their circumstances, they can plan for the future. Back in her room, she's confronted by Fly Feletti, who refuses her earnest plea to leave her and Ace alone. He demands that she help him obtain his share of the bonds, which he tells her Ace does have with him, on threat of seeing her imprisoned for a crime she committed.

After Simms shows that he can have Ace found guilty of a crime in Mexico, the swindler heads for Mardi Gras in New Orleans, with the policeman as well as Ricki in tow. Amid the noise and crowds of the carnival, Ace and Ricki don traditional costumes and succeed in giving Simms the slip. Ricki suggests they depart for South America by ship while they have the opportunity, but Ace tells her he intends to turn over the bonds to Simms. Also on hand in the crowded Mardi Gras atmosphere is Fly Feletti; as the day of celebration nears midnight, Ace and the others will question where their loyalties stand, and what hope they can hold for the future.

Early announcements of the film, as casting and pre-production got underway in the fall of 1945, referred to it by the title "Time for Two." Under the direction of Jules Dassin (1911–2008), what ultimately became known as *Two Smart People* falls short of top-notch entertainment, but remains highly watchable throughout, with a pace that keeps the story moving and some good performances. Billed by MGM as "the glamorous story of crooks in love," the film's handsome look is enhanced by the skillful cinematography of the great Karl Freund (1890–1969), who ably captures Lucille Ball's beauty. An Academy Award winner for *The Good Earth* (1937), Freund would be credited with perfecting the three-camera technique used to shoot Lucy's groundbreaking television series.

Miss Ball (1911–1989) could surely find comedy in the role of a fast-talking swindler, but the script here gives her little chance to be funny. Perhaps the harshest critical reaction accorded *Two Smart People* came from Lucy herself. Looking back some two decades later, from her secure perch as a top-rated sitcom star, she dismissed the film as "a real dog."[18] Lloyd Nolan is briskly competent and matter-of-fact as the policeman who may have more of an edge on Ace than the latter anticipates.

John is well-cast as a suave, sophisticated man who is effortlessly charming, but always on the watch, saying, "I've trusted my life to no one but myself." He's well-paired with Lucy, and demonstrates that he can play a character who may be of uncertain origin, but moves convincingly in a sophisticated venue. Strikingly handsome in his Mardi Gras garb as a pirate, he shows himself well able to handle the action sequences as well as the romantic interludes, and engages the audience sympathy as he finds himself at a turning point in his life.

Leslie Charteris (1907–1993), co-author of the screenplay, is well-equipped to write about charming rogues, having already given the world his famous fictional character of thieving Simon Templar, known as the Saint. Columnist Hedda Hopper (December 1, 1945), who visited the set, wrote, "After watching Lucille Ball and John Hodiak lend their various talents to scenes for 'Time for Two,' I don't have to go to New Orleans to the Mardi Gras. I saw it at Metro."

Reviews: "A smartly contrived and amusing, if completely unbelievable, comedy-melodrama ... will depend on its marquee names to insure fair-plus business.... There are some exciting sequences to satisfy the action fans.... Lucille Ball ... and John Hodiak, as the smooth-talking, devil-may-care swindler, do their utmost to make these roles convincing, and Lloyd Nolan is excellent as the easy-going detective."—Leyendecker, *Film Bulletin*, June 10, 1946

"Romantic melodrama with elements that will capture the favor of men and women equally. In Lucille Ball and John Hodiak the film has a combination that will do plenty of good at the box office.... The film has a casual quality and an easy-going air that make it pleasant to take.... Jules Dassin, who directed well, obtained capable performances from his players."—*Film Daily*, June 6, 1940

The Arnelo Affair (1947)

John Hodiak (*Tony Arnelo*), George Murphy (*Ted Parkson*), Frances Gifford (*Anne Parkson*), Dean Stockwell (*Ricky Parkson*), Eve Arden (*Vivian Delwyn*), Warner Anderson (*Det. Sam Leonard*), Lowell Gilmore (*Dr. Avery Border*), Michael Branden [Archie Twitchell] (*Roger Alison*), Ruth Brady (*Dorothy Alison*), Ruby Dandridge (*Maybelle*), Joan Woodbury (*Claire Lorrison*), Lillian Bronson (*Secretary*), Griff Barnett (*Mr. Adams*), Thaddeus Jones (*Mr. Porterville*)

Director/Screenplay: Arch Oboler. *Producer*: Jerry Bressler. *Story*: Jane Burr. *Director of Photography*: Charles Salerno. *Film Editor*: Harry Komer. *Musical Score*: George Bassman. *Recording Director*: Douglas Shearer. *Art Direction*: Cedric Gibbons, Wade Rubottom. *Set Decorations*: Edwin B. Willis. *Associate*: Thomas Theuerkauf. *Costume Supervision*: Irene. *Makeup*: Jack Dawn.

MGM; released February 13, 1947. B&W; 86 minutes.

Anne Parkson is embroiled in a murder case, thanks to her association with Tony Arnelo. His lady friend Claire Lorrison has been shot and killed, and he blames his infatuation with Anne for having caused him to lose his temper. Anne threatens to go to the police, but Tony points out that there's more at stake for her. She might be able to demonstrate her innocence, but, as he says coolly, "Can you prove that you weren't with me, Mrs. Parkson?"

Flashbacks reveal that, after nearly twelve years of marriage, Anne was settled into a stagnant relationship with a lawyer, Ted Parkson, who pays more attention to his work than his wife. Though she has a cute nine-year-old son, Ricky, and a comfortable middle-class life, Anne is dangerously restless when Ted introduces her to a client, nightclub owner Tony Arnelo. Arnelo is immediately attracted to Anne's beauty, and begins pursuing her, with a request that she use her interior decoration skills to spruce up his home.

Anne tries unsuccessfully to resist the urge to visit Tony, but she's inexorably drawn to him. She enjoys his company, and soon he presents her with a key to his place. Knowing she's teetering on a dangerous precipice, Anne asks Ted to take her away, but he refuses, citing his work. On her next visit to Tony's apartment, she's startled by the arrival of Claire, an actress who's clearly another of his conquests. Claire warns her about the dangers of getting involved with Tony, who appears just in time to hear, and give her face a harsh slap.

After running out on Tony, Anne is shocked the next morning when a newspaper headline reveals that Claire has been murdered. One of the police's few clues is the discovery of a compact that bears Anne's initial. Tony keeps trying to reach her, but Anne refuses to take his calls. Finally agreeing to meet with him, Anne pleads to be left alone, but Tony tells her she belongs to him. When she bolts from his car, he finds a half-written note she'd begun, which will prove incriminating should he share it with the police.

On their wedding anniversary, Ted reassures Anne of his love, but makes the mistake of taking her to Arnelo's for a surprise celebration with friends, including her chic neighbor Vivian. Inside, Tony joins the party, as does Detective Sam Leonard of Homicide, to whom the nightclub owner denies any close acquaintance with the late Miss Lorrison. Anne faints, and spends much of the next day in bed, where Vivian senses she's having trouble with a man, but doesn't get the whole story. Tony calls again, this time to warn Anne to expect a visit from the police, and to be careful of what she tells him. Anne's guilty demeanor doesn't escape Detective Leonard's notice, but she denies any connection with the murder.

Ted is horrified to discover that his wife not only has a key to Arnelo's apartment, but that her compact is the state's key piece of evidence in the murder case. Anne pleads with Tony to relinquish his hold on her, but he's insistent that she belongs to him. Though unsure of the state of his marriage, especially after confronting Tony, Ted's efforts to save Anne kick into high gear as the noose seems to be closing around her neck.

John, top-billed, is well-cast as the corrupt but compelling Tony Arnelo, credible as a man who's ruthlessly single-minded in taking advantage of a woman's vulnerability, and charming enough to make her response credible. "I like what's beautiful," he says simply, clearly the motive behind his pursuit of a married woman. He gives a slightly ironic reading every time he addresses Anne as "Mrs. Parkson," underscoring the fact that she's unable to resist his attentions despite her wedding ring. He arrogantly tells the policeman he's "too good to stick to your design for what you call living—punching a time clock, watching the nickels, tipping my hat to the boss, 'Yes, sir,' 'No, sir,' 'Thanks for the gold watch, but I'm too old to hear it tick.'" It's a strong performance as one of his least sympathetic screen characters.

According to columnist Dorothy Manners (June 13, 1946), John had originally balked at playing such an irredeemable character. "Two months ago," she reported, "Hodiak went on suspension at MGM for supposedly refusing to play a racketeer. Either the reason for this suspension was a mistake in the first place—or John decided that a bad boy can be a good role. Besides, when a fellow marries is no time to be off salary."

George Murphy (1902–1992) is quietly effective as Anne's husband, dull enough to make understandable her growing restlessness, but solidly reliable when push comes to shove. Likewise Warner Anderson (1911–1976), who makes a believable police investigator, unglamorous but dogged in his pursuit of a killer. The beauty of Frances Gifford is more noticeable than her acting prowess, though her task isn't helped by the melodramatic voiceovers she's asked to perform in the first half of the film.

Eve Arden (1908–1990) always perks up any drama in which she's assigned a supporting role, and she has some good dialogue here as Anne's chic, worldly pal Vivian, who notices Tony's obvious interest in her friend and terms him "the man with the four-alarm eyes." She has a strong scene in the final reel wherein she gives Ted a new perspective on how marriage plays out for women. Joan Woodbury (1915–1989), highly experienced with B movies on Poverty Row and elsewhere, makes the most of her single scene as the ill-fated Claire. Dean Stockwell (1936–2021) is an impressive child actor who can play "cute" scenes without letting them get sticky, and Ruby Dandridge (1900–1987) contributes warmth and humor to the role of the Parksons' housekeeper.

Production began in the summer of 1946, with Hodiak clocking back in at MGM after his honeymoon. Producer/screenwriter Arch Oboler (1909–1987) was a highly successful radio writer/producer best known for his contributions to the suspense drama *Lights Out*. He puts his radio experience to work with *The Arnelo Affair*, with some aspects more successful than others.

The film underwent some trimming prior to general release, with footage of actor Frank Wilcox apparently among that which landed on the cutting room floor. A reader wrote in to *Photoplay* (June 1948) to complain that "the previews were better than the picture. There were three or four scenes that weren't even in the movie."

Reviews: "'The Arnelo Affair' is a gripping melodrama almost certain to please theatre-goers generally…. It has excitement, suspense, humor, pace, crisp dialogue, superior photography and first-rate performances…. The film's themes—extra-marital dalliance and circumstantial evidence—offer limitless exploitation angles."—*Film Bulletin*, February 17, 1947

"This is Mr. Arnelo, dear!" A meeting that was to pay off in heartbreak, scandal, the brink of tragedy.

This lobby card for *The Arnelo Affair* (MGM, 1947) shows the uneasy triangle that develops with Anne Parkson (Frances Gifford, right) and the two men in her life: unscrupulous Tony Arnelo (John Hodiak, left) and her husband Ted (George Murphy).

"Arch Oboler, radio's master of suspense, has effectively transposed his technique into the visual medium with 'The Arnelo Affair.' Wisely, too, he's combined some of the best of both radio and film methods to build a mood of sustained tension in what may become one of this season's sleepers.... Hodiak smartly underplays the nitery op's vicious nature concealed by a genteel gloss."—*Variety*, February 12, 1947

Desert Fury (1947)

John Hodiak (*Eddie Bendix*), Lizabeth Scott (*Paula Haller*), Burt Lancaster (*Tom Hanson*), Wendell Corey (*Johnny Ryan*), Mary Astor (*Fritzie Haller*), Kristine Miller (*Claire Lindquist*), William Harrigan (*Judge Berle Lindquist*), James Flavin (*Sheriff Pat Johnson*), Jane Novak (Mrs. *Lindquist*), Anna Camargo (*Rosa*), Ralph Peters (*Pete*), Tom Schamp (*Dan*), Milton Kibbee (*Mike*), Ray Teal (*Bus Driver*), Lew Harvey (*Doorman*), John Farrell (*Drunk in Jail*)

Director: Lewis Allen. *Producer*: Hal B. Wallis. *Screenplay*: Robert Rossen, from the novel by Ramona Stewart. *Directors of Photography*: Charles Lang, Edward Cronjager. *Technicolor Color Director*: Natalie Kalmus. *Associate*: Francis Cugat. *Music Score*: Miklos Rozsa. *Art Direction*: Perry Ferguson. *Special Photographic Effects*: Gordon Jennings. *Process Photography*: Farciot Edouart. *Set Decoration*: Sam Comer. *Costumes*: Edith Head. *Editor*: Warren Low. *Makeup Supervision*: Wally Westmore. *Sound Recording*: Harry Lindgren, Walter Oberst.

Paramount; released August 15, 1947. Color; 96 minutes.

Gambler Eddie Bendix and his cohort Johnny Ryan are on their way to the desert town of Chuckawalla, near Reno. Just outside town, Eddie demands that they stop the car at the bridge where his late wife Angela died. Their car is blocking the bridge when beautiful young Paula Haller passes by. Johnny moves the car, but not before Eddie and Paula take a good look at each other.

Paula's mother, Fritzie, is the proprietor of the Purple Sage in Chuckawalla, where a brisk business in gambling is done. Paula is snubbed by the more socially proper residents of the town, because of her mother's background and dubious livelihood. Fritzie is upset to hear that her 19-year-old daughter has dropped out of yet another school where she didn't fit in. Nor is she pleased to hear that Eddie Bendix, with whom Fritzie has a history, is back in town.

Paula wants to stay in town and work at the bar with her mother, but Fritzie is opposed. Tom Hanson, a young sheriff's deputy, is a former rodeo rider forced to retire due to injury. He's in love with Paula, and would like to settle down with her on a ranch, but she's uncertain what she wants. Eddie, meanwhile, has taken a lease on a nearby ranch, and intends to stay for a while, which isn't regarded as good news by some of the townspeople.

Fritzie isn't pleased when Paula and Eddie chat each other up at one of her dice tables. She calls in Tom, admits she had him investigated by a detective agency, and offers him financing for his ranch if he marries Paula. Despite his feelings for Paula, he doesn't want Fritzie arranging their lives, and knows Paula would also resent this. He tells Paula of the deal Fritzie offered, causing her to pack her bags and run out on her mother, though she later returns.

At the bridge outside town, Paula meets Eddie, and tells him she'd like to get better acquainted. She offers him a ride home to his ranch, where Johnny discourages her from hanging around. Eddie admits his cohort is probably right, that he wouldn't be good for Paula. Still, when she comes back the next day, it's obvious both are attracted. He admits that he knew both her late father and Fritzie back East, when they were bootlegging. When he tries to give her advice, she rebels at being bossed around, and tells him off.

In town, Tom warns Paula to stay away from Eddie. He tells her that, as a sheriff's deputy, he saw the body of Eddie's late wife after her car crash, and Paula resembles her strongly. She seems to be heeding his counsel, but when the gambler pulls up in his car, and offers an apology for his earlier behavior, she readily jumps in.

At Eddie's ranch, he and Paula get along famously, though he has a flare of anger when she brings up his first wife. He tells her he's been associated with Johnny since he was almost as young as she. Paula realizes that she and Johnny are in a competition to see who will control the destiny of the man she loves. Johnny urges Eddie to leave Chuckawalla, but he tells him he's decided to stay.

The romance of Eddie and Paula faces opposite from all sides, including Fritzie, who tells her daughter she will have him arrested if she continues to see him. After a run-in with Johnny, Eddie shows up at Fritzie's

Johnny Ryan (Wendell Corey, background) is none too pleased to find his cohort Eddie Bendix (John Hodiak, center) appreciating the charms of lovely Paula Haller (Lizabeth Scott) in *Desert Fury*.

house, asking Paula to go away with him and get married. Although Fritzie warns her against trusting him, Paula agrees. On their way out of town, they pick up Johnny. During a stop at a roadside café, Paula finally begins to understand Eddie's true nature. But he's unwilling to let her slip away, and a violent confrontation ensues.

Desert Fury is an entertaining melodrama that looks good, but has a somewhat trashy, pulpy tone to its characters and situations. Despite the lavish color photography, it's often described as a Western with *film noir* elements. *Desert Fury* was a mostly faithful adaptation of Ramona Stewart's 1945 novel "Desert Town." The screenplay makes some changes from the book, raising Paula's age from seventeen to nineteen, and altering Eddie's last name from Benedict to Bendix. Someone should have suggested changing the name of the town, Chuckawalla, where it's set, and saving that name for a later comedy. Some of the novel's elements wouldn't have passed movie censorship standards of the 1940s, such as Fritzie (spelled "Fritzi" in the text) owning brothels as well as gambling facilities, and her denunciation of her daughter as "a slut."

Though the film tries to come across as gritty, there's a nagging unreality about it, and viewers are unlikely to forget they're watching a movie, albeit a fairly sexy and entertaining one. Though the actors don't camp it up, it isn't hard to imagine them sharing a chuckle between takes over some of the overheated dialogue and situations. Some viewers may have been led by the title to expect something other than what the film ultimately delivers.

John, borrowed from MGM by Paramount for the role of Eddie, is top-billed onscreen but newspaper ads gave the edge to Miss Scott. Producer Hal Wallis reportedly secured Hodiak's services by granting MGM the rights to an unspecified story. Eddie, John's character, is not unlike the one he'd just played in *The Arnelo Affair,* a man women shouldn't want, but do. He's clearly attracted to Paula, but tries to warn her off: "I'm not the kind of guy for you. You'll get your brains knocked out, kid. You're gonna wish you'd never seen me." The attraction between Hodiak's character and Miss Scott's is presented as largely physical, and she seems to appreciate his bare chest at least as much as Tallulah Bankhead did in *Lifeboat* (though he's lacking tattoos this time around). According to a studio publicity item, "Hodiak bet $5 he could slip a few real dollar bills into phoney money used in gambling scenes … and they would go unnoticed. He won the bet."[19]

During the shoot, Lancaster told set visitor Hedda Hopper (September 9, 1946), "What a part Hodiak's got! He plays a heavy without one redeeming feature." Still, for much of the running time, we don't see Eddie do anything particularly nefarious, and it's mostly left to the actor to suggest a degree of menace that will justify later story twists. Physically, Hodiak doesn't resemble the character as described in Miss Stewart's book, who has "a shock of white hair."[20]

As much as anything, *Desert Fury*'s raison-d'être seems to be as a showcase for the up-and-coming players who were protégés of producer Wallis, including Burt Lancaster and Lizabeth Scott. Lancaster was still in the early stages of his film career, and is credible in the less exciting role of Tom, the good guy Paula is slow to appreciate, though it's somewhat anticlimactic in the wake of his debut in *The Killers* (1946). Tom thinks Paula is in over her head, and warns her, "When you tangle with someone like Bendix, you don't just pick up your jacks afterwards and go home." As his career progresses, Lancaster will have ample opportunity to doff his shirt onscreen, and project a tougher image, but here he's fairly milquetoast alongside Hodiak.

Though her talent comes across clearly, Lizabeth Scott (1921–2015) is too mature both in looks and demeanor for the part of a teenager just growing into womanhood, and doesn't convince as a naïve youngster who needs to be protected from bad influences. She does have star quality, however, and she's costumed and photographed beautifully. As Eddie tells Paula, "You're a strange combination. You can recognize an automatic clip, and you play house like you meant it." She's more effective playing the stronger side Paula inherited from her mother, plain-spoken enough to say to Eddie about Johnny, "If you love me, get rid of him." This is the first film for Wendell Corey (1914–1968), given "introducing" billing in the opening titles. Corey is competent as Johnny, Eddie's longtime mentor, but the two actors are almost exactly the same age, and look it, which undermines his believability as an older, hardened tough guy.

Mary Astor (1906–1987) occasionally seems to be pushing a bit too hard in the role of Paula's hard-boiled mother Fritzie, stabbing the air with her many cigarettes as she emphatically declaims her lines. In her memoir, Miss Astor who was going through a frustrating patch in her career, admitted, "Fritzie was good for my nerves. I could use all my accumulated bitterness and bad temper and do a little exploding." She praised the "strong, good actors," including Hodiak, who served as her "opponents" in her scenes.[21]

Director Lewis Allen later remarked of *Desert Fury* that John "considered it one of the best roles of his career, because it gave him an opportunity for a forceful and interesting characterization. The gambler had a ruthless and hard-boiled front, but inside he was a weak and cowardly person."[22] On the set, however, columnist Jimmie Fidler (November 11, 1946) reported that Allen was dissatisfied with John's performance in the first few takes of a love scene with Miss Scott, complaining, "You tighten up the minute the cameras start turning.... No girl would consider love-making, the way you're doing it, convincing!" A quick rebuttal to Allen's comments came not from the star himself, but by his wife, paying an unannounced set visit, who said, "He made love to me that way in a picture, and I married him!"

Reviews: "Handsome production values, good Technicolor photography, and star names should assure this melodrama of pretty good grosses, but as entertainment it is only fair and, at that, unpleasant.... Not only are the characters unreal, but the reasons for their actions are so indefinite that the spectator becomes befuddled as the story moves from one ugly situation to another."—*Harrison's Reports*, August 2, 1947

"Excellently produced and directed, with a cast whose top names are known in most situations, Desert Fury is a dramatic offering that will attract considerable attention.... The entire production is a credit to Hal Wallis, who again proves he understands what the public wants by his choice of subject-matter and his well-chosen cast. John Hodiak is exceptionally good in the leading role of a crooked gambler and Lizabeth Scott is capable and attractive as the girl who falls for him."—*Showmen's Trade Review*, August 2, 1947

Love from a Stranger (1947)

John Hodiak (*Manuel Cortez*), Sylvia Sidney (*Cecily Harrington*), Ann Richards (*Mavis Wilson*), John Howard (*Nigel Lawrence*), Isobel Elsom (*Auntie Loo-Loo*), Ernest Cossart (*Billings*), Philip Tonge (*Dr. Horace Gribble*), Anita Sharp-Bolster (*Ethel*), Frederic Worlock (*Insp. Hobday*), Billy Bevan (*Taxi Driver*), Colin Campbell (*Bank Teller*), Charles Coleman (*Hotel Doorman*), Eddie Dunn (*New York Detective*), Eugene Eberle (*Bellboy*)

Director: Richard Whorf. *Producer*: James J. Geller. *Screenplay*: Philip MacDonald. *From a Play by* Frank Vosper. *Based on a Story by* Agatha Christie. *Music*: Hans J. Salter. *Orchestrations*: Emil Cadkin. *Musical Director*: Irving Friedman. *Director of Photography*: Tony Gaudio. *Editorial Supervisor*: Alfred de Gaetano. *Film Editor*: Fred Allen. *Art Director*: Perry Smith. *Set Decorations*: Armor Marlowe. *Photographic Effects*: George J. Teague. *Special Art Effects*: Jack R. Rabin. *Assistant Director*: Emmett Emerson. *Costume Designer*: Michael Woulfe. *Makeup*: Ern Westmore, Del Armstrong. *Hair Styling*: Eunice, Helene King. *Sound Director*: J.N.A. Hawkins. *Special Sound Supervision*: Leon Becker. *Sound Mixer*: Percy Townsend.

Eagle-Lion; released November 15, 1947. B&W; 81 minutes.

Cecily Harrington is a young woman of modest means whose life is about to change drastically, as she just won 50,000 pounds in the Irish Sweepstakes. Planning to travel with her friend and roommate Mavis Wilson, Cecily lists their flat for rent. At the agent's office, she bumps into handsome, charming Manuel Cortez, who later turns up at her apartment, as a prospective tenant. He charms the inexperienced young woman into a dinner date, then over the next few days their relationship progresses more rapidly than a woman of her era is supposed to permit.

Though Cecily has a longtime fiancé, Nigel Lawrence, she quickly falls under the spell of the sophisticated Mr. Cortez, and despite the hesitation of her family and friends, she impulsively agrees to marry him. Thrown over in favor of Manuel, Nigel confides to Mavis that Cecily's new husband strikes him as suspicious, though he has no definite grounds for thinking so. A check into Cortez' background turns up nothing, so little that Nigel wonders why the man seems to have no traceable past.

On their honeymoon, Manuel shows Cecily a small, remote cottage where he proposes that they live. Though Manuel appears to be a model husband in most ways, he warns their maid, Ethel, and gardener, Billings, that the cellar of the cottage is to be used by him only; he explains to Cecily that he is conducting research involving some dangerous chemicals. Furiously guarding his privacy, he even lashes out angrily at Cecily when she tries to visit him in the cellar. Patching up their quarrel, he tells Cecily that he has made all the arrangements for them to travel through the Orient, though he doesn't let her see the tickets.

When Cecily turns her ankle in the garden, the local medico, Dr. Gribble, is summoned by Ethel. The injury is a minor one, but the chatty doctor is interested to see that Manuel seems to share his interest in criminology, which the latter's wife considers a grisly hobby. Both read a journal called *Medical Jurisprudence and the Criminal*, which recently published an article on the three-time wife killer Pedro Ferrara. A pencil sketch of the murderer, still believed to be at large, has been removed from Manuel's copy of the journal. Before long, Manuel has succeeded in getting Cecily to sign a power of attorney, and he begins taking control of her financial affairs. While Mavis and Nigel suspect he is a swindler, Manuel has hidden Cecily away in the isolated cottage, and discourages her from inviting visitors. Cecily notices that her meticulous husband has made a note on his calendar of August 31 at 9 p.m., which he says denotes the date on which his research will be concluded.

While Manuel is out of the house, Dr. Gribble returns with his copy of the criminal journal, to win the friendly argument he'd had with Cecily's husband about the sketch it contained. Meanwhile, Nigel has approached Scotland Yard for help, where he too sees a copy of the journal, and the

The role of murderously inclined Manuel Cortez (John Hodiak) in *Love from a Stranger* was just one of the nefarious characters he enacted in 1947. Also pictured in this lobby card is Sylvia Sidney, as his unlucky spouse.

sketch of the murderer on the lam, who looks like Manuel Cortez with a different hair color. Inspector Hobday is persuaded by the new information Nigel has presented that Cecily has married a dangerous man, and agrees to investigate further.

When Cecily spills ink on the envelope that supposedly contains their travel tickets, she opens it and sees that it contains no tickets. On August 31, Cecily has finally grown suspicious of her outwardly charming husband, and takes the opportunity of his absence running an errand to search the cellar. After finding a bottle of hair dye and clippings about the murderer Ferrara, and intercepting a letter showing that Manuel is in the process of converting her money to bearer bonds, and making plans to travel to Scotland, Cecily finally realizes her husband means to kill her—that day.

Trying to remain calm when Manuel returns, she pretends everything is normal as the zero hour approaches, while Nigel and the detective from Scotland Yard make a last-ditch effort to locate and rescue the woman he loves.

Love from a Stranger is a concise little thriller that tells its straightforward story in just over 80 minutes, always moving at a steady clip. Any criticisms a viewer might have are largely outweighed by the fact that it doesn't stick around long enough to wear out its welcome.

Playing his most villainous film character, John exudes charm as the seemingly well-traveled, cultured Manuel Cortez, whose surface polish conceals a deadly nature. "Perhaps I'm a reincarnation of Bluebeard," his character teases his new young wife. The serial murderer Pedro Ferrara, who brands himself Manuel Cortez, is said to have "an extraordinary fascination for women," and Hodiak conveys this quality effectively. His broad smile gets little use here until the final reel, when the escalating battle of wits between him and his terrified wife escalates, his evil grin in close-up showing what lurks under his attractive exterior. The screenwriter and director aren't terribly interested in what makes the sadistic Manuel tick; he's just a plain-out bad guy.

Sylvia Sidney (1910–1999), whose film career stretched from the silent era through *Mars Attacks!* (1999), has an air of fragility that suits the character of Cecily, a sheltered young woman from the 19th century whose innocence Cortez exploits. She skillfully conveys Cecily's infatuation with Manuel Cortez, as well as the terror she feels on what may be the last day of her life, as she bluffs her husband who's intent on murder. Isobel Elsom (1893–1981) enlivens a few scenes as Cecily's scatterbrained Auntie Loo Loo, who tries in vain to prevent her niece from breaking her engagement to marry a man she just met, as does Anita Sharp-Bolster (1895–1985), playing the Cortez household's maid, who's longer on loyalty than brains.

Though her name is downplayed in the opening titles, the original story came from Dame Agatha Christie (1890–1976), the world's best-selling mystery writer. It is the second screen adaptation of Frank Vosper's play *Love from a Stranger*, which in turn was based on Christie's short story "Philomel Cottage." Vosper's play, in which he played the male lead, opened on the London stage in 1936, and was subsequently produced on Broadway. It first was adapted for film the following year, with Ann Harding and Basil Rathbone in the leads.

Most of the character names in *Love from a Stranger* come from Vosper's play, from Cecily Harrington to Dr. Gribble, though the wife-killer was given the new name of Manuel Cortez for this production, having been known as Bruce Lovell onstage. The principal characters in Christie's original story were called Alix King and Gerald Martin. In the story, which has a somewhat different and slightly more ambiguous ending, the nefarious husband's cellar hobby is seemingly nothing more sinister than photography.

In the British Isles, the film saw release under the title *A Stranger Walked In*.

Reviews: "This is a taut, tense story of a maniac wife-killer who carefully plans marriage and the subsequent murder of his wife.... That's all there is to the story, but it has been so well prepared in Philip MacDonald's excellent screenplay ... so superbly directed by Richard Whorf, and so splendidly acted by Sylvia Sidney and John Hodiak with top notch support from every other player that it emerges as an exceptionally believable, exciting melodrama.... It is Mr. Whorf's direction, in most part, that makes this picture as good as it is.... The playing of Miss Sidney and Mr. Hodiak is remarkably restrained for the type of parts they play."—*Showmen's Trade Review*, November 8, 1947

"One of those spine-tingling melodramas which sets its plot early in the first reel and then develops from there.... Although the outcome may well be anticipated by the majority of the audience, director Richard Whorf and producer James J. Geller have introduced sufficient action, suspense and an insight into the mental quirks of the murderer to keep most audiences nervously poised on the edges of their seats."—*Motion Picture Herald*, November 8, 1947

Homecoming (1948)

Clark Gable (*Col. Lee Johnson*), Lana Turner (*Lt. Jane McCall*), Anne Baxter (*Penny Johnson*), John Hodiak (*Dr. Robert Sunday*), Ray Collins (*Lt. Col. Avery Silver*), Gladys Cooper (*Mrs. Kirby*), Cameron Mitchell (*"Monk" Monkevickz*), Marshall Thompson (*Staff Sgt. "Mac" McKeen*), Lurene Tuttle (*Miss Stoker*), Jessie Grayson (*Sarah*), J. Louis Johnson (*Sol*), Eloise Hardt (*Nurse Aldine Bradford*), Art Baker (*Williams*), Peggy Badley (*Nurse Simpson*), Frank Arnold (*Maitre D'*), John Albright (*Corpsman*)

Director: Mervyn LeRoy. *Producer*: Sidney Franklin, in association with Gottfried Reinhardt. *Screenplay*: Paul Osborn. *Original Story*: Sidney Kingsley. *Adaptation*: Jan Lustig. *Musical Score*: Bronislau Kaper. *Director of Photography*: Harold Rosson. *Art Directors*: Cedric Gibbons, Randall Duell. *Film Editor*: John Dunning. *Music Conductor*: Charles Previn. *Recording Director*: Douglas Shearer. *Set Decorations*: Edwin B. Willis. *Associate*: Henry W. Grace. *Special Effects*: Warren Newcombe, A. Arnold Gillespie. *Miss Baxter's Gowns*: Helen Rose. *Hair Styles*: Sydney Guilaroff. *Makeup*: Jack Dawn. *Technical Adviser*: Paul Lund.

MGM; released April 29, 1948. B&W; 112 minutes.

As World War II rages overseas, Dr. Ulysses "Lee" Johnson seemingly has his world perfectly in order. Working as Chief of Surgery at Lafayette

Hospital, he enjoys a prestigious career matched by an affluent home life, with devoted wife Penny and two servants looking after him, and their household unencumbered by children. His college friend Dr. Bob Sunday visits his office to discuss the need for improved health care in the nearby community of Chester Village, which has suffered an outbreak of malaria among its poorer residents. Caught up with plans for his birthday, Lee disappoints his colleague by putting him off.

War news grows worse, and Lee decides he should enlist in the military. The night before reporting for Army duty, he is chastised by Bob, disappointed that his friend never made time to help the people of Chester Village. Bob labels him a "four-flusher," saying angrily, "Get wise to yourself, Lee." Flying overseas for duty, Lee's chat with his friend and fellow doctor Avery is overheard by Lt. Jane McCall, a lovely nurse who thinks Lee lacks the proper attitude toward the obligations for Americans to serve their country. Annoyed, Lee tells her there would be fewer problems in the world if people stayed out of things that didn't concern them. Jane, who's nicknamed "Snapshot" by her colleagues, is a young widow with a 6-year-old boy who annoys Lee with her frank disdain for his self-centeredness, while Lee offends her by suggesting she should be home with her child. They are both discomfited when they learn that they must work together, as she has been assigned to serve as his nurse.

Working 16-hour shifts operating on wounded soldiers, Lee soon acknowledges that Jane is a skilled nurse under trying circumstances, but their personal relationship remains prickly. He recognizes one of the patients he treats as "Monk" Monkevicz, a young man from Chester Village whom he knew back home, and assures the young man he'll recover nicely. Suggesting a cup of coffee after their shift, Lee makes it clear that he wants to win Jane's friendship, but she initially rebuffs him. Later, she brings him coffee, and he apologizes for his insensitivity. Based on his given name of Ulysses, Jane has tagged him "Useless," but slowly they begin to reach a better understanding.

Back at home, Penny Johnson and her mother notice that Lee frequently mentions Jane in his letters, though he claims to find her an irritant. Penny confesses that she's feeling a little jealousy, which Lee assures her is absurd. But he and Jane continue to unbend with one another as each sees a lighter side of the other.

After an impromptu visit to a Roman ruin where they bathe, Lee and Jane return to camp to find more soldiers needing care. Among them, for the second time, is Monk, now suffering from a ruptured spleen, complicated by malaria. Lee is troubled to realize that nothing more can be done for Monk, who dies shortly afterwards. Avery comments that Monk lacked good medical care in his childhood, and Lee realizes that he was part of the community that Bob Sunday had urged him to get involved in helping. Shortly afterwards, another enemy attack on the base leaves Avery fatally injured.

Lee writes to Penny, asking her to pay their condolences to Monk's father. Going to Chester Village to do so, she finds Bob caring for Mr. Monkevicz, who is too ill to see her. She confides in Bob about her fears that she and Lee are growing apart, telling him that her husband admitted being attracted to Jane, but said he had overcome it and they were just friends. Jane worries that wartime service has changed Lee.

With Lee due for leave in Paris, he learns that Jane has been transferred to another unit, and she agrees to keep him posted on her whereabouts. Unexpectedly, he sees her in Paris, and they share a evening marked by a kiss. Their brief interlude is interrupted by news that Germans are aggressively moving in, intending to overtake the city. Both know they will be needed, and cut their leave short to take a dangerous trip back nearer the battlefront. Holed up with Jane overnight, Lee confesses his love for her as they prepare to walk into danger.

After three years in the service, Lee is finally discharged and on his way home. Bob tells a worried Penny that her husband is worth fighting for, but she's afraid he's outgrown her. When Lee gets back home, he is welcomed, but when Penny steels her nerve to ask what happened with Lt. McCall, he shares some unexpected news.

Homecoming is a lengthy but satisfying melodrama that combines the action of the war front with a story of a married man who's drawn to a colleague as they work alongside each other. The film was an adaptation of "The Homecoming of Ulysses," a story by playwright Sidney Kingsley (1906–1995), perhaps best-known for *Dead End*.

Paired here for the third time, top MGM stars Clark Gable and Lana Turner effectively play the story of a love that must remain unrequited. Gable, always endearing to moviegoers, is cast as a flawed man who's not the typical war movie hero, but who undergoes growth in his life as the result of adversity. He ultimately acknowledges, under Jane's influence, that he has always seen his patients as "just cases, not human beings.... I've never cared enough." A deglamorized Miss Turner is believable as the beautiful but tough Army nurse who's much clearer about her aim in life. "I'm a very irritating person," Jane says bluntly, but she is also one whose devotion to her principles is strong. One of the actress' better scenes finds Jane sharing with Lee poignant memories of her brief first marriage, and how her life has changed since being widowed.

Homecoming provided a second opportunity for John to work alongside his wife Anne Baxter, though they don't play a couple here. Nonetheless, they share two strong scenes in which their chemistry comes across plainly. Columnists had fun with the idea of Hodiak, in character, trying to salvage Miss Baxter's marriage to Gable, with Sheilah Graham (October 10, 1947) remarking, "That's the height of unselfishness." John's character, along with Miss Turner's, serves as the voice of conscience that helps bring out a change in Dr. Lee Johnson's life and values. Aside from his friendship with the Johnsons, we learn little about Bob's own private life, though he's clearly a man who takes the Hippocratic oath seriously, and has his priorities straight. Miss Baxter does a fine job of portraying the loyal wife who never stops loving Lee despite the strain in their marriage, eliciting audience sympathy as his relationship with Jane grows. In later years, however, she complained that the film "just was not believable.... The censor would not permit any hints of adultery.... It would have been far more realistic to confront the actual situations that had arisen. So the picture flopped. Big time."[23]

Ray Collins (1889–1965), best-known as Lt. Arthur Tragg on TV's *Perry Mason*, contributes a solid supporting performance as Lee's older doctor friend, but Gladys Cooper (1888–1971) is sadly underused in her brief, undemanding role as Penny's supportive mother. Cameron Mitchell (1918–1994), at the beginning of what would be a long-lasting film career, is cast as the ill-fated young laundryman Monk, whose fate marks a turning point in Lee's life.

Director Mervyn LeRoy (1900–1987), who had scored a triumph several years earlier by producing *The Wizard of Oz* (1939), had stayed busy at MGM during the war years, directing stars such as Greer Garson. He elicits good performances from his cast here, including Miss Turner, whose career he had played a strong role in developing.

This was the first of three films in which John Hodiak will support Clark Gable; the second, *Command Decision*, followed shortly in its wake, and would feature other supporting players who had popped up in *Homecoming*.

Reviews: "*Homecoming* is the picture that Clark Gable should have had for his return to the screen, after his years in service. It is a warm, human, interesting story that is directed with skill by Mervyn LeRoy and acted with understanding and dramatic technique.... Hodiak turns in another capital portrayal as the doctor who is more interested in humanity than glory."—Wood Soanes, *Oakland Tribune*, May 27, 1948

"A showmanly drama out of the top production drawer, film has its sights on solid grosses in all situations.... Performances are of top quality all down the line.... Story line makes a direct play for the tear ducts and has heart.... Miss Baxter does a beautiful smooth job as the understanding wife and John Hodiak as a family friend scores in shorter footage."—*Variety*, April 7, 1948

Command Decision (1948)

Clark Gable (*Brig. Gen. K.C. Davis*), Walter Pidgeon (*Maj. Gen. Roland Kane*), Van Johnson (*Technical Sgt. Immanuel T. Evans*), Brian Donlevy (*Brig. Gen. Clifton I. Garnet*), Charles Bickford (*Elmer Brockhurst*), John Hodiak (*Col. Edward Rayton Martin*), Edward Arnold (*Congressman Arthur Malcolm*), Marshall Thompson (*Captain George Lee*), Richard Quine (*Maj. George Rockton*), Cameron Mitchell (*Lt. Ansel Goldberg*), Clinton Sundberg (*Maj. Homer V. Prescott*), Ray Collins (*Maj. Desmond Lansing*), Warner Anderson (*Col. Ernest Haley*), John McIntire (*Maj. Belding Davis*), Moroni Olsen (*Congressman Stone*), John Ridgely (*James Carwood*), Michael Steele (*Capt. Lucius Jenks*), Edward Earle (*Congressman Watson*)

Director: Sam Wood. *Producer*: Sidney Franklin, in association with Gottfried Reinhardt. *Screenplay*: William R. Laidlaw, George Froeschel. *Based on the Play* by William Wister Haines, produced on the Broadway stage by Kermit Bloomgarden. *Musical Score*: Miklos Rozsa. *Director of Photography*: Harold Rosson. *Art Directors*: Cedric Gibbons, Urie McCleary. *Film Editor*: Harold F. Kress. *Recording Director*: Douglas Shearer. *Set Decorations*: Edwin B. Willis. *Associate*: Jack D. Moore. *Special Effects*: A. Arnold Gillespie, Warren Newcombe. *Makeup*: Jack Dawn.

MGM; released December 25, 1948. B&W; 112 minutes.

Brigadier General K.C. Davis of the U.S. Army Air Force is on duty in England, overseeing a company of military bomber pilots. He is carrying out the top-secret "Operation Stitch," aimed at destroying three factories in Germany where the Nazis are constructing a new type of aircraft with capabilities that exceed those belonging to the Allies.

On his own initiative, Davis goes ahead with the first target to be bombed, which takes his men beyond the point where they can be safely protected by other aircraft. Losses are heavy, and reporters, including "Brockie" Brockhurst, are frustrated by the brass' insistence on keeping the operation secret. Nonetheless, while the weather permits, Davis schedules the second mission for the following day, despite warnings that his men are tired and beginning to rebel. Among those stirring up dissension is decorated young pilot Lucius Jenks, whom Davis confines to quarters when he refuses to take part.

Though losses on the second day are again heavy, Davis believes it is essential to the war effort that Germany's manufacture of these planes be halted. But his superior officer, Major General Roland Kane, is under pressure from top brass to minimize the loss of enlisted men, particularly given the impending visit of members of a Congressional Military Action

Committee. Kane orders a security blackout over the company, and wires Davis to delay the third step of the mission, an attack on the factory at Schweinhofen.

The Congressional envoy arrives just in time to see a returning plane flown by an inexperienced pilot crash and burn on the runway. Davis' friend, Col. Ted Martin, who took part in the initiative, tells him that, thanks to a crewman's error, the pilots bombed the wrong site. Ted, whose wife is expecting a baby any day, suggests that Davis keep this information to himself, as the photos they brought back look like they carried it out as planned. To appease Congressman Malcolm and his allies, who would shortly be voting on funding for air missions, Davis is told to present a medal of honor to Malcolm's nephew, Jenks, but he refuses, intending to charge the rebellious young pilot with desertion.

As Kane and his fellow officers entertain the visitors, Davis tries to tell him privately of the misfired mission, but before he can do so, Brockhurst gleans the news, and has to be sworn to secrecy. Davis chafes at the political pressures that are standing in the way of what he believes must be done. But when Kane finally allows Davis to use his own judgment, warning him that the fallout may be severe, the dangerous plan goes forward as scheduled. He is shaken by the news that Ted Martin was killed during the operation, just after a telegram announced the birth of his son. Jenks is finally offered the medal he was to receive, but angrily refuses it. Davis must wrestle with his conscience about the suicide missions to which he has knowingly consigned his men, and question whether he has failed as a leader.

An unusual war film for the period, *Command Decision* takes its theme from the challenges facing Army men who must make difficult decisions under pressure. It's easy enough to tell that the screenplay is adapted from a Broadway play, which in turn was based on author William Wister Haines' 1947 novel. The result is a film that is inevitably talky, taking place largely at Davis' headquarters, and lacking in all but a few bits of action. There is no comedy relief, unlike many war movies, though it would certainly seem out of place here, and no romantic interest at all. The rights to Haines' novel and play were purchased at the instigation of star Clark Gable, who sought the lead role of "Casey" Davis. He gives a strong performance as a man who finds the weight of leadership heavy on his shoulders; Gable's reaction is understated but very effective when he receives the news of his friend Ted's death. Popular young actor Van Johnson has a surprisingly minor supporting role as Davis' aide, while Walter Pidgeon (1897–1984) and Brian Donlevy (1901–1972) also appear. Poster art showed most of the main cast members sporting grins that would be hard to spot in the sober film that unreeled.

Hodiak is reduced to sixth billing here for the part of the ill-fated Ted Martin, described as "the greatest combat leader in the Army force." Once again, he works well opposite Gable, and he makes his character sufficiently likable and admirable that viewers feel the loss when Ted dies just as his eagerly awaited son is born.

Director Sam Wood told an interviewer, "It took 48 days to do the shooting, but I did three months preliminary work on it. In all my picture making I have models made of every scene, so I can plan my action. Then I have an artist who draws every scene and fits in the dialogue so that when I begin I know exactly what I am going to do with each scene. In that way I save many retakes." Asked if he allowed his cast to view dailies, Wood responded, "No. You know how it is, one might see a shadow on his face he didn't like and want a retake."[24]

MGM may have been uncertain as to the box office appeal of this more than usually cerebral war story, as suggested by the extent to which executives packed the cast with names. But as columnist Bob Thomas (April 20, 1948) noted of the all-star cast, "With less pictures being made,

Command Decision (1948) is the second of three times that Hodiak (right) supported MGM star Clark Gable.

the film minds figure they might as well double or triple up their stars in single movies," adding that many of MGM's players were working in either this or *Words and Music*.

Reviews: "'Command Decision' is a literate war drama ... [Its] footage is long, but the story comes through with a sock that grips. The stars, and even the minute bits, turn in worthy thesping to keep everything about the film on the class level.... Clark Gable walks off with a picture in which everyone of the cast stands out.... Sam Wood's direction is articulate in endowing the film with the toughness of war and, at the same time, a sentiment that will click with the femmes. There are no phony touches in the drive for drama."—*Variety*, December 29, 1948

"Clark Gable ... has his strongest assignment in this feature since he returned from the service himself.... Van Johnson as Gable's aide, Brian Donlevy as his succeeding officer, and John Hodiak are others with important work to do.... *Command Decision* is strictly a vital picture of men and war and will have to appeal on that basis. Its audience may be somewhat restricted on that account. But it deserves attention."—Edwin Schallert, *Los Angeles Times*, December 27, 1948

The Bribe (1949)

Robert Taylor (*Rigby*), Ava Gardner (*Elizabeth Hintten*), Charles Laughton (*J.J. Bealer*), Vincent Price (*Carwood*), John Hodiak (*Tug Hintten*), Samuel S. Hinds (*Dr. Warren*), John Hoyt (*Gibbs*), Tito Renaldo (*Emilio Gomez*), Martin Garralaga (*Pablo Gomez*), Fernando Alvarado (*Flute Player*), Julian Rivero (*Diego*), William Haade (*Walker*), Ernesto Molinari (*Bartender*), Alberto Morin (*José*), Peter Cusanelli (*Rhumba Dancer*), Robert Cabal, Richard Lopez (*Bellboys*)

Director: Robert Z. Leonard. *Producers*: Pandro S. Berman, Robert Z. Leonard. *Screenplay*: Marguerite Roberts. *Based on the Short Story by* Frederick Nebel. *Musical Score*: Miklos Rosza. *Director of Photography*: Joseph Ruttenberg. *Art Directors*: Cedric Gibbons, Malcolm Brown. *Film Editor*: Gene Ruggiero. *Song*, "Situation Wanted": Nacio Herb Brown, William Katz. *Recording Director*: Douglas Shearer. *Set Decorations*: Edwin B. Willis. *Associate*: Hugh Hunt. *Special Effects*: Warren Newcombe, A. Arnold Gillespie. *Miss Gardner's Costumes*: Irene. *Hair Styles*: Sydney Guilaroff. *Makeup*: Jack Dawn.

MGM; released February 3, 1949. B&W; 98 minutes.

Rigby, a government agent, has been dispatched to the Central American island of Los Trancos, where his assignment is to investigate a racket involving war surplus materials. Valuable American planes are being shipped overseas and sold illegally. His boss, Gibbs, alerts him to the two key suspects: Tug and Elizabeth Hintten, a married couple.

Rigby tracks down Liz Hintten at Pedro's, a canteen in the town of Carlota where she sings. He pays her a visit in her dressing room; she assumes he's a masher and asks him to leave. Before he does, her husband Tug arrives on the scene, drunk. He offers Rigby a drink, and explains that he is a former Air Force man who lost his job with an airline. Moments later, he passes out. Wanting to get closer to them, Rigby helps Liz carry her inebriated husband home to bed. She tells Rigby that, after seven months, she and Tug would like to leave the island, but are too deeply in debt to do so.

Though Rigby wasn't tipped off to him as a suspect, he can't help noticing that a portly man he dubs "Pie Shape" always seems to be hovering nearby. Rigby hires a boatman, young Emilio Gomez, to help him tour the nearby islands and search for evidence. After their first day out at sea, Tug invites Rigby to dinner with his wife, then asks him to see her home. He persuades her to go for a swim before returning home, and their mutual attraction leads to a kiss. After one kiss, however, Liz pushes Rigby away.

Liz (Ava Gardner) tends to dissolute husband Tug (John Hodiak) in *The Bribe* (MGM, 1949).

Also on hand in Carlota is the mysterious Carwood, with whom Rigby chatted on his flight out. Though Carwood had said he was destined for Peru, he turns up to visit Rigby, saying his accounts of the good fishing on the island intrigued him. Shortly after Carwood's arrival, Rigby is approached by "Pie Shape," whose real name is J.J. Bealer, and offered a $10,000 bribe to leave the island immediately. Rigby declines.

While he's unsure of Carwood's motives, he agrees they should go out fishing together. On Emilio's boat, Rigby is on the verge of making a major catch when his new friend uses his moment at the steering wheel to pitch Rigby overboard. Emilio dives in to help his employer, but there are sharks in the water, and the younger man loses his life. Back on land, a sorrowful Rigby visits Emilio's father to express his condolences, and Mr. Gomez offers to take his son's place on the boat, suspicious that Carwood killed Emilio intentionally.

Liz rushes to see Rigby after hearing of the accident, and is relieved to see he was not the man who died. She tells him that she has been a failure as Tug's wife, that she does not love him, and has decided to leave him. Just then, Bealer turns up to inform her that Tug has been taken ill, and is at his cottage. The doctor Bealer summoned tells Liz that Tug has a serious heart condition, which is why he lost his job as a pilot. He is unable to reassure her about her husband's long-term outlook. Liz tells Rigby she cannot go through with her plans to leave Tug while he lies ill.

With Tug still incapacitated, Rigby follows his boat, tracking down the location where the airplane engines are being held. He knows it is his responsibility to report his findings, but hesitates on Liz's behalf. After failing once again to bribe Rigby by raising the stakes, Bealer drives home the point that Liz will be implicated if he files a report, as the boat being used by him and his associates is registered in her name.

Unsure he can depend on Rigby's cooperation, Bealer visits Liz, alerting her that her husband is a criminal, and Rigby a policeman. "It's your husband's life—against a cop's job," he warns, saying that Tug would not survive being jailed. Bealer provides Liz with a bottle of knockout drops, wanting her to render Rigby unconscious long enough for the smugglers to cover their tracks and escape to safety. Rigby asks Liz to be frank about everything, but when she complies, he doesn't disclose his role in law enforcement, leaving her mistrustful.

The Bribe is a serviceable crime drama with some effective moments, and good performances, though it never rises to the heights it might have. Ava Gardner's biographer Lee Server fairly described it as "another hodgepodge of other, better movies" that left the viewer "constantly feeling as if he had walked in at the middle of the picture."[25]

For most of its first hour, *The Bribe* utilizes a flashback format, as Rigby struggles with the dilemma of turning in the woman he loves. Though it's hardly difficult to imagine a man falling in love with Ava Gardner in her prime, she and Robert Taylor are given little material with which to explain how their relationship goes from zero-to-sixty so quickly. While the love between Rigby and Liz inflames rapidly, so, apparently, did the attraction between the two actors, with Taylor and his leading lady enjoying a tryst off-screen as well as on.

John's disappointingly small role as Tug Hintten gives him only a few scenes in which to strut his stuff, but he makes a strong impression nonetheless as the broken man whom Rigby describes as "leaking his life out, every time his heart pumped." He allows us to understand why Liz still has some feelings for him, as well as why his descent into the bottle has lost him her respect. He told columnist Harold Heffernan (June 25, 1948), "Here I am again in a third straight role that attracts some audience sympathy.... People are supposed to feel sorry for me because I'm suffering from a heart ailment. They know that's why I'm trying to drink myself under the table all the time."

Charles Laughton (1899–1962) delivers a colorful performance as the nefarious Bealer, who dispatches villainy with a gleam in his eye, but claims he's only doing so to finance a foot operation he needs. Claiming he was once an honorable type himself, he says, "Get smart, Mr. Rigby. Everybody grafts nowadays. It's the way people operate."

According to a column item, Vincent Price (1911–1993) gave full measure to the scene in which Carwood smothers John's character with a pillow, taking the lethal action "so vigorously that the bed collapsed—not part of the script."[26]

Reviews: "The marquee value of this melodrama's five-star cast will, no doubt, be of considerable help in drawing patrons to the theatre, but as entertainment it is no more than fair. It should, however, easily satisfy those who do not mind a story that lacks realism and is, at times, wildly melodramatic.... The players do their best, but their efforts are not enough to overcome the artificiality of the plot."—*Harrison's Reports*, February 5, 1949

"It would be difficult as well as decidedly unrealistic to minimize the cast power on display in this standard melodrama which falls back on formula for its punches. Robert Taylor, Ava Gardner, Charles Laughton, John Hodiak and Vincent Price are names for any showman to conjure with.... Chiefly, what keeps *The Bribe* bound to the ground is the familiar ring it strikes with many predecessors although the attraction should give a satisfactory, if unspectacular, account of itself."—*Motion Picture Daily*, February 4, 1949

Malaya (1949)

Spencer Tracy (*Carnahan*), James Stewart (*John Royer*), Valentina Cortesa [Cortese] (*Luana*), Sydney Greenstreet (*The Dutchman*), John Hodiak (*Kellar*), Lionel Barrymore (*John Manchester*), Gilbert Roland (*Romano*), Roland Winters (*Bruno Gruber*), Richard Loo (*Col. Genichi Tomura*), Ian MacDonald (*Carlos Tassuma*), Tom Helmore (*Matissan*), David Fresco (*Barracuda Ed*), James Todd (*Carson*), DeForest Kelley (*Lt. Glenson*), Bill Kennedy, Jack Shea (*Interns*), Eddie Lee (*Japanese Aide*), Matt Moore (*George*), Frank Wilcox (*Naval Officer*)

Director: Richard Thorpe. *Producer*: Edwin H. Knopf. *Screenplay*: Frank Fenton. *Based on an Original Story by* Manchester Boddy. *Musical Score*: Bronislau Kaper. *Director of Photography*: George Folsey. *Art Directors*: Cedric Gibbons, Malcolm Brown. *Film Editor*: Ben Lewis. *Music Conductor*: André Previn. *Recording Supervisor*: Douglas Shearer. *Set Decorations*: Edwin B. Willis. *Associate*: Henry W. Grace. *Special Effects*: A. Arnold Gillespie, Warren Newcombe. *Miss Cortesa's Costumes*: Irene. *Men's Costumes*: Valles. *Miss Cortesa's Hair Styles*: Sydney Guilaroff. *Makeup*: Jack Dawn.

MGM; released December 27, 1949. B&W; 94 minutes.

In 1942, publisher John Manchester of the *Los Angeles Record* is authorized by the White House to seek much-needed rubber through "informal means." He summons free-lance reporter John Royer to his office, who suggests that the best source for the war materiel is Malaya. "With the right kind of money, and the wrong kind of man, I can get that rubber for you," Royer tells the publisher.

Set up in a temporary apartment, Royer soon has a visitor—federal agent Kellar, who knows not only his background but the facts about his meeting with Manchester. Kellar warns Royer that the mission he's undertaking—to take gold into Malaya, and smuggle out rubber—is treacherous. Royer can take on the project only with help from a man named Carnahan, whom Kellar informs him can currently be found at Alcatraz. At the prison, Royer makes his proposal to his old friend Carney, who's told he will be released from confinement if he accepts the assignment. Royer, whose younger brother was killed by Japanese forces, has revenge on his mind as well as the stated mission.

In Malaya, Carney takes Royer to see "The Dutchman" at his saloon, where the ex-inmate is also reunited with his lady friend, Luana, who sings there. The Dutchman, who has cultivated a friendly relationship with Colonel Tomura of the Japanese army, provides Royer and Carnahan with men to help their mission—"good, honest riffraff," and a motor launch. He also furnishes the names of three plantation owners with whom they may

Newspaper reporter John Royer (James Stewart, right) has a not entirely welcome visit from G-man Kellar (John Hodiak) in *Malaya* (MGM, 1949).

be able to make a deal. They visit the three sites, where they make it clear that they intend to either buy the rubber they have stockpiled, or steal it. At one, Col. Tomura shows up, and it's clear that he's suspicious of the two men.

After the first two exchanges have taken place, Royer has 150,000 tons of rubber he must still smuggle out of the country. His cohorts, including Carney, think he should he satisfied with that and get out of the country as soon as possible. But Royer knows the third plantation owner, Gruber, has a large supply as well, and is determined to get it, though the Nazi sympathizer is not trustworthy. As Royer sets out, Carney creates a ruckus that distracts Col. Tomura and his men, and is arrested. The Dutchman persuades Tomura to release Carney to his custody.

Gruber tells Royer that there is an ambush of Japanese forces awaiting him downriver should he try to complete the mission, but Royer won't be dissuaded. Before he gets to what he expects to be the danger point, he and his men are attacked, and Royer is killed by the enemy. Col. Tomura suggests to Carney that, for the right amount of money, he might be persuaded to look the other way as the rubber exchange is completed. Aside from completing the mission, Carney takes on a few other pieces of unfinished business—avenging Royer's death, completing the mission, and seeing to Luana's future.

"It's the spot that's so hot it sizzles with excitement!" proclaimed newspaper ads of the film, originally announced as "Operation Malaya." *Malaya* is elevated somewhat by strong cast values. It does offer some strong action sequences, but also a bit more talk than many viewers likely wanted.

With co-star billing below the title, Hodiak plays a federal agent, Kellar, of whom Royer says, "Anything you say, he knows already." For his part, Kellar tells Royer wearily, "My professional opinion is that you're going to make me lose a lot of sleep." Hodiak holds his own with two of the strongest leading men in Hollywood, Spencer Tracy and James Stewart.

Most of John's performance can be found in the film's first half-hour; he vanishes from the story once the scene changes to Malaya. He resurfaces just before the final curtain falls, to play a brief scene with Sydney Greenstreet that wraps up the story. Publicity for the film tried to put the best face on Hodiak's assignment to such a minor role. Producer Edwin H. Knopf explained that once the lead roles were cast, "Then, with two big names like Tracy and Stewart in the bag, we got really ambitious. We submitted the script to John Hodiak. He said he was willing to play a third part, as long as Tracy and Stewart were in the picture."[27]

Valentina Cortese (1923–2019), billed here as "Cortesa," appears about half an hour into the film as Luana, who has a romantic history with Carnahan. Miss Cortese, who had become a Fox contract player the previous year, makes her American film debut in *Malaya*. Luana's rendition of "Blue Moon" recurs in several scenes. Her pairing with Tracy doesn't really convince, but she's beautiful and engaging in the role. Off-screen, she married up-and-coming actor Richard Basehart in 1951. Sydney Greenstreet (1879–1954), in his final film role, commands attention whenever he appears on-screen, sleepy-eyed and low-key as he is. Hawaiian-born Richard Loo (1903–1983), busy playing enemy agents in numerous American films of the 1940s, furnishes subtle menace as Tomura.

According to MGM publicity, *Malaya* "necessitated the use of the largest set ever constructed on the studio's lot. The set, comprising thirty-seven acres, was transformed into a Malayan jungle where much of the action … takes place…. The original M-G-M 'jungle,' built for early Tarzan films, served as the base … but was enlarged four times its previous size."[28]

Columnist Hedda Hopper (February 18, 1949) published a tongue-in-cheek complaint about *Malaya*'s focus on male characters, with only Miss

Cortese representing womanhood. "What have they got against our sex?" she asked. "Yet it's the little woman who decides what movie to see, and drags her male with her."

Reviews: "This lengthy, slightly fantastic, but nevertheless entertaining Metro melodrama qualifies as an above-average boxoffice attraction generally on the strength of an all-star cast that glitters with highly-rated marquee names.... Better grosses will be a certainty in action houses where such improbable adventure vehicles usually delight the regular patrons.... Unfortunately, the plot fails to measure up to a standard befitting the film's top-notch cast.... John Hodiak and Lionel Barrymore do their bit in surprisingly inconsequential roles."—*Film Bulletin*, January 16, 1950

"The cast is far superior to the material at its disposal. And although the opening shot of a letter from the late President Roosevelt mentioning 'informal' methods of procuring new rubber in wartime might lead you to expect a drama of the documentary type, 'Malaya' ... paints a distinctly peculiar picture of the means stooped to, with high Governmental approval ... [Still], there's plenty of excitement in this account ... colorful characterizations, hard-hitting lines and plenty of hair-trigger tension.... Appearing briefly, Hodiak and Barrymore, particularly the former, make the most of their respective roles."—Mildred Martin, *Philadelphia Inquirer*, December 29, 1948

Battleground (1949)

Van Johnson (*Holley*), John Hodiak (*Donald Jarvess*), Ricardo Montalbán (*Johnny Roderigues*), George Murphy (*"Pop" Stazak*), Marshall Thompson (*Jim Layton*), Jerome Courtland (*Abner Spudler*), Don Taylor (*Standiferd*), Bruce Cowling (*Wolowicz*), James Whitmore (*Kinnie*), Douglas Fowley (*"Kipp" Kippton*), Leon Ames (*Chaplain*), Guy [Herbert] Anderson (*Hansan*), Thomas E. Breen (*Doc*), Denise Darcel (*Denise*), Richard Jaeckel (*Bettis*), Jim [James] Arness (*Garby*), Scotty Beckett (*William J. Hooper*), Brett King (*Lt. Teiss*), George Chandler (*Mess Sergeant*), Jerry Paris (*German Sergeant*), John Mylong (*German Major*), Michael Browne (*Levenstein*), Neville Brand (*Singing Soldier*), Jim Drum (*Supply Sergeant*), Lillian Clayes (*Old Woman*), Tommy Walker (*Mechanic*), Nadine Ashdown, Janine Perreau (*Little Girls*)

Director: William A. Wellman. *Producer*: Dore Schary. *Associate Producer/Story and Screenplay*: Robert Pirosh. *Director of Photography*: Paul Vogel. *Art Directors*: Cedric Gibbons, Hans Peters. *Film Editor*: John Dunning. *Musical Score*: Lennie Hayton. *Recording Supervisor*: Douglas Shearer. *Set Decorations*: Edwin B. Willis. *Associate*: Alfred E. Spencer.

MGM; released December 1, 1949. B&W; 118 minutes.

The men of the 101st Airborne Division, weary from their tours of duty, are eagerly anticipating their imminent three-day leave in Paris. Just before they are due to leave, they are disappointed by a change of plans that finds them transported to the Belgian town of Bastogne. On arrival, they are greeted by two little girls, and an attractive young woman, Denise, whom they take to be the children's mother. Denise offers them hospitality, and explains that the two girls are war orphans for whom she is caring. Holley, a womanizer, dances with Denise, and gives her his romantic attentions.

Though the soldiers' presence in Bastogne is supposed to be unannounced, leaflets dropped from the sky make it clear that their arrival is known to the enemy. Assigned to guard the area against German infiltration, the men of the 101st soon learn that enemy forces are close at hand. Clad in American uniforms, fluent in English, and armed with Army passwords, the Germans make it difficult for the soldiers to know who can be trusted.

Jarvess, Holley, and Rodrigues are sent out on an exploratory mission to reconnoiter. They encounter German troops, see through their attempt to pose as Americans, and a confrontation ensues in which Rodrigues is shot. His colleagues hide the wounded Rodrigues under a disabled tank, promising to send help for him.

Back at camp, Holley learns that his fellow officer has been injured and removed to an Army hospital, leaving him in charge of the unit. Several of the men go back to rescue Rodrigues, but he has died alone in the snow. With fog clouding the skies, and air support unable to penetrate the area, Holley and his compatriots realize that they are surrounded, badly outnumbered, and ill-equipped to defend themselves.

A deadly confrontation with the enemy ends with the men of the 101st able to take several Germans prisoner. Back in Bastogne, they enjoy a brief respite, and a reunion with Denise. Then Nazi officers show up to give them two hours to leave the area, telling them there will be heavy casualties for them and the people of the city if they do not. Their official answer, delivered to the Nazi leader's face, is "Nuts!"

Battleground is, as an opening card announces, a tribute to the fighting men who served in the Battle of the Bulge, and would become known as "The Battered Bastards of Bastogne." Grittily realistic for its era, the screenplay focuses on the enlisted men waging battle on the ground, rather than officers. Multiple characters are developed through brief vignettes that depict most of them as cynical, inclined to gripe as real men would do, but ready to rise to the occasion when they are tested under fire. The film demonstrates how the soldiers cope with cold, illness, and the strain of being in near-constant danger. Small moments illustrate the strange new world in which the men live, as when one soldier pauses alongside his just-shot comrade only long enough to claim his gun, then moves on.

Van Johnson acquits himself well in the starring role of Holley. The actor was facing the possibility of a career slump as he aged out of the boyish roles that had made him a bobbysoxer idol a few years earlier. Holley steals a few eggs in Bastogne, and carries them along as the soldiers march, carefully guarding them until he has the chance to enjoy them, which is regularly postponed.

Second-billed, Hodiak plays Donald Jarvess, a newspaper columnist who became caught up in his own patriotism, and is now having second thoughts about his eagerness to serve. "I was too good," he tells Holley of his journalistic work. "I wrote a piece about the real meaning of the war—the fight against fascism, why every American had to get in there and pitch in. Logic was magnificent; couldn't resist it. Next thing I knew, I was in a troop train waving bye-bye to my wife." Now engaged in the conflict, Jarvess resents that he feels less up-to-date on war news than he was when he was getting the first look at newspaper wire service reports from the front. Later, under pressure, he mutters, "Man gets hit, he at least has the right to know what country he's dying in." Though he's more highly educated than many of his fellow soldiers, which they don't let go unnoticed, he proves to be an effective member of the unit.

Ricardo Montalban (1920–2009) contributes a strong performance as the Mexican-American soldier Johnny Rodrigues, who is delighted by his first look at snow close up, but comes to a tragic end. Newcomer Denise Darcel (1924–2011) has the only significant female role in the film, with her work sufficiently well-received that she was given additional screen time. Marshall Thompson (1925–1992) is a standout as the greenest of the unit's men, one who takes a few missteps initially but gradually wins the respect and camaraderie of his fellow soldiers. Much critical praise came to James Whitmore (1921–2009), still in his twenties, for his supporting role as the tobacco-spitting commander. His work merited an Academy Award nomination as Best Supporting Actor.

Producer Dore Schary, who came to MGM as Vice President of Production after resigning his position at RKO, began working on *Battleground* at his previous job, and his new employer bought the screen rights. Some at MGM, including Louis B. Mayer, thought moviegoers were tired of war pictures, and were dubious about *Battleground*'s prospects, giving it the satiric title "Schary's Folly." Preparations for it began in 1948, with early casting announcements suggesting that either Robert Mitchum or Robert Taylor would play the starring role. At least one column item stated that it would be shot in Technicolor, which didn't happen.

Trade papers ultimately announced that William Wellman

(1896–1975) had been signed to direct, with production expected to be underway by spring. Schary was pleased with Wellman's work, later writing, "Bill came in twenty days under schedule and about a hundred thousand under budget—but what was important, he came in with a powerful, well-paced picture full of action and humor."[29] Of working with the director and largely male cast, John told an interviewer, "It's just like working with one big family. We all have so much fun. Wellman is always wise-cracking and it helps to relieve the tension."[30]

To keep costs down, much of the film was shot on the MGM lot. More than twenty real-life soldiers who had served in the 101st Division were recruited to work as extras and bit players in the film, and the actors went through a simulated boot camp in preparation for their roles. By that time, Taylor had dropped out of the leading role, giving way to Van Johnson. Screenwriter Robert Pirosh was awarded a Bronze Star for his own military service, on which he drew to script *Battleground*. Later active in television, he created the World War II drama *Combat!* (ABC, 1962–67).

First screened in New York in November 1949, the film had its West Coast premiere in Los Angeles on December 1, with its leading stars in attendance, before going into wider release a few weeks later. Those early playdates qualified it for consideration the following spring at the Academy Awards. *Battleground* received multiple nominations, including Best Picture and Best Director. Pirosh took home a statuette for his story and screenplay, as did Paul Vogel for his

On the set of *Battleground* (1949), director William A. Wellman reviews the script with his second-billed star, John Hodiak.

cinematography. Its popular success, with a multi-million-dollar profit, proved the naysayers wrong, and helped speed Mayer's demise at MGM.

Reviews: "*Battleground* ranks with the best of the war melodramas yet produced. It is a superior picture, one that pays a deserving tribute to the American troops who fought in the Battle of the Bulge.... The story is rich in characterizations, skillfully portrayed by the competent cast."—*Harrison's Reports*, October 1, 1949

"*Battleground* assumes to be the story of an infantry platoon, and it has the quality of being well concentrated on its theme and idea.... It has many haunting scenes.... And its characters are just such a mixture as one might find in a group of men in the Army, with their eccentricities exaggerated.... The film is splendid in its war front sequences.... Johnson, Hodiak, ill-fated Montalban, Murphy and, rather specially, Marshall Thompson are fine."—Edwin Schallert, *Los Angeles Times*, December 2, 1949

Ambush (1950)

Robert Taylor (*Ward Kinsman*), John Hodiak (*Capt. Ben Lorrison*), Arlene Dahl (*Ann Duveral*), Don Taylor (*Lt. Linus Delaney*), Jean Hagen (*Martha Conovan*), Bruce Cowling (*Tom Conovan*), Leon Ames (*Maj. C.E. Breverly*), John McIntire (*Frank Holly*), Pat Moriarity (*Sgt. Mack*), Charles Stevens (*Diablito*), Chief Thundercloud (*Tana*), Ray Teal (*Capt. J.R. Wolverson*), Robin Short (*Lt. Storrow*), Richard Bailey (*Lt. Tremaine*), Marta Mitrovich (*Mary Carlyle*), Ray Bennett (*Orderly*), Heinie Conklin (*Quartermaster*), William Haade (*Joe*), Lane Chandler (*Doc Horton*), Florence Lake (*Mrs. Wolverson*), Peter Prouse (*Cpl. Evans*), Cap Somers (*Sutler*), James Harrison (*Sgt. Isaacs*), Cliff Clark (*Capt. Harcourt*), Hank Mann (*Barber*)

Director: Sam Wood. *Producer*: Armand Deutsch. *Screenplay*: Marguerite Roberts, based on the story by Luke Short. *Director of Photography*: Harold Lipstein. *Art Directors*: Cedric Gibbons, Malcolm Brown. *Film Editor*: Ben Lewis. *Musical Score*: Rudolph G. Kopp. *Recording Supervisor*: Douglas Shearer. *Set Decorations*: Edwin B. Willis. *Associate*: Ralph S. Hurst. *Women's Costumes*: Walter Plunkett. *Hair Styles*: Sydney Guilaroff. *Makeup*: Jack Dawn. *Technical Adviser*: Col. Charles E. Morrison, USA.

MGM; released January 13, 1950. B&W; 89 minutes.

It's 1878, and Ward Kinsman is prospecting in Arizona, near the foot of Bailey Mountain. It's considered a dangerous occupation thanks to the heavy presence in the area of a rogue band of Apache Indians, escaped from their reservation, led by Diablito. Most recently, a wagon train was attacked by him, and all the passengers killed, with the possible exception of Mary Carlyle, daughter of a now-deceased general.

Ward is summoned back to the Cavalry post by Major Breverly, who wants him to undertake a mission to locate and rescue Mary, if she is still alive. He is urged on by Mary's beautiful sister Ann. Ward considers that such a mission would cost a heavy loss of soldiers' lives, and tells Ann frankly that Diablito may have already killed her sister. The major's associate, Captain Ben Lorrison, although romantically involved with Ann, agrees with Ward's opinion.

Meanwhile, Lt. Linus Delaney has fallen in love with Martha Conovan, a laundress who's married to the abusive and hard-drinking Tom. She resists her would-be suitor's advances, as her religion tells her she is married for life. When the pay wagon arrives at the base, Tom uses much of his salary to get drunk in the saloon, begrudgingly giving Martha a little for groceries. Ward punches Tom, but not before the drunk soldier attacks Major Breverly with a pitchfork.

With the major in sick bay, Capt. Lorrison assumes command of Fort Gamble. Ordered to follow Diablito and get Mary safely home, he sets out with a troupe of men. They succeed in finding some women and children the Indian warriors left behind, as well as an elderly man, Tana, who claims that he hates Diablito and does not support his mission. Tana and an Indian woman are taken captive and returned to the fort. They say that Mary is still with the band of Indians that went ahead.

Ben thinks Tana can be useful in tracking down Diablito, but Ward does not trust him. Ward is told by the commanding officer to stop interfering in Army affairs, but he finds it difficult to do so when Ben tells Linus it is his fault the major was injured, and wants him transferred out of the unit. Ward and Ben attempt to settle their differences with a fistfight off-base, which the latter wins handily. Nonetheless, Ward agrees to continue acting as guide in the pursuit of Diablito and his men.

Before the expedition heads out, Ben proposes marriage to Ann, who asks him to wait until he returns for her answer. Later, Ward tells Ann that she will not marry Ben, and stakes his own claim with a kiss. Meanwhile, Tom Conovan overpowers a guard and escapes from his imprisonment, going on the lam.

Ben and his men set out on the course he chose strategically to locate the Indians and their captive. They soon learn that, while they have some 60 fighting men, the Indians are closer to 200 in number. Ward finds the body of Tom Conovan. When Tana lives up to Ward's suspicions by running away, Ward chases him down, ultimately killing him.

Ward makes a plan to augment the confrontation Ben is facing with the Indians, by stirring up a stampede of the Native Americans' horses. Though this works, the Indians set a trap for Ben and the other men who head off in pursuit of them, and the result is a brutal attack in which many lives are lost. Ultimately, it is Ward ends up in a deadly confrontation with Diablito.

Running free of her captors, Mary is taken into the care of Ward and the other soldiers. After heavy losses, the Army men return to camp where Ann, Martha, and the other enlisted men anxiously await news of Mary, and the fates of those who bravely went to war with the Indians.

From the opening titles, when we see sobering footage of the deadly fate that befell members of a wagon train, it's clear that *Ambush* means to be a grim, adult Western, not shying away from depicting the stark violence of the era. Screenwriter Marguerite Roberts adapted a short story by Luke Short (1908–1975), whose popular fiction had previously been the basis for films like *Coroner Creek* and Pine-Thomas' *Albuquerque* (both 1948). Production of the film got underway in late May 1949.

Top-billed Robert Taylor, of course, emerges as the film's ultimate hero, though he loses that fight with Lorrison. He's believable as the prospector who lives by his wits, and who has learned from experience to have instincts that he recognizes and takes seriously. Arlene Dahl (1925–2021) makes a fine leading lady, though the film lacks the Technicolor photography that would complement her beauty in other Westerns. Cinematographer Harold Lipstein frames her beautifully in multiple close-ups and bust shots, her lovely face bathed in light, and she makes her character's concern for her sister touching.

Hodiak, in his second film with Taylor, is interestingly cast as Captain Ben Lorrison, a by-the-book Army man, who isn't lacking for daring and strength, but ultimately overplays his hand in his pursuit of an Indian warrior. The older Frank Holly sums up Ben thusly: "I guess I just naturally distrust a perfect man. He's too good. He never makes mistakes and he don't understand nobody else making 'em. And he don't like no man overly much."

While that assessment doesn't prove entirely accurate, John gives the role gravitas, despite a screenplay that doesn't favor him. Though he seems to have more chemistry with the leading lady than the ostensible star, Hodiak winds up with the short end of the stick. Still, it's a sizable and interesting role for him, a better one than his next MGM Western will offer. Many of his fans' ears undoubtedly perked up when Ben, returning to camp, remarks that he's "been dreaming about a shower for three days," and indeed he does scrub up in a revealing scene moments later.

Jean Hagen (1923–1977), two years prior to being seen in her classic role as the unforgettable Lina Lamont in *Singin' in the Rain* (1952), delivers a subtle, understated performance as the wronged wife of Tom Conovan. The subplot of a battered and mistreated wife, which originated in Short's book, is somewhat unusual for the period.

This was the final released film of director Sam Wood (1883–1949), who died of a heart attack prior to its release. Wood's death cut short a productive career dating back to the silent era, one that encompassed the making of genuine classics like *Kings Row* (1942) as well as directing two superior Marx Brothers films, *A Night at the Opera* (1935) and *A Day at the Races* (1937). Producer Armand Deutsch (1913–2005), a very wealthy man who inherited family money, went on with his wife to become part of the Reagans' "Kitchen Cabinet" in the 1980s as well as a prominent arts patron.

Early announcements of *Ambush* dropped names like James Stewart and Van Heflin among those who were supposedly under consideration for key roles. Syndicated columnist Hedda Hopper (May 15, 1949) reported that John had only one day of rest after completing *Battleground*, before plunging into filming *Ambush*. Location shooting took place near Albuquerque, New Mexico, where a large troupe of MGM employees traveled, and dozens of local residents were hired to take part in battle scenes.

According to columnist Louella O. Parsons (July 15, 1949), John interrupted his location work on *Ambush* to fly back to Los Angeles when his father was unexpectedly hospitalized. The elder Mr. Hodiak's condition was reported to be serious but not life-threatening.

Reviews: "Above-average entertainment of its kind, despite its shortcomings. Where it misses fire is in the U.S. Cavalry-versus-Indians story, which is somewhat confusing because of the maze of plots and counter-plots, and which is developed at rather a slow pace.... Strengthened by a cast whose marquee value should give it a lift at the box-office."
—*Harrison's Reports*, December 31, 1949

"A slowly-developing western ... that will find favor with the youngsters, and with adults who like 'horse opera' with hard riding and fighting, capably acted. Several fight sequences arouse considerable excitement.... Hodiak acts the role of the opinionated and brash captain with self-righteous restraint.... Miss Dahl is charming to look at, as usual, and gives a nice performance."—*Showmen's Trade Review*, December 24, 1949

A Lady Without Passport (1950)

Hedy Lamarr (*Marianne Lorress*), John Hodiak (*Peter Karczag a/k/a Joseph Gombush*), James Craig (*Frank Westlake*), George Macready (*Palinov*), Steven Geray (*Frenchman*), Bruce Cowling (*Archer Delby James*), Nedrick Young (*Harry Nordell*), Steven Hill (*Jack*), Robert Osterloh

(*Lt. Lannahan*), Trevor Bardette (*Lt. Carfagno*), Charles Wagenheim (*Ramón Santez*), Renzo Cesana (*A. Sestina*), Esther Zeitlin (*Beryl Sandring*), Carlo Tricoli (*Mr. Sandring*), Marta Mitrovich (*Elizabeth Alonescu*), Don Garner (*Dimitri Matthias*), Richard Crane (*Navy Flyer*), Nita Bieber (*Dancer*)

Director: Joseph H. Lewis. *Producer*: Samuel Marx. *Screenplay*: Howard Dimsdale. *Adaptation*: Cyril Hume. *Suggested by a Story by* Lawrence Taylor. *Music*: David Raksin. *Director of Photography*: Paul C. Vogel. *Art Directors*: Cedric Gibbons, Edward Carfagno. *Film Editor*: Fredrick Y. Smith. *Recording Supervisor*: Douglas Shearer. *Set Decorations*: Edwin B. Willis. *Associate*: Ralph S. Hurst. *Special Effects*: A. Arnold Gillespie. *Hair Styles*: Sydney Guilaroff. *Makeup*: Jack Dawn.

MGM; released August 3, 1950. B&W; 74 minutes.

Hailed by a man in a passing car on a New York street, Ramón Santez panics and runs into traffic, where he's hit and killed by a taxi. Ramón had flown in from Miami the previous day, but the coroner tells police after examining the corpse that he was likely from Cuba. Found in the dead man's possession was half a $1000 bill. Immigration authorities are notified of the case.

Pete Karczag, a U.S. Immigration officer, confers with the police in Havana, who call his attention to a man named Palinov, owner of the Gulf Stream Café. Pete visits the American Embassy, posing as Joseph Gombush, a Hungarian trying to gain entry into the U.S. When he's refused a passport, "Joseph" purposely makes a scene. Afterwards, on the street, he's offered a drink by Palinov's compatriot. At the café, he's chatted up by Palinov himself, who claims his "soft heart" compels him to help those having difficulty emigrating. The undercover Immigration officer passes the initial test, but Palinov notes that he will bear further checking.

Another patron of the café is lovely Marianne Lorress, a Viennese woman who was also turned away by the Embassy. Palinov tells her his fee for getting her safely to Charleston, South Carolina, will be $1000. "Joseph" and Marianne are introduced to each other by Palinov, who claims she too is Hungarian. "Joseph" bluffs his way through a conversation in which she's said to be the niece of Budapest's mayor, but out of her earshot he boosts his own credentials by telling Palinov she's a liar.

At the police station, Pete is shown a series of sketches of people believed to be dealing illegally with Palinov, one of whom is Marianne. He tracks her down to a café where she's on the verge of being arrested, charged with taking a job as a cigarette girl without a work permit. Pete poses as her boyfriend, with whom she had an argument, and gets her out of the clutches of the police.

Taking her back to his own hotel, Pete books a room for her, but she rebuffs him when he asks for a kiss. He finds himself attracted to Marianne, who shows him the number tattooed on her arm from her stay at the Buchenwald concentration camp. Going back to his own room, Pete is attacked and beaten by intruders, making him wonder if Marianne can be trusted. The attackers find his police ID. The next day, however, Pete and his lady friend share a walk through the sights of Havana, and Marianne tells him her father is already in the U.S. as an illegal alien, and that he can offer her a home if she can make it there. Afterwards Pete types a resignation letter to his boss, Frank Westlake, telling him he plans to stay in Cuba for personal reasons.

Marianne suggests that "Joseph" make a deal with Palinov to travel on the same flight with her, but the slimy smuggler tells him he's aware of his real identity. Pete warns him that he is on his trail, saying, "Don't let anyone else squash you underfoot. Save yourself until I get ready."

Reporting to Westlake that his cover has been blown and the situation is escalating, Pete learns only that the pilot taking the aliens out of Cuba is named James. Immigration officials in Miami identify the pilot in question, but Pete and his Cuban police contact are unable to learn from where the flight will depart, and Palinov tells Marianne to be ready to leave that night. Westlake tells Pete they can catch the plane after it crosses the U.S. border, which means that Marianne and her fellow aliens will be caught and arrested.

James throws off his pursuers by

Immigration officer Pete (John Hodiak) finds himself in an awkward position—in love with *A Lady Without Passport* (1950). Hedy Lamarr plays the lady in question.

changing planes, but he's identified at a Jacksonville airport when he stops to refuel and has to take off without the needed gasoline. With a Navy pilot tracking him, James is forced to make a crash landing in the Everglades. The pilot and Palinov launch a raft into the nearby river, abandoning the other passengers to cope as best they can. When Pete and his boss arrive, Westlake makes it a priority to locate the passengers on foot, but Pete tells him, "The girl's in a spot and I put her there." He takes the launch and heads for a potentially deadly confrontation with the smuggler, while Marianne will have to decide whether she's safer with Palinov, who warns her Pete intends to arrest her.

A Lady Without Passport is a modestly entertaining drama that benefits from location shooting in Cuba and crisp black-and-white cinematography. John gives a solid performance as Pete, who is dedicated to his mission but finds his sympathies engaged by Marianne. He and Hedy Lamarr aren't given much screen time to establish their romantic rapport, but convey it more than adequately, with him visibly moved despite his devotion to his work when she tells him she has been on the run for ten years. Hodiak skillfully shows the conflict Pete is feeling between his job and this woman, and his interest in her welfare. Pete tells her not to expect American life to be totally idyllic, saying soberly, "A little thing like an accent, a foreign name, can set you apart. There's always someone who laughs." Miss Lamarr, as Marianne, assures him that she can take this in her stride if she makes her way to safety. John's frequent colleague James Craig appears here in the supporting role of Pete's boss.

According to Hedda Hopper (December 16, 1949), Hedy Lamarr, despite the lure of a $125,000 paycheck, initially balked at co-starring with Hodiak, "insist[ing] that a star of her caliber be signed." Miss Hopper sneered, "I'm surprised she didn't ask them to find her a rich husband, too." At that point, she reported that "the deal is dead," but that didn't last.

Director Joseph H. Lewis (1907–2000) won latter-day acclaim from film historians, especially for his modestly budgeted crime drama *Gun Crazy* (1949). Though *A Lady Without Passport* has not come in for a similar amount of acclaim, critic Myron Meisel has termed it "perhaps the loveliest of Lewis' neglected works."[31] In Lewis' capable hands, the excitement and activity remain frequent throughout, the story moving rapidly enough to keep viewers engaged, though it provides more satisfaction for action fans than romance lovers.

The filmmakers acknowledge two officials of the U.S. Immigration and Naturalization Service in the opening titles for technical assistance and cooperation. The screenplay makes clear not only Palinov's wrongdoing, but the fact that some of his passengers besides Marianne are seeking entry to the U.S. for dishonest reasons. The film was shot under the working title "Visa." Columnist Hedda Hopper (January 21, 1950) noted, "John Hodiak, unhappy a few years ago because he didn't get enough work, is about to cry, 'Uncle!' 'Visa' is his fifth in a year."

Reviews: "Take it or leave it.... Either way you won't get hurt.... Under direction by Joseph H. Lewis, the action film is fast, smooth and suspenseful. Performances by conscientious players are another most helpful factor. John Hodiak works awfully hard and succeeds in making his man ... a likable and convincing character."—Wanda Hale, *New York Daily News*, August 4, 1950

"Rather routine stuff. There are some suspenseful moments, but the plot is of the programmer variety that will satisfy only avid action fans. Undoubtedly, the marquee value of Hedy Lamarr and John Hodiak will tend to hike grosses somewhat, but their fans are likely to be disappointed."—*Film Bulletin*, July 11, 1950

The Miniver Story (1950)

Greer Garson (*Kay Miniver*), Walter Pidgeon (*Clem Miniver*), John Hodiak (*Spike Romway*), Leo Genn (*Steve Brunswick*), Cathy O'Donnell (*Judy Miniver*), Reginald Owen (*Mr. Foley*), Anthony Bushell (*Dr. Kanesley*), Henry Wilcoxon (*Vicar*), Richard Gale (*Tom Foley*), Peter Finch (*Polish Officer*), William [James] Fox (*Toby Miniver*), Cicely Paget-Bowman (*Mrs. Kanesley*), Ann Wilton (*Jeanette*), Paul Demel (*José Antonio Campos*), Alison Leggatt (*Mrs. Foley*), Brian Roper (*Richard*), Sam Kydd (*Removal Man*)

Director: H.C. Potter. *Producer*: Sidney Franklin. *Screenplay*: Ronald Millar, George Froeschel. *Based on Characters Created by* Jan Struther. *Music*: Herbert Stothart. *Adaptation*: Miklos Rozsa. *Conductor*: Muir Mathieson. *Director of Photography*: Joseph Ruttenberg. *Art Director*: Alfred Junge. *Film Editors*: Harold F. Kress, Frank Clarke. *Recording Director*: A.W. Watkins. *Photographic Effects*: Tom Howard. *Miss Garson's Costumes*: Walter Plunkett. *Additional Costumes*: Gaston Mallet.

MGM; released October 26, 1950. B&W; 104 minutes.

An opening card tells us, "This is the story of a woman after a war—who lived and hoped and struggled through the anxious years, and now saw them end and another peace begin."

It's May 8, 1945, and Kay Miniver, still separated from her husband and children, is one of thousands of Britishers in London listening to Winston Churchill's radio announcement that the Germans have surrendered, and the war is over. She shares a ride home with young Tom Foley, a neighbor who tells her he spent time with her daughter Judy in Cairo, where she was serving as driver to an officer, Steve Brunswick. Tom shows Kay a drawing he did of her daughter, and she senses that he has feelings for Judy.

Back in their village, Kay is greeted by American colonel Spike Romway, who's been stationed in the village. He tells her his unit will be departing shortly, and invites her to a farewell party at the local pub that evening. At the pub, Spike tells Kay that, although their acquaintance was fairly short, and they both are married, he has fallen in love with her. He assures her that he doesn't expect her to return his feelings.

Along with Judy, the Minivers' son Toby returns home, after living in America with a foster family during the conflict. Last to arrive for the reunion is Kay's husband Clem. On their first evening together as a family, Judy tells her father she fell in love with Steve Brunswick, although he's older than she, and married to a pianist. Tom drops by later hoping to see her, but she's gone out with Steve. Kay tells Clem they will have to wait to see how the situation develops.

Clem is worried when Kay experiences a dizzy spell, but she makes light of it. Unbeknownst to him, Kay has known for a few months that she is seriously ill. She implores her physician, Dr. Kanesley, to tell her how long she has to live; he reluctantly informs her that she will likely die within six months to one year.

Visiting Clem at the office where he practices as an architect, Kay suggests he could use a young draftsman, and mentions Tom's drawing skills. Clem is intrigued by a possible job in Brazil, and

In *The Miniver Story* (MGM, 1950) a lonely Mrs. Miniver (Greer Garson) attracts the attentions of an American soldier (John Hodiak).

tells Kay if it comes through they should relocate there. He thinks Kay is exhausted after the war, and needs a change of scene.

Tom comes to the rescue when Steve's car breaks down, and gives Judy a lift home. He makes his fondness for her known, but she tells him she's committed to Steve. Tom kisses her, but agrees they can continue as friends. Kay receives a letter from Spike in America, while Clem gets a response to the proposal he submitted for the job in Brazil. He has invited the firm's representative to dinner, upsetting Kay, who fears that rationing will make it difficult for her to be a proper hostess.

When Steve leaves behind his coat at the Minivers, Kay seizes the opportunity to visit him at his London flat, and get better acquainted with the man her daughter hopes to marry. The man she meets is temperamental, selfish, and freely admits he argued passionately with his current wife. Though the Brunswicks have begun divorce proceedings, Kay realizes she may not live long enough to see her daughter married. As they talk, she helps Steve see that he should stay with his wife.

Kay admits to Clem's assistant Janet that she doesn't want to go to Brazil, and Janet advises her to speak up, but she still hasn't told him the truth about her health. Janet comments to Mrs. Miniver that her husband finds the view from his office window depressing. She impulsively finds him a new office, and shows him some sketches that Tom made, demonstrating that he would make a fine apprentice. Meanwhile, Judy is heartbroken when Steve breaks off their relationship. Kay tells her that wartime relationships are often temporary, and should be. To prove her point, she shares with her daughter the letter that Spike wrote her from the United States, in which he told Kay that he was happy to be back with his wife.

At a community dance, Judy renews her relationship with Tom Foley, and Kay finally finds the right moment to break the news of her health to her husband. As Kay's time grows short, she finds comfort in knowing that her family will survive and prosper after she's gone.

As box office takings in the early 1950s became slimmer, movie studios struggled to survive the advent of television. MGM executives thought a sequel to their popular and Academy Award–winning *Mrs. Miniver* (1942) would be a surefire winner, even eight years later. Both Greer Garson and Walter Pidgeon were still under contract to the studio, and available to reprise their roles from the original film, as did Henry Wilcoxon in the minor role of the town vicar. Not invited back from the original cast was Miss Garson's ex-husband, actor Richard Ney, who had played her older son in *Mrs. Miniver*. Original director William Wyler gave way to H.C. Potter (1904–1977), whose previous credits included *The Farmer's Daughter* (1947), with Loretta Young.

The two stars headed for London in late summer 1949 for production of *The Miniver Story* to get underway. It proved to be a long and somewhat difficult shoot, with illness among the cast and crew slowing things down. They were still overseas as the new year dawned, with MGM reportedly sending Victor Saville to England to take over for Potter and finish the film. Before shooting began, John told an interviewer of Garson and Pidgeon, "I am looking forward to working with both of them. They are fine artists."[32]

Ultimately, the film that resulted lacks a strong sense of narrative drive; it offers viewers a reunion with a family they had loved and admired, but the postwar concerns of the Minivers simply aren't as compelling and urgent as what they had already experienced. Miss Garson and Pidgeon give thoughtful performances as the two members of what her character terms "a rather perfect marriage."

The Miniver Story offers John one of his smallest roles in an MGM feature, despite his third billing. He appears in only two major scenes as Kay Miniver's admirer; he's billed above performers like Cathy O'Donnell (1923–1970) who get far more screen time. It's likely, though, that some of his footage may have been cut, as some of MGM's poster art for the film depicts at least one Garson–Hodiak scene that doesn't appear in the finished product. The script makes it clear that Mrs. Miniver's relationship with his character remains platonic and respectful, though he pledges his love for her.

Young actor James Fox (born 1939), billed here as William, makes his film debut stepping into the role of Toby Miniver. He gives an energetic and likable performance, and it's a pity the story doesn't take more advantage of him. Leo Genn (1905–1978), like Hodiak, has only a few scenes in which to bring out his character, the older love interest of Judy Miniver, but makes him memorable even if Judy's attraction for him is somewhat difficult to understand.

While it's well-acted and directed, and modestly entertaining, *The Miniver Story* proved a disappointment for the studio, failing to recoup its costs and sustaining a loss reported by film historian Scott Eyman as in excess of $2 million.

Reviews: "The Miniver Story fails to measure up to the original Jan Struther story.... The sentimental love story will find its most appreciative audiences among the feminine contingent. The static pace and abundance of dialogue make this ... a poor prospect for the action houses.... A comparatively unimportant role of an American officer is ably played by John Hodiak."—*Film Bulletin*, October 22, 1950

"This bitter-sweet sequel to 'Mrs. Miniver' abounds in the kind of sentimentality that will probably moisten the eyes of the femme trade.... For the most part, it is well-made, but the pace is disturbingly slow for the lack of enough light moments to quicken the tempo and provide relief from the overly-generous serving of pathos. Garson and Pidgeon, heading a competent cast, turn in sensitive performances."—*The Exhibitor*, October 11, 1950

Night Into Morning (1951)

>Ray Milland (*Phillip Ainley*), John Hodiak (*Tom Lawry*), Nancy Davis [Reagan] (*Katherine Mead*), Lewis Stone (*Dr. Horace Snyder*), Jean Hagen (*Girl Next Door*), Rosemary DeCamp (*Annie Ainley*), Dawn Addams (*Dotty Phelps*), Jonathan Cott (*Chuck Holderson*), Celia Lovsky (*Mrs. Niemoller*), Gordon Gebert (*Russ Kirby*), Harry Antrim (*Sam Andersen*), Katherine Warren (*Margaret Andersen*), Whit Bissell (*Monument Salesman*)
> *Director*: Fletcher Markle. *Producer*: Edwin H. Knopf. *Screenplay*: Karl Tunberg, Leonard Spigelgass. *Director of Photography*: George J. Folsey. *Art Directors*: Cedric Gibbons, James Basevi. *Film Editors*: George White, Robert Watts. *Music*: Carmen Dragon. *Recording Supervisor*: Douglas Shearer. *Set Decorations*: Edwin B. Willis, Alfred E. Spencer. *Special Effects*: Warren Newcombe. *Hair Styles*: Sydney Guilaroff. *Makeup*: William Tuttle.
> MGM; released June 8, 1951. B&W; 84 minutes.

Phillip Ainley, who teaches English at a state university, enjoys a pleasant suburban life as a happily married man with wife Annie and 10-year-old son Timmy. But his comfortable existence is plunged into chaos when a furnace explosion at his home kills Annie and their son. The middle-aged professor remains publicly stoic through their funeral and the days beyond. But Phillip, who's moved into a hotel, begins spending too much time in the bar, and privately feels suicidal thoughts.

He receives ready support from his best friend, fellow professor Tom Lawry, and Tom's fiancée Katherine Mead, who works as secretary to their department chair, Dr. Snyder. Katherine, who was widowed only weeks into her first marriage, knows from painful experience what Phillip is suffering, while Tom is sympathetic though he has never lived through such a serious loss. Phillip's in-laws, still grieving, urge him to consider marrying again and having a second family, something he can't fathom after twelve happy years with Annie. Phillip pays surreptitious visits to his burned-out former home, and insists on returning to work, though he acts oddly with his students.

With Dr. Snyder's approval, Phillip's friends and colleagues offer him chances to get away for a few weeks, and Tom invites his friend to move into his apartment. As the days go by, Tom and Katherine worry about Phillip's slide into alcoholism. She accompanies Phillip to buy his family's gravestones, and has more cause for concern when a traffic episode with another driver causes him to erupt in anger.

Though Tom, too, wants to help his friend, he begins to be disturbed by the amount of time and thought his fiancée is giving to the bereaved widower. Phillip rejects the advances of a lonely neighbor, and Katherine tries to reassure Tom that she is not romantically interested in anyone but him.

A second, more serious traffic accident, with Phillip at the wheel and a young student, Dotty, as a passenger, earns him a night in jail, a $500 fine, and the loss of his driver's license for a year. Phillip's colleagues still want to be supportive, and his department chair refuses his offer to resign. Dotty and her fiancé, Chuck, are distressed when he flunks Mr. Ainley's class, jeopardizing a job he's already been offered once he graduates. Despite Katherine's pleading, Phillip insists the grade was justified, and refuses to change it.

Having told his friends he's been offered a temporary teaching post at Yale, Phillip starts trying to make amends to those he's hurt, giving a neighborhood boy Timmy's bicycle, agreeing to give Chuck a makeup test, and changing his will to benefit Tom and Katherine. While her fiancé is encouraged that Phillip may be coming out of his misery, Katherine instinctively realizes that his behavior signals his intention to end his life. Against Tom's wishes, which results in his saying they should go their separate ways, Katherine races to Phillip's side, hoping she can intervene before another tragedy strikes.

Shot under the title "People in Love," *Night into Morning* is an engrossing drama about grief, a subject rarely explored in depth in movies of the period. Karl Tunberg and Leonard Spigelgass' script moves at a rapid pace, holding the viewer's attention, despite the somber subject matter. The film carefully steers clears of maudlin touches, giving more weight to the occasional moments when strong feelings come to the surface. Director Fletcher Markle (1921–1991) elicits fine performances from his lead actors. Ray Milland (1907–1986), who had already earned an Academy Award for playing an alcoholic in *The Lost Weekend* (1945), is excellent here as Phillip Ainley. Milland's stuffed-shirt demeanor is well-suited to playing a dignified, erudite English professor, and makes it only the more shocking and moving when the control he's desperately trying to hold onto slips. One of his strongest scenes finds him going back to his ruined house, calmly offering his son's bike to the boy's best friend, then erupting into a tirade that terrifies the child and sends him running.

Not yet married to Ronald Reagan, future First Lady Nancy Davis

Filmography 141

PREVIEW SCENE OF
PEOPLE IN LOVE
starring RAY MILLAND, JOHN HODIAK, NANCY DAVIS,
LEWIS STONE, ROSEMARY deCAMP

Originally announced as "People in Love," *Night into Morning* (MGM, 1951) was perhaps not the light entertainment most summertime moviegoers wanted. Starring (left to right) are Ray Milland, Nancy Davis (Reagan) and John Hodiak.

(1921–2016) gives a strong performance as Katherine Mead, a young woman who has fought her way back from devastating grief brought on by the death of her first husband. "I died with Dan," she tells Phillip, but she empathizes with what he's suffering, and can foresee the danger he's in. Whatever one's opinions of the Reagans' politics, it's difficult to deny that Miss Davis's dramatic talent is clearly on display here. She has a striking moment when Katherine rushes into Ainsley's classroom during a lecture, with the house fire visible in the distance, and cries out in alarm, "Phil, it's your house!" Near the end of the film, Katherine makes one last-ditch effort to get through to Ainsley, and Miss Davis' playing of this critical scene can't be faulted. It's not surprising that Nancy Reagan would later say, "It may well have been the best picture I ever did." Of her co-star Hodiak, Mrs. Reagan later recalled, "I had known Johnny when he worked in radio in Chicago. Now he was a rising star in pictures."[33]

John Hodiak's second-billed role as Tom Lawry isn't as challenging as Milland's or Davis', nor does he play such a well-fleshed-out character, but he contributes solidly to the success of the film. Though he and Miss Davis seem slightly mismatched, he's believable as the man who helped her realize, after her own bereavement, that she could love again. "Katherine's the expert on these matters," he grumbles as his fiancée proves to be more help to his best friend that he himself can. Director Markle recalled that John teased the young actress about her love of rehearsal, to which she replied, "Johnny, you'll be so glad when we start shooting that we've explored every possible way of doing this scene. Come on, get off your rump and let's do it again."[34] Markle noted that, with some difficulty, he persuaded MGM executive Dore Schary to permit the film company a rehearsal period before shooting got underway, promising that it would save time and cut costs, which it did. The film was completed four days ahead of schedule.

Reviews: "*Night into Morning* is an example of a carefully produced and well acted drama which can experience, at best, only moderate box office success because of its heavy, somber story.... Nearly everyone has experienced the tragedy of death, and such misfortune so intimately portrayed on screen is not the type of entertainment today's moviegoers seem to prefer.... Ray Milland, playing the professor, is the kind of capable actor who can not [*sic*] give a bad performance, and his characterization ... is thoughtful and sincere. John Hodiak inevitably has trouble with the spot of Milland's friend, a teacher who fails to recognize the problem. Nancy Davis brings warmth and animation to the role of Hodiak's fiancée."
—*Film Bulletin*, June 4, 1951

"One of the darkest experiences that the human spirit can be forced to endure—that is, the death of a loved one and the adjustment subsequent thereto—is considered with decent compassion and simple dramatic clarity in 'Night into Morning' ... Mr. Milland's performance is quiet and sure, and Fletcher Markle's forthright direction conceives the aspects of personal tragedy in their prosaic forms.... John Hodiak is calm and competent as his somewhat baffled friend, and Nancy Davis does nicely as the fiancée."—Bosley Crowther, *New York Times,* June 11, 1951

The People Against O'Hara (1951)

Spencer Tracy *(James Curtayne),* Pat O'Brien *(Vincent Ricks),* Diana Lynn *(Ginny Curtayne),* John Hodiak *(Louis Barra),* Eduardo Ciannelli *(Sol "Knuckles" Lanzetta),* James Arness *(Johnny O'Hara),* Yvette Duguay *(Katrina Lanzetta),* Jay C. Flippen *(Sven Norson),* William Campbell *(Frankie Korvac),* Richard Anderson *(Jeff Chapman),* Henry O'Neill *(Judge Keating),* Arthur Shields *(Mr. O'Hara),* Louise Lorimer *(Peg O'Hara),* Ann Doran *(Betty Clark),* Emile Meyer *(Tom Mulvaney),* Regis Toomey *(Fred Colton),* Katharine Warren *(Mrs. Sheffield),* Celia Lovsky *(Mrs. Korvac),* Charles Bronson *(Angelo Korvac),* Peter Mamakos *(James Korvac),* Richard Bartlett *(Tony Korvac),* Bill Fletcher *(Pete Korvac),* Michael Tolan *(Vincent Korvac),* Paul Bryar *(Det. Howie Pendleton),* Maurice Samuels *(Papa Lanzetta),* William Schallert *(Intern),* John Sheehan *(Postal Clerk),* Ned Glass *(Preliminary Hearing Judge),* Mae Clarke *(Receptionist),* Dan Foster *(Assistant D.A.),* Fred Essler *(Augie),* William Self *(Narcotics Squad Technician),* Jim Toney *(Ofcr. Abrams),* Don Dillaway *(Morty),* Lou Lubin *(Eddie),* Angi O. Poulos *(Carmen Vasullo),* Frank Sully *(Fishmonger),* Joyce Otis *(Thelma),* Kay Scott *(Secretary)*

Director: John Sturges. *Producer*: William H. Wright. *Screenplay*: John Monks, Jr., from a novel by Eleazar Lipsky. *Director of Photography*: John Alton. *Art Directors*: Cedric Gibbons, James Basevi. *Film Editor*: Gene Ruggiero. *Music*: Carmen Dragon. *Recording Supervisor*: Douglas Shearer. *Set Decorations*: Edwin B. Willis, Jacque Mapes. *Special Effects*: A. Arnold Gillespie, Warren Newcombe. *Miss Lynn's Costumes*: Helen Rose. *Hair Styles*: Sydney Guilaroff. *Makeup*: William Tuttle.

MGM; released September 7, 1951. B&W; 102 minutes.

Late one evening, a car carrying two men arrives at the home of Bill Sheffield, and moments later Sheffield is shot. Police quickly learn that the car belongs to a young man, Johnny O'Hara, and lift fingerprints from the rearview mirror that belong to small-time hood Frankie Korvac. Meanwhile, Johnny is breaking off his relationship with a young woman, telling her it would be dangerous for her to continue seeing him.

Questioned in the district attorney's office, Frankie admits to driving the vehicle, but says Johnny fired the gun that killed Sheffield. When Johnny returns home the following morning, he is arrested, and later arraigned on charges of murder and robbery (Sheffield's suitcase, supposedly containing gold, was taken). Johnny's mother calls old family friend Jim Curtayne, a lawyer who has switched from handling criminal cases to civil actions, much to the relief of his adult daughter Ginny. Jim tries to find another lawyer for Johnny, but his family is unable to raise an adequate retainer, so he agrees to take the case himself.

Johnny tells Assistant District Attorney Louis Barra that Bill Sheffield was his boss, and owed him money for overtime work at his fish market. He admits that a gun recovered by police is his, a war souvenir, and identifies the suitcase, which he previously saw, closed, in Sheffield's office. Johnny claims that, at the time of the incident, he was working overnight at the fish market, but the security guard doesn't back his story.

Barra thinks he has an open-and-shut case on his hands, one that will advance his career, but having Jim to defend the accused complicates matters. Ginny Curtayne, thinking her father is safely out of the criminal work that stressed him into alcoholism, agrees to marry her boyfriend Jeff Chapman, but she's dismayed to read in the newspaper that he has taken the O'Hara case. The elder Curtayne assures her he can handle the pressure, but she feels she must postpone her wedding plans.

Jim soon learns that Johnny's alibi was false, and cautions him never to lie to his lawyer. Johnny says he was out walking that night, but has no witnesses. Jim asks him about a lady friend, but Johnny denies having one.

Gangster "Knuckles" Lanzetta summons Jim to his office, claiming he wants to help Johnny, but Jim refuses his assistance. Lanzetta tells Jim that the murder victim was suddenly flush with money just before he died. After their meeting, the two men walk outside, where Lanzetta introduces Jim to his pretty younger wife, who is the woman Johnny was with on the night of the murder. Jim visits the Korvac family, but fails to convince them Frankie should change his story.

As the trial opens, Frankie continues to insist that Johnny organized the robbery, enlisted his help in carrying it out, and told him of a fence who would give them good money for Sheffield's gold. On cross-examination, Jim brings out Frankie's own criminal past, but he finds himself struggling to provide the best representation for his client. Facing memory problems, and fearing he is letting Johnny down, Jim is ready to take a drink in the evening, but Ginny's intervention prevents him.

Jim confides to an old crony, Det. Vince Ricks, that he's disappointed by his own performance in court. Ricks warns him that ADA Barra has been approached by a witness who claims to have seen Johnny at the murder scene. The witness in question, a sailor named Sven Norson, is disappointed with the financial rewards he's been promised by Barra for testifying, and implies he's open to a better offer. Still drinking, Jim asks him his price, and writes him a check for $500.

Though he accepted the bribe, Norson sticks to his story on the witness stand, implicating Johnny. As Barra stands nears him, Jim can see that he's clutching the check he wrote. Jim's client is convicted, and he faces repercussions for trying to bribe a witness.

Jim learns that his old friend Toby has died, and delivers the eulogy at his funeral. Afterwards, he learns that a young woman tried to visit Johnny in prison, falsely claiming to be his sister. Jim goes back to the O'Hara apartment and searches his client's belongings, finding an Italian-English dictionary and the receipt for a postal box. Inside the box is a letter awaiting Johnny, with feminine handwriting that leaves Jim convinced his client has a woman in his life that, for some reason, he has chosen to keep secret.

Returning to the fish market, Jim confronts Mrs. Lanzetta. She admits that she was with Johnny on the night of the murder, but was too afraid of her husband to speak up. Jim takes her to Barra's office, but when Johnny is brought in, he denies her story, to protect her. Jim continues to question her, and she recalls a morning when her husband saw a photo of Sheffield's suitcase, and reacted strongly. The suitcase is examined by narcotics officers, who find some $200,000 worth of dope in its lining. Jim uses Lanzetta to spread the word that he will be at the Sheffield home that evening with the suitcase. He's then fitted for a wire that he hopes will gather evidence to clear his client, at the cost of considerable danger to himself.

The People Against O'Hara is a smart, compelling mystery that effectively combines courtroom drama, action, and suspense. It was adapted from Eleazar Lipsky's novel of the same name, which appeared under Doubleday's "Crime Club" imprint in 1950. Director John Sturges (1910–1992) elicits fine performances from his cast, without letting the story sink into melodrama. *The People Against O'Hara* was a relatively early credit for the man who would go on to make *Bad Day at Black Rock* (1954, with Tracy), and *The Great Escape* (1963), among other noteworthy films. The sharp black-and-white photography of New York streets by cinematographer John Alton (1901–1996) contributes strongly to the film's mood and atmosphere.

According to Tracy's biographer James Curtis, the meaty lead role here, as an attorney struggling with alcoholism, was "a grim and uncomfortable job for a man of his particular history."[35] Nonetheless, the actor is compelling as Jim Curtayne, a flawed man who ultimately rises to the occasion when he's called upon to do so. Tracy was pleased when he was able to demand that his old friend Pat O'Brien (1899–1983) be cast in the supporting role of Detective Ricks.

Once again supporting top MGM star Tracy, Hodiak delivers a fine, understated performance as the up-and-coming assistant district attorney,

Louis Barra. His character is an ambitious man, who perceives that convicting Johnny O'Hara will bring favorable publicity to him and his office. As Ricks comments noncommittally, "You can start packing your bag for the governor's mansion." In Lipsky's novel, Barra is described as "a powerful man with massive shoulders and a thick neck. His nose was strongly curved, his hair lay sleek and gleaming black."[36] On the printed page, he has a wife, but that's more than we learn about Barra's home life in the film.

Initially, Barra seems to be the younger man who will prove that Jim Curtayne is past his prime, but subsequent events will lead to a growing sense of mutual respect between the two men. Hodiak eschews showy acting to give a credible portrait of a prosecutor whose drive to get ahead doesn't ultimately outweigh his code of ethics. Diana Lynn (1926–1971) is effective in the scene where she finds her father getting ready to take a drink, and confronts him angrily, calling herself "the nagging daughter of an incurable alcoholic," before bursting into tears a moment later.

Only a few months earlier, James Arness (1923–2011) had appeared as the title character in 1951's *The Thing (From Another World)*. He gets more of an acting showcase here, as Tracy's enigmatic young client Johnny O'Hara. Lipsky had stipulated that the character was a "young giant,"[37] and Arness, who stood 6'7" tall, certainly fit the bill. It appears that director John Sturges blocked some scenes so as to make this less distracting; the actor is often seen seated. In the courtroom scene, when he walks alongside Hodiak, he towers over his co-star. Another future leading man, Charles Bronson (1921–2003), is unbilled for his small role as one of small-time hood Frankie's brothers.

Hodiak will play a prosecutor again the following year, in *The Sellout*. At around the same time, Raymond Burr gave a strong performance as a district attorney in *A Place in the Sun* (1951), which a few years later would result in his being invited to audition for his career-altering role in TV's *Perry Mason*. Had Hodiak still been alive by the time that show was being cast, he too might well have been on the list of actors considered.

Reviews: "Combining elements of courtroom drama, personal conflict and action, this is an interesting, entertaining entry. The high powered quartet of Tracy, O'Brien, Lynn, and Hodiak turn in solid performances, and this should make a difference at the boxoffice [*sic*]. The direction, crisp, builds to a climax taut with suspense."—*The Exhibitor*, August 29, 1951

"Spencer Tracy and his costars furnish enough marquee strength to help get *The People against O'Hara* rolling initially, but entertainment values do not have enough punch to give it any sustained drive.... A basically good idea for a film melodrama is cluttered up with too many unnecessary side twists and turns, and the presentation is uncomfortably overlong.... As the three costars, O'Brien, Hodiak and Diana Lynn ... have comparatively shorter footage, but each comes through excellently."—*Variety*, August 22, 1951

Across the Wide Missouri (1951)

Clark Gable (*Flint Mitchell*), Ricardo Montalban (*Ironshirt*), John Hodiak (*Brecan*), Mariá Elena Marqués (*Kamiah*), Adolphe Menjou (*Pierre*), J. Carrol Naish (*Looking Glass*), Jack Holt (*Bear Ghost*), Alan Napier (*Capt. Humberstone Lyon*), George Chandler (*Gowie*), Richard Anderson (*Dick Richardson*), Timothy Carey (*Baptiste DuNord*), Frankie Darro (*Cadet*), Gene Coogan (*Marcelline*), Bobby Barber (*Gardipe*), Michael Dugan (*Gordon*), Maurice Brierre (*French Trapper*)

Director: William A. Wellman. *Producer*: Robert Sisk. *Screenplay*: Talbot Jennings. *Story*: Talbot Jennings, Frank Cavett. *Music*: David Raksin. *Director of Photography*: William Mellor. *Technicolor Color Consultants*: Henri Jaffa, James Gooch. *Art Directors*: Cedric Gibbons, James Basevi. *Film Editor*: John Dunning. *Recording Supervisor*: Douglas Shearer. *Set Decorations*: Edwin B. Willis, Ralph S. Hurst. *Special Effects*: Warren Newcombe. *Costume Designer*: Walter Plunkett. *Hair Styles*: Sydney Guilaroff. *Makeup*: William Tuttle. *Indian Technical Adviser*: Nipo T. Strongheart.

MGM; released October 21, 1951. Color; 78 minutes.

Flint Mitchell, earning his living as a fur trapper in the Old West, is eager to enter Blackfoot Indian country, where beavers are plentiful. Stockpiling supplies and fresh horses for his next expedition, Flint expresses an interest in buying the pony that belongs to a young Indian woman, Kamiah, but she tells him through a translator that she and the animal will not be separated. She inquires if he has a wife, or is interested in one, but he says no.

Flint encounters his old friend Brecan, who lives full-time with the Blackfoot Indians. Brecan tells his pal that Kamiah is a Blackfoot who was kidnapped as a child by the Nez Percé, and their chief Looking Glass considers her his daughter. Deciding that having a Blackfoot wife would help him gain access to the Blackfoots' trapping ground, Flint bids to become Kamiah's husband, as does Brecan, who wants to return her to her own people. She and her father accept the trade Flint is offering, and she becomes his wife.

With some thirty men in his brigade, Flint launches his venture into Indian country, but the scouts they send ahead are immediately killed by Indian braves. Flint asks Kamiah if there is an alternate route into the region, and she tells him of one. It requires difficult travel over mountaintops, but the troupe ultimately arrives. They build a stockade and begin trapping beaver, keeping out a watchful eye for any Indians who may attack.

Out alone one day, Flint is surrounded by Indians, led by the fierce Ironshirt. He manages to escape, but Ironshirt plans an attack on the trappers' fort, beginning with the theft of several horses. Flint goes to the Blackfoot village, where Kamiah's grandfather, Bear Ghost, acknowledges him as her husband. Having fallen genuinely in love with his wife, Flint has a new regard for the Indians' culture, and hopes for friendly relations. However, Ironshirt is still angry, especially when he's forced to return the trappers' horses.

Kamiah tells Flint she is expecting his child. He arranges a ceremonial meeting with Bear Ghost to share the good news. But one of Flint's men, avenging his brother's death at the hands of Indians, shoots and kills Bear Ghost. His death leaves Ironshirt the tribe's new leader, eager to avenge the death of Bear Ghost.

When spring comes around, the trappers are ready to leave with their lucrative collection of furs. But an outburst of violence from Ironshirt's men leads to tragedy for Flint, and ultimately a one-on-one confrontation with the Blackfoot leader.

The only actor billed above the title, Clark Gable (1901–1960) isn't photographed to look his best here, as Technicolor seems to give a reddish tint to his lined face. He was reportedly ill during the shoot, and some of the 50-year-old actor's heroics, such as his ability to outrun a number of healthy-looking young Indian braves, come across as implausible.

Though no credit is given onscreen, MGM bought the rights to Pulitzer Prize–winning historian Bernard DeVoto's nonfiction book of the same title, published in 1947. The film had originally been announced as far back as early 1948, at which time it was said to be a vehicle for Spencer Tracy. Screenwriter Talbot Jennings (1894–1985) was an Academy Award nominee whose credits included *Northwest Passage* (1940) and *Anna and the King of Siam* (1946).

Given co-star billing are Ricardo Montalban as Ironshirt, believable as the fierce Indian warrior, and Hodiak as Flint's friend Brecan. Making a strong entrance just a few minutes into the film, Hodiak, decked out in a long black wig and pigtails, has a few key scenes with Gable before disappearing for a lengthy stretch. His character remains with the Blackfoot Indians, his background unexplored in the release print, and he appears intermittently throughout the second half of the film but has relatively little to do.

Mexican-born actress/singer María Elena Marqués (1926–2008), as Kamiah, is making the first of two appearances in Westerns opposite Hodiak as an Indian woman. They will work together again in *Ambush at Tomahawk Gap*. With an "introducing" credit here, she generally attracted solid notices even when the film overall didn't. For most of the film, her character and Gable's cannot speak without an interpreter; actor Adolphe Menjou (1890–1963) is saddled with the job of translating other characters' dialogue, which slows the momentum of the film.

Cinematographer William C. Mellor (1903–1963) reported that shooting location footage for *Across the Wide Missouri* was a daunting task. "About the only advantages we had over those early trappers," he wrote, "were a camera and walkie-talkie-cum-telephone connection with [MGM studios in] Culver City."38 He noted that, high up in the mountains, they experienced a "daily routine of rain, sleet and snow."

John Hodiak as Brecan in *Across the Wide Missouri* (MGM, 1951). Like his castmates, Hodiak lost some significant footage when studio executives chopped William A. Wellman's film to 78 minutes.

The film's brief running time (for an "A" feature) reflects the substantial revisions it underwent between shooting in the summer of 1950, and its release more than a year later. According to the director's son, studio executives "would not support this offbeat Western, and it became the most butchered of all Wellman's films up to this point. While the director was out of town on the location of his next picture, there were numerous reedits and much restructuring."39 The cutting of the film necessitated the addition of narration by actor Howard Keel (1919–2004), voicing Flint's adult son, to bridge some of the resulting story gaps.

Wellman said that

the film was intended to avoid depicting the Indians as pure villains, and to fairly represent their side of the story. Ironshirt, he said, "was a hero. He was defending his property and the rights of his people. But writers, both for the screen and novels, have rarely stressed this point. I guess you can't have two 'heroes' in one story."[40] Though Flint initially feels entitled to invade the Blackfoot land, and plunder its resources, he has a change of heart, as Keel's narration states, "Suddenly they were no longer savages. They were people, who laughed, and loved, and dreamed."

For all its shortcomings, *Variety* (January 2, 1952) listed *Across the Wide Missouri* as #13 on its list of "Top Grossers of 1951," reporting grosses of $2,800,000. Nonetheless, it proved a disappointment for Hodiak fans, who surely expected a more prominent appearance by him.

Reviews: "A modest Indian-vs.-white adventure film.... The picture unwinds at a leisurely pace that makes its surprising 78-minute running time seem long.... Satisfactory in supporting roles are Ricardo Montalban.... John Hodiak, Adolphe Menjou and James Whitmore.... The film is one of the lesser directorial achievements by Wellman."—*Film Bulletin*, October 22, 1951

"There is much about this outdoor Technicolor melodrama that is worthwhile, but it is handicapped by an uneven story and on the whole shapes up as no more than fairly satisfactory entertainment.... On the credit side are some fine action sequences.... On the debit side is the choppy, episodic story, as well as a number of dull passages during which the characters sit around and do nothing but talk, talk, talk."—*Harrison's Reports*, September 22, 1951

The Sellout (1952)

Walter Pidgeon (*Haven Allridge*), John Hodiak (*Charles "Chick" Johnson*), Audrey Totter (*Cleo Bethel*), Paula Raymond (*Peggy Stauton*), Thomas Gomez (*Kellwin C. Burke*), Cameron Mitchell (*Randy Stauton*), Karl Malden (*Capt. Buck Maxwell*), Everett Sloane (*Nelson Tarsson*), Jonathan Cott (*Ned Grayton*), Frank Cady (*Bennie Amboy*), Hugh Sanders (*Judge Neeler*), Griff Barnett (*J.R. Morrison*), Burt Mustin (*Elk Ludens*), Whit Bissell (*Wilfred Jackson*), Roy Engel (*Sam Slaper*), Jeff Richards (*Truck Driver*), Vernon Rich (*County Clerk*), Bob Stephenson (*Bailiff*), Cy Stevens (*Court Stenographer*)

Director: Gerald Mayer. *Producer*: Nicholas Nayfack. *Screenplay*: Charles Palmer. *Story/Associate Producer*: Matthew Rapf. *Director of Photography*: Paul C. Vogel. *Art Directors*: Cedric Gibbons, Arthur Lonergan. *Film Editor*: George White. *Music*: David Buttolph. *Recording Supervisor*: Douglas Shearer. *Set Decorations*: Edwin B. Willis, Ralph

S. Hurst. *Special Effects*: A. Arnold Gillespie. *Montage Sequence*: Peter Ballbusch. *Hair Styles*: Sydney Guilaroff. *Makeup*: William Tuttle. MGM; released May 30, 1952. B&W; 83 minutes.

Haven Allridge, editor/publisher of the *St. Howard Post-Intelligencer*, visits the nearby town of Bridgewood to have dinner with his daughter and son-in-law. On the way home, he stops to offer a ride to Wilfred Jackson, a man with a candy stand in the lobby of the newspaper headquarters, when he sees him waiting at a bus stop. Almost immediately, he's pulled over by Bridgewood police, where, thanks to his inability to produce his license, he learns about the peculiar form of justice carried out by the sheriff. After a brief stay in a cell, where the other prisoners beat Jackson, both men are hauled into the town's kangaroo court. Allridge is on the verge of being assessed a fine on trumped-up charges when Sheriff K.C. Burke is alerted that he's the father-in-law of county prosecutor Randy Stauton.

His family connections winning him release, Allridge talks to his son-in-law about taking action against the corrupt sheriff, but Randy is hesitant to take on the powerful man. Angered, Allridge splashes the sordid story all over the front pages of his newspaper, reporting not only the facts of his and Jackson's case but also others reported by readers.

Outside the St. Howard city limits, Sheriff Burke retaliates by taking punitive steps against the paper and its supplies being transported through the county. Word of the public's desire for a cleanup job in Bridgewood reaches the state Attorney General's office, where young lawyer "Chick" Johnson is assigned to visit the area and investigate a possible case for prosecution, with the help of policeman Buck Maxwell.

Johnson arrives in town to find that Haven Allridge is suddenly AWOL, and the newspaper's exposes have abruptly ceased. The affidavits Allridge collected from the sheriff's victims are now missing from his office. Few people are willing to talk to the state prosecutor, except for a friendly young woman in a bar, Cleo, whom he correctly guesses is in Burke's employ. Taking a liking to Johnson, Cleo admits she was told to bring him to Burke's illicit gambling club, Amboy's. He decides he might get some valuable information, and lets it be thought he was lured there by her charms. He's approached by Burke's lawyer, Nelson Tarsson, who, failing to secure Johnson's cooperation with a bribe, warns him that he will have difficulty proving any charges against his client.

One by one, the potential witnesses against Burke respond to threats and intimidation, recanting their stories. By placing pressure on crooked club proprietor Bennie Amboy, Johnson and Maxwell learn that Haven Allridge hasn't been seen since the night he was taken upstairs for a meeting at Amboy's. That night, Allridge was pressured to turn over the affidavits and cease his investigative reporting. When he refused to cooperate, violence ensued and Amboy admits he hasn't seen Allridge since.

Allridge abruptly resurfaces at his daughter's home, telling her he's been doing a job in Detroit, and will be going back there. Johnson promptly subpoenas him to be the star witness at the hearing which will determine whether or not a criminal case against Burke and his cohorts will go forward. A subdued Allridge warns the young lawyer not to call him as a witness, as he will not cooperate.

Johnson considers canceling the hearing and returning to the state capitol, disgusted that his most important witness seems to be developing cold feet, but is urged by Captain Maxwell to persist. Returning to his hotel, the prosecutor finds an unsigned note that alerts him, "They got Cleo in the jail!" He strong-arms his way into the prison, decks the guard, and is about to leave with a grateful Cleo when there's a confrontation with Burke and his men. Maxwell's intervention allows them to leave safely, and Cleo boards a train headed out of town.

The Sellout: Can prosecutor Chick Johnson (John Hodiak, left) count on newspaperman Haven Allridge (Walter Pidgeon) to do the right thing?

At the hearing, Johnson calls Allridge, who initially declines to answer any but the first question he's asked, in which he acknowledges being a newspaperman. He's asked to stay in the courtroom, and looks on as multiple other witnesses give in to fear, and refuse to incriminate Burke. Although the still-jailed Wilfred Jackson testifies truthfully about his experience, the evidence is slim enough that the outcome of Johnson's case looks bad, until he gets last-minute help from an unexpected source.

Shot under the title "County Line," *The Sellout* has been described by author Larry Langman as "absorbing but preachy,"[41] and the validity of both adjectives is reflected in the mixed reviews it received upon initial release. The early scenes lead us to believe that Walter Pidgeon is playing our hero, a crusading newspaperman, who explains to his son-in-law his credo as a journalist: "When I cashed my first $12 check as a kid reporter, I took on the newspaperman's chore of playing watchdog to a free society, and it's my job to bark my lungs out whenever I see a burglar prowling around." But it soon begins to seem that he's instead playing the title character, and the main good-guy baton is passed to Hodiak, as prosecutor Chick Johnson.

Hodiak, who inherited the role after Robert Walker declined it, anchors the film with his strong performance as what the scheming sheriff describes as a "smart kid from the Attorney General's office," who during his stay in Bridgewood and environs develops a new appreciation for the work he's considered giving up for a more lucrative job. He shows that he can throw a punch like an action hero, but also convinces as a tenacious lawyer and prosecutor. As the situation grows tense in the courtroom, he mutters to Maxwell, "Here we go off the high board. I hope there's water in the pool."

Pidgeon effectively plays the heroic stance Allridge takes early on—when he's being railroaded into a court fine, and the judge tells him "Ignorance of the law is no excuse," Pidgeon retorts, "You're doing all right"—but also does well as the man whose fright begins to take hold of him as his family is threatened.

Twenty years before he began patrolling *The Streets of San Francisco* in that popular ABC series, Karl Malden (1912–2009) gives a realistic performance as the police captain who disagrees with Johnson on his methods, before the two men develop a more solid working relationship. Audrey Totter (1917–2013) has a few good moments as the somewhat cynical Cleo, who may get a second chance to improve her lot in life with Chick's help. Modern-day viewers may chuckle to see that one of Burke's conniving cohorts looks a lot like Sam Drucker of TV's Hooterville, but character actor Frank Cady's (1915–2012) performance as the man who cracks under pressure is quite good.

Scenarist and associate producer Matthew Rapf (1920–1991), getting one of his earliest professional credits here, went on to become a successful television producer, with series including *Ben Casey* (ABC, 1961–66) and *Kojak* (CBS, 1973–78) on his resume. Actress Paula Raymond (1924–2003) seen as Peggy, was asked about Hodiak by film historian Dan Van Neste, and described her co-star as "Charming! I liked him enormously. He was a total professional."[42] This was the final film released from John's lengthy tenure as an MGM contract player.

Reviews: "While it tells a familiar story of corruption, 'The Sellout' tells it with more than usual dramatic emphasis and effect.... The story is old hat, but it achieves a convincing tone through Gerald Mayer's restrained direction and the playing of a veteran cast.... John Hodiak makes the most of his sides as the sleuth-prosecutor."—*Film Bulletin*, December 31, 1951

"What could have been an acceptable program melodrama comes out a wordy little lesson in civic consequences.... The script gets on a soapbox with a lot of ponderous dialog clichés that mean nothing.... Very few requirements are made on the cast by the script and Gerald Mayer's direction. Development and performances are routine despite a few attempts at being different."—*Variety*, December 19, 1951

Battle Zone (1952)

John Hodiak (*MSgt. Danny Young*), Stephen McNally (*Sgt. Mitch Turner*), Linda Christian (*Jeanne*), Martin Milner (*Cpl. Andy Sayer*), Dave Willock (*Smitty*), Jack Larson (*Cpl. James O'Doole*), Richard Emory (*Lt. Mike Orlin*), Philip Ahn (*South Korean Guerrilla Leader*), Carleton Young (*Colonel*), John Fontaine (*Lt. Pilot*), Todd Karnes [Karns] (*Officer*), Gil Stratton, Jr. (*Marine Runner*), Charles Bronson (*Private*), Harry Lauter (*Marine Intelligence Officer*), Dorothy Patrick (*Danny's Girl*), Peter Adams (*Marine Truck Driver*), Lee Choon Wha (*Korean Farmer*), William Cabanne (*Sentry*), Cosmo Sardo (*Bartender*), Billy Lechner (*Photo Interpreter*), Herb Jacobs, Gregory Walcott (*Riflemen*), Lee Graham, Tom Irish, Alvy Moore, Robert Nichols, Bob Sanford (*Marines*)

Director: Lesley Selander. *Producer*: Walter Wanger. *Screenplay*: Steve Fisher. *Associate Producer*: William *Photography*: Ernest Miller. *Film Editor*: Jack Ogilvie. *Production Manager*: Allen K. Wood. *Assistant Director*: Henry Hartman. *Research*: Lester A. Sansom. *Technical Supervision*: Capt. John M. Terry. U.S.M.C. *Art Director*: David Milton. *Recording*: Charles Cooper. *Set Continuity*: Gordon Otto. *Special Effects*: Ray Mercer. *Music*: Marlin Skiles.

Allied Artists; released October 26, 1952. B&W; 81 minutes.

In the early days of the Korean War, former newsreel photographer Danny Young gives up his civilian job to re-enlist as a non-commissioned officer in the Marines. Reporting for duty at Camp Pendleton, he finds his friendly rival, Sgt. Mitch Turner, who's become a career military man. Although Mitch is in charge of the Photographic Unit, Danny enjoys telling him that he will be working independently, with his own assignment from higher-ups.

Danny is still carrying a torch for Jeanne, an Italian-born Red Cross worker with whom he quarreled before they went their separate ways. Unaware of her current circumstances, he's delighted when she calls him and asks for a meeting there in San Diego. Danny doesn't realize that Jeanne is now the fiancée of Mitch, and doesn't react well when she breaks the news. She explains that she tried to contact him some time earlier, sought out Mitch to help, and then fell in love with him.

Within days, Danny, Mitch and Jeanne are all dispatched with their units to Korea, where the Marines are actively battling against enemy invasions. As is his wont, Danny goes right up to the battle zone to capture the best possible footage. Meanwhile, he bets Mitch a month's pay that he can get another date with Jeanne. Although she shares a friendly drink with him, Jeanne makes it clear that her loyalty is to Mitch. Danny tells her that she has mistaken security for love, and that he's not giving up on her.

Though Mitch explains to his cameramen that there is often value in footage taken behind the scenes, Danny devotes himself to capturing action footage, even when it places him into jeopardy. Despite Mitch's best efforts to leave him behind, Danny continues to track Mitch and his men as they go from snow country to hotter climes.

The enlisted men have been hoping that the war is winding down, and are disheartened when it's learned that Chinese Communist forces are invading the country in large numbers. Some 200,000 refugees and others are need of immediate evacuation. Mitch and Danny talk about the fact that American military intelligence is fast becoming obsolete thanks to the enemy's new efforts. Mitch has made plans to go undercover behind enemy lines, and Danny agrees to come along.

Danny and Mitch are unaware that there's a traitor within their ranks, whose actions put them in peril. While the officers they left behind find their film footage invaluable, a deadly confrontation with the North Korean invaders leaves several men dead, and Danny wounded. Back at camp, the two sergeants come to a new mutual respect, and Jeanne resolves the question of which of them will play into her future.

Made on a reported $200,000 budget, *Battle Zone* is John Hodiak's first film gig as a freelancer, shot after his initial Broadway sojourn, in *The*

Chase. He plays a role familiar to action movie fans—the military man who rebels against authority, and bends the rules every chance he gets, but delivers the necessary heroics when the need arises. For much of the film's running time, Danny and Mitch primarily wield movie cameras rather than weapons, as *Battle Zone* is devoted to showing the importance of the work war photographers do. As Danny, Hodiak is arrogant not only about his romantic prowess, confident he can win back Jeanne's hand, but about his wartime skills, looking down on Mitch's approach to covering the Marines' offensive:

> **MITCH:** Listen, Sergeant, there's been something I've been meaning to ask you.
> **DANNY:** What, how to shoot a war?

In the opening titles, the production company acknowledges the Department of Defense, the Marines, and the people of Camp Pendleton for production cooperation and assistance. While shooting at Camp Pendleton, John posed for pictures with numerous young Marines that were sent for publication in their hometown newspapers.

An early casting announcement in the *Los Angeles Times* (May 26, 1952) stated that Edmond O'Brien had been signed for the leading role in *Battle Zone.* About a month later, however, the same publication's Edwin Schallert noted that O'Brien "found himself facing two commitments at the same time" and withdrew, with John, recently returned from his Broadway sojourn, stepping into the role.

Stephen McNally (1911–1994) is cast as Mitch. A solid, unglamorous actor, he ably incorporated both heroes and villains into his onscreen repertoire. Linda Christian (1923–2011) was Mexican by birth, but is credible here as an Italian woman. She was at this time the wife of film star Tyrone Power, though they would divorce in 1956. Among the young actors featured as enlisted men are Jack Larson (1928–2015), better known as Jimmy Olsen on TV's *The Adventures of Superman,* and Martin Milner (1931–2015), whose credits include two hit series, *Route 66* and *Adam-12.* Alvy Moore (1921–1997), always remembered as Hank Kimball on TV's *Green Acres,* has a tiny role as well.

Director Lesley Selander (1900–1979) does a skillful job of integrating actual documentary footage of the Korean War into scenes that show his principal players at or near the front line. A veteran of numerous Westerns, he will again direct John in another wartime saga, *Dragonfly Squadron* (1954). Under Selander's guidance, *Battle Zone* is well-equipped to satisfy the audience for which it was intended, despite the trite romantic subplot. In the view of film historian Robert J. Lentz, "*Battle Zone* comprises a compact history of the first year of the war. It is not a detailed

Red Cross worker Jeanne (Linda Christian) is a lady with at least two admirers, one of them Danny (John Hodiak), in *Battle Zone* (1952).

history, but it is accurate and thoughtfully illustrates the war's various stages in an easy to understand fashion."[43]

Walter Wanger (1894–1968) was, by necessity, something of an absentee producer for *Battle Zone*. During production, he was serving a four-month prison sentence for the December 1951 incident in which he shot his wife Joan Bennett's agent Jennings Lang, with whom he believed she was having an affair. According to columnist Louella O. Parsons (June 14, 1952), the film "was put into work before Walter started his sentence at the prison farm. Carrying on in Walter's absence is Walter Mirisch." Wanger's secretary reportedly paid daily visits to him in prison so that he could maintain his involvement in the film during shooting. Wanger was released from jail in September 1952, about six weeks prior to the film's opening night.

Reviews: "An interesting film that should do okay at the box office. Film has strong marquee power ... and boasts some exciting actual war footage.... Hodiak, McNally and Miss Christian all turn in well-shaded performances."—*Independent Film Journal*, October 18, 1952

"A fine representation of the Korean War that is authentic, compelling and bears rare conviction. John Hodiak, Stephen McNally and Linda Christian perform well under the excellent direction of Lesley Selander.... This appears to be a money-maker for all situations.... There is plenty of action in this neatly balanced production which has effectively emphasized a genuine and plausible story."—*Motion Picture Daily*, October 15, 1952

Ambush at Tomahawk Gap (1953)

John Hodiak (*McCord*), John Derek (*Kid*), David Brian (*Egan*), Maria Elena Marques (*Navajo Girl*), Ray Teal (*Doc*), John Qualen (*Jonas P. Travis*), Otto Hulett (*Stranton*), Percy Helton (*Marlowe*), Trevor Bardette (*Twin Forks Sheriff*), Steve Clark (*Prison Wagon Driver*), John Doucette (*Burt*), Gail Robinson (*Frank Egan*), Harry Cording (*Stableman*), John War Eagle (*Indian Chief*)

Director: Fred F. Sears. *Producer*: Wallace MacDonald. *Story and Screenplay*: David Lang. *Director of Photography*: Henry Freulich. *Art Director*: Walter Holscher. *Technicolor Color Consultant*: Francis Cugat. *Film Editor*: Aaron Stell. *Set Decorator*: Louis Diage. *Assistant Director*: James Nicholson. *Sound Engineer*: George Cooper. *Musical Director*: Ross DiMaggio.

Columbia; released May 5, 1953. Color; 73 minutes.

Four ex-prisoners from the Yuma Territorial Prison are dropped off in the town of Twin Falls after serving a five-year sentence for stagecoach robbery. Three of them—leader Egan, Doc, and the Kid, are members of the gang responsible for the crime; the fourth is McCord, an innocent bystander who was mistaken for their cohort and wrongly convicted.

Their presence in Twin Falls, the sheriff makes plain, is not welcome, telling them they are allowed to stay for no more than an hour. In the local saloon, McCord promptly punches Egan, saying, "I've been waiting to do that for five years." After the brawl that ensues, the gang members leave McCord behind and head out. People in Twin Falls know that there are Apache Indians in the surrounding hills, but don't see any reason to warn the ex-prisoners to whom they sold horses and weapons. McCord barters his saddle for a rifle and a horse from a man, Stranton, who tells him that the fourth gang member, Egan's brother Frank, was killed after cheating in a poker game at Tomahawk Gap.

McCord follows the three gang members and comes to the rescue when they are attacked by Indians. Afterwards, he tells them that Frank is dead, and that he intends to follow along as they retrieve the $10,000 he hid from the robbery. He makes it plain that he expects to be reimbursed for serving the dead man's prison time, with a share of the proceeds.

En route, the men find a young Indian woman alone, who defends herself by firing a shot that wounds the Kid's arm. Egan wants to leave him behind, but Doc insists on tending to him, with the help of the woman, hoping the Kid can be persuaded to go straight.

On arrival in Tomahawk Gap, the troupe finds that it has become a ghost town. A windstorm prevents Egan from immediately searching for the bankroll, while Doc removes the bullet from the Kid. Egan attempts to assault the woman, but is interrupted by the arrival of a stranger, the last remaining resident of the town. Jonas P. Travis announces that he is the caretaker of the town's graveyard, and objects when the men begin digging at a gravesite where they expect to find the stolen money. They find a cashbox, but it's empty.

Not wanting to stay in the town too long, the men hurriedly tear it apart in search of the stolen money. Unexpectedly, Stranton appears, planning to recoup the money and return it to the Army, and warning that Army men are heading there. The bandits overpower him, but while under guard, he uses a broken mirror to signal the Apaches, waiting nearby. McCord urges the other men to keep going a bit longer in search of the money.

Egan becomes the first of the gang to get an arrow in the back, just as he's attacking the Indian woman again. The men head out of town, leaving her behind because Jonas lies that it was she who signaled the Apaches, but they are soon forced to turn back when they realize they are surrounded. The remaining ex-convicts are forced into a bloody confrontation with Indian fighters, which only one of them will survive.

After serving a prison term for a crime he didn't commit, McCord (John Hodiak) is ready to settle a few scores in *Ambush at Tomahawk Gap* (Columbia, 1953).

A modestly budgeted but well-made Western, *Ambush at Tomahawk Gap* is a bit more violent than usual for the period, with a relatively high body count despite its short running time. Although sagas of the Old West will become increasingly commonplace on television as the decade progresses, Columbia hedges its bets against the newer game in town with a more adult story and good-quality color photography that couldn't yet be found on most small screen Westerns.

Top-billed John Hodiak demonstrates that he's well-suited to the Western genre, riding, shooting, and taking part in multiple action sequences, though his character McCord is usually the one urging the others not to use their guns. David Brian (1914–1993) capably enacts the role of the violent and bloodthirsty Egan. The two are at odds for much of the film, but McCord isn't intimidated. Early on, he tells Egan he intends to find his brother and see him imprisoned, despite his rival's warning:

EGAN: He'll kill you.
MCCORD (coolly): He'll have to.

Though at least one reviewer at the time of the film's release complained that it offered no one for whom to root, Hodiak's McCord is shown to have a moral code of his own. Having been unjustly jailed, he calculates the amount of money he would have earned at his honest job during those five years, and demands only that as compensation. His final scene shows him making a dangerous move against the Indians that costs him dearly.

David Lang's well-constructed screenplay is economical with names throughout; the old codger Travis, when he introduces himself, becomes one of the only characters whose full moniker we learn. (The first names of the protagonists, including Hodiak's McCord, are never divulged, nor is the name of the young Navajo woman they meet.) Always a reliable supporting player, John Qualen (1899–1987) has a good character role here as Travis, who protests in vain as the bandits invade the ghost town and hunt for the missing money. John Derek (1926–1998) and Mexican-born actress/singer María Elena Marqués provide the love interest, as the Kid and the Navajo captive. Miss Marqués, who speaks no English dialogue in the film, is making her second screen appearance with Hodiak, as she was previously seen in *Across the Wide Missouri*. Hers is the only female role in the film. The other men show less interest in her character than might be expected after a five-year stretch in prison, with only Brian's character predisposed to take advantage of her, though he's unsuccessful in doing so. Ray Teal (1902–1976), who would cross over to the right side of the law as the sheriff on TV's *Bonanza*, plays the older gang member who hopes to persuade the Kid to make a new start in life while he can. Always a busy character actor, Teal is making his fourth appearance in a Hodiak feature.

Ambush at Tomahawk Gap is an entertaining Western drama with plenty of action and some good performances. It is efficiently directed by Fred F. Sears (1913–1957), who like Hodiak would die young after making only a few more films. It received a "B" rating from the National League of Decency, so tabbed due to "excessive brutality." It demonstrates one arena into which Hodiak's career might have gone had he lived longer, as he easily could have followed fellow movie actors like John Payne and Rod Cameron into lucrative employment as the star of a Western TV series.

Reviews: "Here is a delight for Western film fans. Although made along formula lines, this action-filled story, made in color by Technicolor, is far superior to the ordinary fun of outdoor films. It is brisk, straightforward and morally meaningful. The competent cast is headed by John Hodiak.... Fred F. Sears is the director, responsible for keeping things in a state of suspense right up to the final ironic shot."—*Motion Picture Daily*, May 8, 1953

"A hard-hitting blood-and-thunder western that will please action fans who like their sagebrush epics brutal [sic] and savage.... The picture's title is a strong exploitation item and the star names of John Hodiak, John Derek and David Brian should help at the box office. Still another plus item is the excellent Technicolor photography."—*Independent Film Journal*, May 2, 1953

Mission Over Korea (1953)

John Hodiak (*Capt. George Slocum*), John Derek (*Lt. Pete Barker*), Audrey Totter (*Kate*), Maureen O'Sullivan (*Nancy Slocum*), Harvey Lembeck (*Sgt. Maxie Steiner*), Richard Erdman (*Pvt. Swenson*), William Chun (*Kilamson Lee*), Rex Reason (*Maj. Jim Hacker*), Richard Bowers (*Singing Soldier*), Ralph Ahn (*Radio Operator*), Walter "Pee Wee" Flannery (*George Slocum, Jr.*), Susan Hawkins (*Slocum's Little Girl*), Tyler McVey (*Col. Colton*), John Pickard (*Maj. McGuire*), Todd Karns (*2nd Lt. Jerry Barker*), John Crawford (*Tech Sergeant*), Sumner Williams (*Jeep Driver*), Norma Randall (*Blonde*), Al Choi (*Maj. Kung*)

Director: Fred F. Sears. *Producer*: Robert Cohn. *Screenplay*: Jesse L. Lasky, Jr., Eugene Ling, Martin M. Goldsmith. *Story*: Richard Tregaskis. *Director of Photography*: Sam Leavitt. *Art Director*: George Brooks. *Set Decorator*: Frank Tuttle. *Assistant Director*: James Nicholson. *Sound Engineer*: George Cooper. *Musical Director*: Mischa Bakaleinikoff. *Technical Adviser*: Capt. Paul F. Hopkins.

Columbia; released July 10, 1953. B&W; 84 minutes.

Army Captain George Slocum, a pilot involved in military reconnaissance, is summoned from his base at Kimpo, Korea to a meeting in

Japan, which affords him a welcome opportunity for a brief reunion with his wife Nancy and children. While there, he promises to look up his buddy Jerry Barker's kid brother Pete, who's now a lieutenant. On arrival, Pete, who was expecting Jerry, buzzes George's plane as a prank. George chews him out, but comes to his defense when the young pilot is called on the carpet.

En route back to Kimpo, enemy action causes George and Pete to be instructed to fly on to Seoul, though they are low on fuel. Passing over Kimpo, a grim sight awaits them—the base has been attacked, with heavy losses of men. One of the injured is Jerry, who shortly afterwards succumbs to his injuries. A bitter Pete, already showing signs of being a hothead, vows revenge for his brother's death, saying of the enemy, "I want to pay them off in napalm." Despite George's warnings, Pete flies his plane low to fire at opposition soldiers, which results in the young pilot being injured and his vehicle damaged.

George is instructed to fly a load of supplies to American forces under attack. Leaving the base, George allows young Kilamson Lee, a civilian

Captain George Slocum (John Hodiak) is happy to be reunited with his wife (Maureen O'Sullivan) and young son (Walter "Pee Wee" Flannery) in *Mission Over Korea* (1953).

known to the soldiers he hero-worships as "Clancy," to ride along. Once again going against orders, Pete tries to bomb an enemy tank, causing his plane to be shot down. George is relieved when Pete, whom he was forced to leave behind, is brought safely back. Though sympathizing with Pete's grief over his brother's death, he warns him he won't tolerate another incident of insubordination.

A surprise attack on the base leaves George critically wounded. Pete commandeers the unit's last remaining plane to fly George to a hospital for emergency surgery, but shortly after arrival, the captain dies of his injuries. Nancy, a nurse with whom Pete has previously had a flirtatious relationship, tells him he must now step up to the plate, that the mission George was carrying out is too important not to be fulfilled. Pete faces a test of his mettle as he takes command of the men in his unit.

Mission Over Korea is an adequate, if unexceptional, programmer that pays tribute to the American forces who served in the war. The film's pressbook described its lead characters as "the 'seeing eye dogs' of the Artillery—the gallant guys who go behind enemy lines to spot the targets for our big guns!" Like *Battle Zone* the previous year, it tells the story of Army men who support the men on the ground with their information-gathering abilities, yet find themselves at mortal risk. Though performances are generally good, its main appeal is likely to be to action or aviation buffs, who will enjoy the plentiful combat footage.

Film historian Robert J. Lentz critiqued the film as "suffer[ing] from the normal B-movie maladies of a formulaic script, contrived situations, actors of less than exceptional talent and a general lack of imagination," but did acknowledge its "very authentic feel as far as the military situation goes."[44] Producer Robert Cohn stated in a newspaper interview that the director and two cameramen spent eight weeks on location in Korea. "We shot 85,000 feet of completely realistic film," Cohn said, "and most of it was so much better than the action prescribed by the script that we rewrote the screenplay to fit the action shot."[45] Serving as the film's technical adviser was Korean War veteran Captain Paul Hopkins, who explained, "When most men go into combat, their only knowledge of warfare has been from what they've seen in the movies. That's why the Army wants war pictures to be done as accurately as possible."[46] Script feedback from Hopkins and his Army colleagues resulted in reducing the number of guerrillas killed by two American soldiers, thinking five more credible than the nine originally specified.

This is John's second film in less than a year for director Fred F. Sears, though it's a step down for both from *Ambush at Tomahawk Gap*. He's more than capable of filling the role of another military man in wartime, though he gets no standout scenes here.

While the cast list includes two actresses whose names had value on a marquee, their screen time is limited. Maureen O'Sullivan (1911–1998), playing George Slocum's loyal wife, is in the film for no more than ten minutes. She manages to make an impression in those few moments, and plays well off Hodiak, but it's really just an extended cameo. Faring slightly better is Audrey Totter as Kate, a dedicated Army nurse who tells Pete of the imperiled soldiers for whom she cares, "They're all great guys, and they all mean something to somebody."

John Derek (1926–1998), a young Columbia contract player being given the star buildup, is cast in the stereotypical war movie role of the hotheaded maverick, which he plays competently. Richard Erdman (1925–2019) makes the most of his featured role as Private Swenson, which finds him playing his opening scene wearing only a towel. Swenson, who describes himself as "just a little guy from East Los Angeles," is none too happy to find what he let himself in for, saying sadly, "I had to open my big mouth and enlist." He's paired with Harvey Lembeck (1923–1982), and the two give the film a few lighter moments. The on-screen Army cadre receives a welcome touch of diversity by the brief appearance of African American GI man and singer Richard Bowers, who sings "Forgive Me," which charted briefly.

The film's pressbook provided suggested language for a 30-second radio spot promoting the film: "See Korea as the flying-eyes of the artillery see it! Follow the big men in small planes on the greatest adventure of all! Thrill with the hill-hopping, flak-happy hellions for excitement, action and love at the front in 'Mission over Korea.' It's Columbia Pictures' cavalcade of glory starring John Hodiak, John Derek, Audrey Totter, and Maureen O'Sullivan! 'Mission over Korea' is sky-high with thrills! For Korea's greatest ack-ack action-packed adventure, see 'Mission over Korea' starting tomorrow at the State Theatre."

Reviews: "Although it has a better-than-average cast, *Mission Over Korea* is an ordinary war melodrama that does not rise above the level of program fare. Its cliché-ridden story offers little that is novel, and the characterizations are trite.... What appears to be considerable actual combat footage has been worked into the proceedings, but even this fails to impress because of the routine story treatment and the lack of forceful drama."—*Harrison's Reports*, July 25, 1953

"*Mission Over Korea* is a sock title and the basic idea of the picture is a good one, but somewhere along the line something went terribly wrong ... for the picture is an average war melodrama telling a familiar story. The performances are able, but material limits them.... It has a great deal of exploitation value in its title and subject matter, which will aid in its selling."—*Independent Film Journal*, August 8, 1953

Conquest of Cochise (1953)

John Hodiak (*Cochise*), Robert Stack (*Maj. Tom Burke*), Joy Page (*Consuelo de Cordova*), Rico Alaniz (*Felipe*), Fortunio Bonanova (*Minister*), Edward Colmans (*Don Francisco de Cordova*), Alex Montoya (*Jose Garcia*), Steven Ritch (*Tukiwah*), Carol Thurston (*Terua*), Rodd Redwing (*Red Knife*), Robert E. Griffin (*Sam Maddock*), Poppy Del Vando (*Señora de Cordova*), John Crawford (*Capt. Bill Lawson*), Edward Hearn (*Gen. Gadsden*), Tyler MacDuff (*White Water*), Joseph Waring (*Running Cougar*), Daniel Nunez (*Ranch Hand*), Chris Willow Bird, Herman Hack, Gil Perkins, Tony Urchel (*Apache Braves*), Victor Adamson, Buck Bucko, Tex Holden (*Townsmen*), Bill Coontz, Billy McCoy (*Troopers*), Art Felix, Bob Folkerson (*Comanche Braves*)

Director: William Castle. *Producer*: Sam Katzman. *Screenplay*: Arthur Lewis, DeVallon Scott. *Story*: DeVallon Scott. *Associate Producer*: Herbert Leonard. *Director of Photography*: Henry Freulich. *Technicolor Color Consultant*: Francis Cugat. *Art Director*: Paul Palmentola. *Film Editor*: Al Clark. *Set Decorator*: Sidney Clifford. *Assistant Director*: Sam Nelson. *Sound Engineer*: Josh Westmoreland.

Columbia; released August 30, 1953. Color; 70 minutes.

Although the war between the U.S. and Mexico is over, representatives of the two countries are still negotiating the ownership of the land surrounding Tucson. A treaty that will make it U.S. territory is under discussion in Mexico City. In the meantime, both Americans and Mexicans living in the region are under attack by Apache and Comanche Indians.

Major Tom Burke of the U.S. Cavalry is assigned by his general to undertake a mission seeking peace with the Indians. He is warned that his troops will be substantially outnumbered by the Indians, and that Cochise, chief of the Comanches, is a formidable opponent. In Tucson, he is invited to be the guest of Don Francisco de Cordova and family at his hacienda. Don Francisco is hopeful that peace can be achieved with Burke's help, but Felipe, whose wife was killed by Indians, does not believe they can be trusted.

Cochise accepts a meeting with Major Burke, hears his proposal, and tells him the tribe will give him their answer in six days, saying, "I will be for peace, but my people may be for war." Major Burke is attracted to Don Francisco's beautiful daughter Consuelo, and tries to court her with champagne, but without success.

Running Cougar speaks for the Comanches who are opposed to seeking peace with the white man. He leads a war party that attacks the de Cordova hacienda and other homes, with violence breaking out. Cochise comes to the defense of the family against the onslaught, during which

Running Cougar is killed. A vengeful Red Knife, Running Cougar's brother, declares that there can be no peace with the white men. Cochise and his woman, Terua, leave for Tucson so that he can talk further with Major Burke, but en route she is killed by Felipe, who has been urged to target Cochise by Sam Maddock, a Tucson saloonkeeper who has his own reasons for opposing the peace treaty.

Cochise, grieving Terua, realizes that his people need reassurance from the Americans, and decides Burke must be compelled to visit their camp. To insure this, Consuelo is taken hostage by the Indians. She treats Cochise with respect, and he grows to admire her.

Major Burke meets with Cochise, and is given four days to prove his assertion that Terua was not killed by an American soldier. If he is unable to do so, Cochise and his tribe will go to war against the white man. Burke learns that Felipe was responsible for the death, and takes him to Cochise, promising he will get a fair trial. When Consuelo confirms the truth of Burke's account, Cochise pledges to stop the imminent battle. When Felipe tries to battle the Indians, he is killed.

Cochise's Comanche counterpart disagrees with his belief that the treaty with the Americans has been upheld. Cochise is sentenced to death by the Comanches, but Major Burke and his men attempt to stop the proceedings.

Though *Conquest of Cochise* offers Hodiak top billing, and a sizable role, it isn't among his more noteworthy films. Its main selling points are the action and battle scenes. With only limited help from the screenplay, John gives the Indian character strength and dignity, bringing out his integrity as well as the challenges faced by his tribe because of the white man. He is a man who responds to reason, but also tells Consuelo, "Survival is our religion." It's debatable, however, whether it is, as the studio pressbook claimed, "a drastic departure from anything he has ever attempted before on the screen," given earlier roles such as the one he played in *Across the Wide Missouri*. Studio publicists said he rode three similar-looking horses onscreen, depending on whether the scene called for jumping, running, or standing still while the human actors spoke.

Hodiak demonstrates a stronger screen presence than that of Robert Stack (1919–2003), who gives an adequate but uninspired performance as his American ally. Joy Page (1924–2008), playing Consuelo, made her film debut as a teenager, playing a refugee in *Casablanca* (1942). The characters played by Hodiak and Miss Page develop a romantic connection that culminates with Consuelo's teaching the Indian warrior the American custom of kissing, though they will have a bittersweet ending.

The character of Cochise figured into other films during this decade,

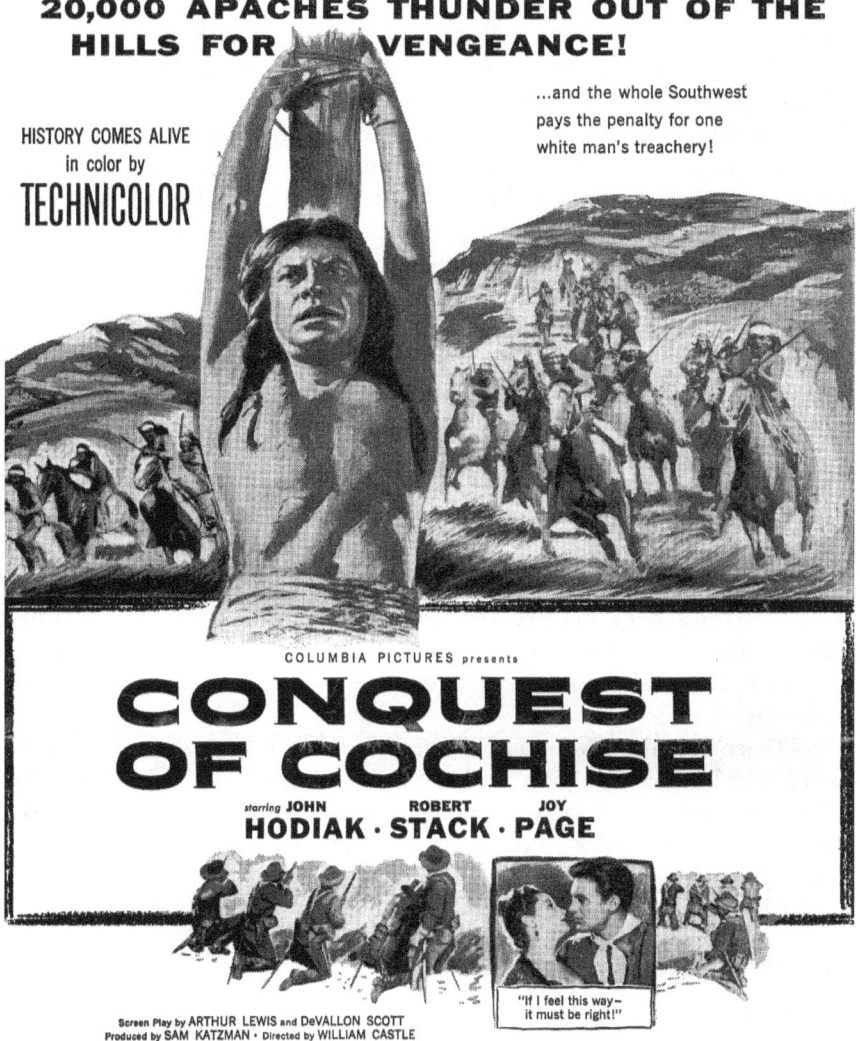

Newspaper ads for *Conquest of Cochise* (1953) depicted the harrowing scene in which the Native American leader (John Hodiak) is threatened with a violent death.

including *Broken Arrow* (1950), in which Jeff Chandler played the role. Rock Hudson played the title role in *Taza, Son of Cochise* (1954).

Producer Sam Katzman (1901–1973) was a longtime maker of low-budget B movies, and would expand his output in the 1950s to include monster movies and teenage musicals. He readily conceded that profit was the main motive of his output, and actors grew accustomed to his habit of making movies with great speed. According to an item in the *Motion Picture Herald* (November 29, 1952), *Conquest of Cochise* was only one of seventeen films on Katzman's production roster for 1953.

Director William Castle (1914–1977) would go on to greater notoriety a few years later, when he began producing horror films. Castle recalled in his memoirs that Katzman balked not only at the number of Indians he wanted onscreen, but also at paying the extra fees necessary to get the performers to shave their heads, suggesting instead that they be fitted with bathing caps painted brown. The result failed to impress Columbia studio head Harry Cohn (1891–1958), who phoned the director and demanded, "Who in the hell authorized the scene where one hundred fucking Indians go swimming—and with bathing caps!"[47] Screenwriter DeVallon Scott (1910–1997) would go on to contribute scripts to TV's *Broken Arrow*, in which Cochise was a featured character.

Though shot prior to *Mission to Korea,* this was Hodiak's final film released before beginning his Broadway run in *The Caine Mutiny Court-Martial,* which opened in January 1954.

Reviews: "'Conquest of Cochise' is a first-rate outdoor drama that will do okay in the general market. The film has some fine Technicolor photography and is loaded with action. It boasts a strong story [and] a freshness in its story line that should please audiences."—*Independent Film Journal*, September 5, 1953

"There's plenty of action here not only involving soldiers vs. Indians but also Indians vs. Indians, and the use of Technicolor helps, too. The story is fairly interesting, and the direction, acting, and production are okeh. This should make an okeh entry for the duallers."—*The Exhibitor*, August 26, 1953

Dragonfly Squadron (1954)

John Hodiak (*Maj. Matthew Brady*), Barbara Britton (*Donna Cottrell*), Bruce Bennett (*Dr. Stephen Cottrell*), Jess Barker (*Dixon*), Gerald Mohr (*Capt. MacIntyre*), Chuck Connors (*Capt. Warnowski*), Harry Lauter (*Capt. Vedders*), Pamela Duncan (*Anne Taylor*), Adam Williams (*Capt. Wyler*), John Lupton (*Capt. Woody Taylor*), Benson Fong (*Capt. Liehtse*), Richard [Dick] Simmons (*Col. Wolf Schuller*), John Hedloe (*Capt. Wycoff*), Frank Ferguson (*Col. Conners*), James Flavin (*Doctor*), Fess Parker (*Texan Lieutenant*), James Hong (*South Korean Pilot Trainee*)

Director: Lesley Selander. *Writer/Producer*: John Champion. *Photography*: Harry Neumann. *Supervising Editor*: Lester A. Sansom. *Film Editor*: Walter Hannemann. *Production Manager*: Allen K. Wood.

Music Editor: Eve Newman. *Assistant Director*: Rex Bailey. *Technical Supervision*: Col. Dean Hess, USAF. *Art Director*: David Milton. *Unit Manager*: Edward Morey, Jr. *Special Effects*: Augie Lohman. *Recording*: Charles Cooper. *Makeup Artist*: Norman Pringle. *Set Decorator*: Robert Priestley. *Set Continuity*: Ted Schilz.

Allied Artists; released March 21, 1954. B&W; 82 minutes.

Major Matthew Brady is a grounded pilot in the U.S. Air Force. His superior officer awakens him in the middle of the night to tell him of a new assignment: he's to oversee the flight training of South Korean officers, using American planes, to aid the war effort. Given only a few hours to leave, Brady has a drink in the officers' club, where a pushy reporter, Dixon, asks if he's still grounded, and mentions the stories he's heard about Brady and "another man's wife."

Brady arrives at the Kongju Air Base, where he finds Dr. Stephen Cottrell and his wife Donna. She is the woman with whom Brady was previously involved, during a period when she believed her husband had been killed in Indochina. Donna wrote him a letter breaking off their relationship when she learned Dr. Cottrell was still alive, and Brady says he has tried to forget her. She admits that she told her husband about being involved with another man, but she has recommitted herself to Dr. Cottrell. Donna also tells her ex-lover that her husband, a gifted surgeon, can no longer operate due to the torture he underwent from the enemy, which left his hands badly burned. Later, she tells her husband that she longer finds Brady appealing, reaffirming her love for him.

Responsible for the medical care of the enlisted men, Dr. Cottrell expresses concern about the ambitious training plan Brady has made. The major tells the company members they will have 25 days to complete their training, and should expect to be flying on active duty immediately afterwards. Knowing the situation in Korea is rapidly escalating, Brady pushes his team hard, so much so that some of the Air Force men apply for transfers. Brady is unsympathetic except in the case of Captain Woody Taylor, whose wife is pregnant, and has been with him in Korea for some two years.

When one of the Korean soldiers makes his first flight attempt, he's intimidated by Russian planes hovering nearby. Not wanting the situation to escalate into direct confrontation, Brady uses a rocket to explode one of their own fuel tanks, and the resulting fireball causes the enemy aircraft to retreat. Though the men are shaping up under Brady's training, Captain Vedders holds a grudge against Brady, because he blames him for the death of his friend Johnny McKay.

The Cottrells and Brady are invited to dinner at the home of the

Major Matthew Brady (John Hodiak) loves another man's wife (Barbara Britton) in *Dragonfly Squadron* (1954).

Taylors, on the same day that Brady has to break the news to the young couple that their transfer was denied. Before dinner is over, Dr. Cottrell is summoned to the base hospital to check on a patient. Before leaving, he admits to his wife that his liking for Brady is growing, despite himself. In his absence, Donna urges Brady not to come back to the area again, and gives him a loving kiss she says will explain why.

Brady is ready to send more of the Korean pilots into the air, though his second-in-command, Captain MacIntyre, is hesitant, feeling they are being rushed. He suggests excusing one of the pilots, who's known to have gone AWOL the night before to visit his hospitalized sister, and is not well-rested, but Brady refuses to take his advice. Brady explains that Vedders' animosity stems from an incident in which his pal McKay's plane was attacked, and the pilot fatally injured. Brady, his co-pilot, apparently bailed out to save himself, was diagnosed as suffering from "no gravity tolerance," and has been grounded ever since.

The novice pilot crashes his plane and is killed, for which Brady's men blame him. But when an investigation shows that the plane was sabotaged, they realize he doesn't deserve their disapproval. Dixon, the reporter, resurfaces, wanting to get insider information about the war in exchange for not playing up the story of the pilot's death; Brady responds with a punch.

Word is spreading that an invasion by Russian forces is imminent. Brady's company is given twelve hours to prepare for evacuation. However, a general tells Brady that the United Nations may sanction the U.S. forces' taking a more active role to defend the area. Donna and her fellow Red Cross workers are to be transported out over land, but Dr. Cottrell feels he is needed, and opts to stay. When the officers fly out prior to the evacuation, Brady chooses to stay behind and aid the men on the ground.

A battalion of fighting men arrives to take a stand, but they have already suffered serious losses. Captain Warnowski, in charge of the unit, thinks their cause is hopeless, but Brady is determined to do his best to see that as many lives as possible are saved. Separated from Brady, Donna, too, finds herself in peril as the workers try to make their way to safety. As they await reinforcements, Brady and his men find themselves in the midst of war, short on weapons and in deadly danger.

John is reteamed here with his director from *Battle Zone* as he fights the Korean War onscreen for the third time. Once again, he projects quiet strength and intelligence in the role of a military leader, one whose grounding prevents his doing the work he once did, and handles action scenes with aplomb. His leading lady, Barbara Britton (1920–1980), makes a believable military nurse, and ably depicts the feelings that both she and Brady are trying to suppress. Early on, when she's trying to reassure her husband that she has recommitted herself to him, she downplays her earlier attraction to Brady, saying nonchalantly, "He's really very average."

Hodiak's casting was announced by trade papers in August 1953, with production scheduled to begin the following month. According to an item in the *Motion Picture Herald* (August 29, 1953), *Dragonfly Squadron* was one of fifteen upcoming films from Allied Artists that would boast "important name casts that have not been available to the company heretofore." It was the only one expected to be released in 3-D. Though it was filmed in that process, interest in the fad seemed to be dwindling by the time it was ready to premiere, and Allied Artists made it possible for theater managers to choose whether they wanted it "flat" or enhanced.

Chuck Connors (1921–1992), pursuing his second career after leaving professional sports, has a significant featured role in the last segment of the film as the military captain who clashes with Brady about what can be done in a situation that looks as if it may be fatal for them all. He was still a few years away from his successful role as the star of TV's *The Rifleman*. Bruce Bennett (1906–2007) is cast as a rather stuffy, reserved man who suffers by comparison to Matthew Brady, and gives a low-key performance that provides what the film needs.

Dragonfly Squadron is most like a traditional war movie in its final reel, when Brady and his men find themselves fighting for survival on the ground. In its earlier scenes, director Selander charts a steady course through the scenes depicting the training of pilots, interspersed with the personal dramas of the men and women dedicated to the cause. He maintains a steady pace that holds viewer interest, with the film less reliant on stock footage than *Battle Zone* was. The larger budget furnished by Allied Artists pays off, with a film that bears little resemblance to the company's earlier product under the Monogram name.

The film was shown to military personnel at the Pentagon, garnering their approval, for which the production company thanked them in the opening titles. Said film historian Robert J. Lentz, "*Dragonfly Squadron* could have been one of the most authentic, realistic and dramatic of all Korean War films, but it isn't ... it is shapeless rather than focused, vague rather than precise, and is not particularly interesting."[48] Though filmed prior to his Broadway success, it opened while Hodiak was treading the boards in New York, and represented his final lead role on film.

Reviews: "The story is familiar, and there is quite a bit of talk for an action film, but the action is there, along with some good stock footage. Performances are good. Where war films are patronized, this will round out the bill nicely."—*The Exhibitor*, February 10, 1954

"From a production point of view, this war melodrama is worthy of a major studio, for the characters are believable, and the dangers to which they are subjected hold the spectator in tense suspense.... The romance is fairly interesting.... John Hodiak does good work as a major."—*Harrison's Reports*, March 6, 1954

Trial (1955)

Glenn Ford (*David Blake*), Dorothy McGuire (*Abbe Nyle*), Arthur Kennedy (*Barney Castle*), John Hodiak (*D.A. John J. Armstrong*), Katy Jurado (*Consuelo Chavez*), Rafael Campos (*Angel Chavez*), Juano Hernandez (*Judge Theodore Motley*), Robert Middleton (*A.A. "Fats" Sanders*), John Hoyt (*Ralph Castillo*), Paul Guilfoyle (*Cap Grant*), Elisha Cook, [Jr.] (*Finn*), Ann Lee (*Gail Wiltse*), Whit Bissell (*Sam Wiltse*), Richard Gaines (*Dr. Johannes Schacter*), Barry Kelley (*Jim Brackett*), Charlotte Lawrence (*Eunice Webson*), Joe McGuinn (*Sgt. O'Flair*), Rodney Bell (*Lew Bardman*), George Ford, Charles Tannen (*Bailiffs*), Dorothy Green (*Mary Ackerman*), Grandon Rhodes (*Prof. Bliss*), John Rosser (*Assistant District Attorney*), Sheb Wooley (*Butteridge*), George

Bruggeman (*Photographer*), Michael Dugan (*Pine*), Eddie Baker (*Electrician*), Robert Bice (*Abbott*), Steve Carruthers (*Court Clerk*)
 Director: Mark Robson. *Producer*: Charles Schnee. *Screenplay*: Don M. Mankiewicz, from his novel. *Associate Producer*: James E. Newcom. *Director of Photography*: Robert Surtees. *Art Directors*: Cedric Gibbons, Randall Duell. *Set Decorators*: Edwin B. Willis, Fred MacLean. *Special Effects*: Warren Newcombe. *Assistant Director*: Robert Saunders. *Music*: Daniele Amfitheatrof. *Film Editor*: Albert Akst. *Recording Supervisor*: Wesley C. Miller. *Hair Stylist*: Sydney Guilaroff. *Makeup*: William Tuttle.
 MGM; released October 7, 1955. B&W; 145 minutes.

Young law professor David Blake is threatened with losing his teaching job at a state university because he has no courtroom experience. His supervisor, who wants to keep him, suggests to the dean that David spend his summer break working with a law firm. After several refusals, David is taken on by lawyer Barney Castle, to be paid only for his expenses. He is assigned the job of defending Mexican-American teenager Angel Chavez, who is accused of killing a young woman, Marie Wiltse, during a beach party at night in the town of San Juno. David will take the responsibility of arguing the case in the courtroom, while Barney devotes himself to raising the funds needed to defend Angel, whose family is nearly penniless.

Angel, who was discovered at the murder scene with scratches on his face, admits he knew Marie from school, and that they were kissing. But he says Marie ran from him and collapsed. David and Barney and secretary Abbe Nyle quickly learn that Marie suffered from a long-term case of rheumatic fever, which may have weakened her heart to the point of causing an attack. Nonetheless, because she was only sixteen, Angel was committing a felony, if he can be shown to be in the midst of engaging in statutory rape, and can be legally held accountable for her death. His mother Consuelo promises to cooperate with Barney and his associates in every way, knowing that there is substantial prejudice against non-white people in San Juno.

Local district attorney John J. Armstrong is an ambitious young man with his sights on higher office. He floats to Barney and David the possibility of allowing a plea deal for manslaughter, with a relatively short prison sentence. But David believes his new client is innocent, and Barney declares the state's case weak, and when the deal is declined Armstrong heatedly tells them he will charge the teenager with first-degree murder.

Marie's grieving parents are persuaded to hold a quiet, private sunrise funeral for their daughter, but it is invaded by local activists including Ralph Castillo, who believes firmly in the separation of the races. It

D.A. Armstrong (John Hodiak, standing) finds himself at odds with the legal team of Barney Castle (Arthur Kennedy, left), David Blake (Glenn Ford) and Abbe Nyle (Dorothy McGuire) in *Trial* (MGM, 1955).

becomes apparent that there is a bloodthirsty element of the townspeople who long to see Angel hanged, and jailer "Fats" Sanders has to fend off a lynch mob that's ready to take justice into their own hands. He persuades the mob to disperse, promising that Angel will be executed legally, and that he will never again run for office if he isn't.

David prepares for the trial with Abby's help, and they grow closer, exchanging a tentative kiss. Meanwhile, Barney travels to New York, where he quickly establishes the "Fund for Angel Chavez," and goes about making the young man a *cause célèbre*. David and Angel learn that the judge who will preside over the trial is African American; they worry that the ethnic aspects of the case will pressure Judge Motley to go overboard proving the defendant is not receiving favorable treatment because of his minority status. It takes some three weeks to select a jury, as David uses data provided by private investigators to weed out potential jurors who have racist associations, or are friends of "Fats" Sanders.

Barney demands David's presence in New York, where he has created a sizable fundraising machine, trading favors with other activist organizations with liberal ideals. David is expected to speak at a rally before a large crowd, but he is angered to see that among Barney's political bedfellows are members of the All People's Party. Barney acknowledges that many of its members are Communist, but reminds David that it takes money to defend an indigent client. David refuses to recite the rally speech Barney prepared for him, and returns to California.

He tells Abby that he has fallen in love with her, but that he blames her for not warning him about what the rally in New York would be like. David has been subpoenaed by a committee investigating Communist activities, but replies responding that he will be unable to appear until the trial has concluded. He realizes that Barney is a Communist, and that Abby was previously, as she admits, "the perfect fellow traveler," which she attributes to her youth and naiveté.

At the trial, a cardiologist testifies that the victim suffered a heart attack provoked by "violent exertion," which David does his best to call into question. Having determined not to put his client on the stand, David is about to rest his case when Barney asks Judge Motley to allow them a recess to confer. Barney insists that Angel testify, and Abby accuses him of making the young man a Communist martyr, believing his conviction and death will work to the party's advantage.

After Armstrong's skillful cross-examination of Angel's testimony, a verdict of guilty is returned. Just before the judge is ready to pronounce sentence, David asks to be heard, although Barney has dismissed him from the case, and convinced Consuelo that he bungled her son's case. Caught up in the fervor of the moment, Barney oversteps his bounds with the judge, giving David one final chance to save his young client from a deadly fate.

Trial is a stirring and engrossing drama that builds social and political issues into an intriguing courtroom story. Don M. Mankiewicz's screenplay pointedly sets the story several years in the past, to 1947, giving the audience a bit of separation from the problems of modern society that he confronts. Similar themes were covered a few years earlier in the Pine-Thomas film *The Lawless* (1950), directed by Joseph Losey.

Glenn Ford (1916–2006) heads the cast with a thoughtful performance as the trained lawyer who comes to terms with the real-life complexities of practicing law in an imperfect world. This is his second socially oriented film with young Rafael Campos (1936–1985), with whom he appeared earlier the same year in *Blackboard Jungle*. Dorothy McGuire (1916–2001) is well-cast as the intelligent, conscientious legal secretary, who comes to terms with her own misguided beliefs of the past as she grows closer to David. It's a role not dissimilar to her acclaimed performance in *Gentleman's Agreement* (1947), where she played a woman not so free of antisemitism as she believes. Miss McGuire scores strongly in the scene in which she poses as the accusing counsel for the investigating committee who, she asserts, will twist David's motives and actions into a damning condemnation of him.

Trial has a certain air of déjà vu for admirers of John's work who have already seen *The People Against O'Hara*. Once again, it's a drama about a lawyer facing an uphill battle to defend a young client against the odds, and once again Hodiak plays the politically ambitious district attorney; his "Jack Armstrong" (the name's resemblance to that of a radio hero is the subject of a joke), is described by Barney as "yesterday's football captain, tomorrow's governor." In Don M. Mankiewicz's novel from which *Trial* was adapted, it's said of Armstrong, "All he cares about is that he's got to be a Senator in fifteen years so he can serve two terms and still be young enough to be a possible President." Barney adds that, by offering to strike a plea deal, "His proposition is for us to trade away our guy's freedom for his own political advantage."[49]

Hodiak conveys this characterization clearly without making Armstrong a cartoonish villain, establishing him as a man who is not completely unscrupulous, though he's at odds with our hero. In his last film for MGM, Hodiak is particularly effective when Angel Chavez goes under the D.A.'s intense cross-examination, with director Mark Robson (1913–1978) using close-ups of both him and Rafael Campos to heighten the tense exchange.

Other good supporting performances come from Juano Hernandez (1896–1970), as the principled judge who refuses to be made a token because of his race, and Katy Jurado (1924–2002), as Angel's mother and most impassioned defender. John Hoyt (1905–1991) makes his racist character chilling with only a few moments onscreen.

The film was released only a couple of weeks prior to Hodiak's death.

Reviews: "A powerful movie [that] probes the ugly passions roused against a Mexican boy charged with a girl's murder.... It's as much a shocker as 'Blackboard Jungle' ... But it will have wider appeal, because its problem is more generally known and understood ... [Don M.] Mankiewicz himself made an excellent screen play of his compelling novel ... [Rafael] Campos, as the defendant, John Hodiak, as the prosecutor; Dorothy McGuire.... Katy Jurado ... and Robert Middleton are credits to the cast."—Corbin Patrick, *Indianapolis Star*, October 7, 1955

"With all [its] (1) storytelling and (2) political insight given strong scripting, directing and acting the result is powerful entertainment. 'Trial' is bound to move people and turnstiles.... From beginning to end the viewer's emotions are engaged.... A believable prosecutor, anxious to win but not bloodthirsty about it, gets just the right amount of aggressiveness in the interpretation of John Hodiak."—*Variety*, August 3, 1955

On the Threshold of Space (1956)

Guy Madison (*Capt. Jim Hollenbeck*), Virginia Leith (*Pat Lange*), John Hodiak (*Maj. Ward Thomas*), Dean Jagger (*Dr. Hugo Thornton*), Warren Stevens (*Capt. Mike Bentley*), Martin Milner (*Lt. Mort Glenn*), King Calder (*Lee Welch*), Walter Coy (*Lt. Col. Dick Masters*), Ken Clark (*Sgt. Ike Forbes*), Donald Murphy (*Sgt. Zack Deming*), Barry Coe (*Communications Officer*), Helen Bennett (*Mrs. Lange*), David Armstrong (*Radio Technician*), Donald Freed (*Paramedic Officer*), Jo Gilbert (*Secretary*), Juanita Close (*Nurse*)

Director: Robert D. Webb. *Producer*: William Bloom. *Writers*: Simon Wincelberg, Francis Cockrell. *Associate Producer*: Barbara McLean. *Music*: Lyn Murray. *Conductor*: Lionel Newman. *Director of Photography*: Joe MacDonald. *Art Direction*: Lyle R. Wheeler, Lewis H. Creber. *Set Decorations*: Walter M. Scott, Stuart A. Reiss. *Special Photographic Effects*: Ray Kellogg. *Film Editor*: Hugh S. Fowler. *Wardrobe Direction*: Charles LeMaire. *Orchestration*: Bernard Mayers. *Assistant Director*: Ad Schaumer. *Makeup*: Ben Nye. *Hair Styling*: Helen Turpin. *Sound*: W.D. Flick, Harry M. Leonard. *CinemaScope Lenses*: Bausch & Lomb. *Technical Advisors*: Malcolm C. Grow, Arthur M. Henderson, Edward G. Sperry, U.S.A.F. *Color Consultant*: Leonard Doss.

20th Century–Fox; released March 29, 1956. Color; 98 minutes.

Air Force Captain Jim Hollenbeck, a pediatrician in private life, recently attended jump school, so as better to understand how enlisted men are affected by the missions they undertake. He's dispatched by his boss, Lt. Col. Dick Masters, to Florida, where a recent test of an ejector seat ended with a broken shoulder for the man who made the jump. Realizing his medical knowledge, combined with first-hand experience, will be helpful, Jim offers to take his place in a second attempt. The broken arm he sustains as a result verifies that the injuries were attributable to a design flaw in the ejector seat, rather than human error.

Jim is nearing the end of a stint in the U.S. Air Force, and ready for his upcoming wedding to Pat Lange, another Air Force employee. But he's intrigued by the description of another project getting underway, one that will attempt to place a man in a hot-air balloon some twenty miles off ground. To work with Dr. Hugh Thornton on the new initiative will require him to re-enlist, and he talks it over with Pat, who gives him her support.

Jim and Pat are wed, but their honeymoon is interrupted with the news that Lt. Col. Masters was killed in a traffic accident. Taking the late Masters' place is Major Ward Thomas, who considers the program's efforts to research future space travel speculative, and tells Jim that other

Air Force activities will be given higher priority. As Jim's work continues, Pat begins to fear that her husband is becoming addicted to the thrill of danger.

Major Thomas is angry when newspapers report on Jim's experimentation, saying his exploits are in danger of causing a ban on human testing. Dr. Thornton agrees to accept responsibility for future experimentation, which Thomas insists be done initially on either dummies or animals rather than Air Force men. After more testing goes smoothly, Jim and Lt. Mort Glenn participate in another test of the gondola, as Pat watches nervously. At the critical moment when he's to jump, Lt. Glenn chokes. Against Major Thomas' orders, Jim jumps in his place. Afterwards, Jim is told by his boss that he's grounded. He considers Major Thomas overly cautious, but is informed by Pat that Thomas himself intends to undertake the next test at supersonic speed. Major Thomas' medical history includes a retinal hemorrhage, which may be aggravated by the test, but he goes forward nonetheless. He makes it safely through the test, but is blinded momentarily. Apologizing to his superior officer for underestimating him, Jim offers his resignation, but Major Thomas tears it up. Soon, Jim is awaiting the opportunity to carry out the ultimate test of the new equipment himself, as Pat waits fearfully.

On the Threshold of Space (1956) offered John his final film role, truncated slightly because he died unexpectedly during production.

Eight years John's junior, Guy Madison (1922–1996) capably plays the starring role of Captain Jim Hollenbeck. For much of the film, Madison handles the heroics, while John seems to be playing the typical commanding officer who oversees things from his comfortable office. Sporting eyeglasses, John clashes with Madison's character, accusing him of "risk[ing] the entire future of the program against a few columns of cheap publicity for himself." But, at 41, John isn't ready for Morris Ankrum roles. The second half of the movie finds his character, based on the real-life exploits of Col. John P. Stapp, becoming more active. John gives Major Thomas a moment or two of determinedly concealed panic when he reports, "I can't see." But as his vision gradually comes back into focus, he relaxes, saying lightly, "Well, I guess I won't need a seeing-eye dog after all." The two men are at loggerheads initially, but gradually come to a mutual understanding and respect.

On the Threshold of Space marked John's final onscreen appearance. He was due to report to the set on the day of his death. Because of his untimely passing on October 19, 1955, his role in the film had to be truncated slightly, and a few of his scenes omitted. Virginia Leith (1925–2019), at this time being given a "rising star" buildup by the studio, is adequate as Madison's wife, a role considerably more dignified than the one that will become her best-remembered, as a disembodied head in *The Brain That Wouldn't Die* (1963).

Martin Milner, previously seen alongside John in *Battle Zone*, appears as the Air Force officer whose last-minute panic puts Jim into danger, while Dean Jagger (1903–1991) brings his usual professionalism to the role of Dr. Thornton.

Movie audiences in the mid–1950s seemed fascinated by the largely untapped potential for space exploration, and B-movie producers obliged them with multiple sci-fi adventures depicting intergalactic travel and aliens from other planets. *On the Threshold of Space* is targeted at more adult viewers, especially those who are technology junkies, to depict the real-life actions that are bringing space travel closer to reality.

Fantasy and Science Fiction's reviewer (September 1956) wrote, "Threshold is a triumph of excellent gadgets over poor acting, poor writing, and poor direction…. But it must be said, in fairness, that the late John Hodiak turned in the finest performance of his career as the counterpart of Colonel Stapp."

Producer William Bloom said of his film, "The public demands freshness. It is a vital commodity. The public's taste has become jaded and the formula story doesn't excite them anymore. That's why stories with new facets and ideas that will intrigue the public are important." He acknowledged the "splendid cooperation" of Air Force officials, who permitted shooting on two bases.[50]

Reviews: "Top results can be expected from this brilliantly photographed ... color production based on the spectacular space-speed tests now being conducted by the U.S. Air Force. Concentrating on the role of the human guinea pigs who test men and equipment at high altitudes and incredible speeds, Threshold generates great suspense and excitement.... In leading roles, Guy Madison and Virginia Leith are appealing as the chief guinea pig and his understanding wife—with John Hodiak and Dean Jagger lending solid support."—*Independent Film Journal*, March 17, 1956

"From the subject of medical research designed to prepare man for space travel and investigation, 20th-Fox has fashioned an absorbing, highly exciting, film. If the film's inherent exploitables are developed, its boxoffice outlook is promising.... The Simon Wincelberg–Francis Cockrell script is sharp and tense, in an almost documentary style. Guy Madison is appealing as the young officer who risks some of the most daring experiments. The late John Hodiak and Dean Jagger also are impressive."—*Film Bulletin*, March 19, 1956

Selected Radio Performances

This compilation of John Hodiak's work on radio, though more detailed than those previously offered, is of necessity incomplete, but it documents as fully as currently possible his work in the medium. Not only done decades ago, his radio work consisted primarily of live performances. Some have survived to be heard in the 21st century; many others have not.

Radio performers, being unseen by audiences, and not required to memorize scripts, could and did appear in far more broadcasts than would be typical of television actors. It was commonplace for a radio actor in demand to appear on multiple programs on the same day, and to hold down continuing roles in more than one series simultaneously. Hodiak often did so.

His radio career breaks down into three phases, beginning with his roughly three-year stint in Detroit, where he became a regularly featured player in the dramatic programs at station WXYZ. Relocating to Chicago in the late 1930s, he built a solid career encompassing several shows heard nationwide, and had recurring roles in multiple popular series, mostly soap operas and adventure shows. After moving to Hollywood in 1943, he continued to perform regularly as a guest star, as did many motion picture actors, on established shows of the day.

Hodiak has a star on the Hollywood Walk of Fame for his radio work.

Detroit, 1936–1939

John Hodiak scored his first professional acting gigs as a performer on Detroit's WXYZ radio. Included among his credits were these shows originating from the station:

The Lone Ranger. Debuting in 1933, the iconic saga told the story of a heroic former Texas Ranger, John Reid, triumphing over outlaws in the

Old West with the help of his Indian friend Tonto and horse Silver. John Hodiak appeared in multiple episodes, playing both heroic and villainous parts.

The Green Hornet. The success of *The Lone Ranger* prompted WXYZ executives to develop other action shows with a strong youth appeal. This popular series debuted in 1936. Like *The Lone Ranger*, it quickly went beyond the Detroit station to a regional and then national hookup. Hodiak worked regularly in this series as well.

Ann Worth, Housewife. WXYZ's late morning soap opera, according to the station's advertising, offered "life's mirror held before every American family." It originally starred Joan Vitez, who was replaced in 1937 by Lenore Collins. Scripted by Tom Dougall, the show went out over the Michigan Radio Network but never nationwide. John appeared in one or more unspecified roles. The daily serial was sponsored by the Mills Baking Company.

Ned Jordan, Secret Agent. "As president of a vast railroad enterprise, J.P. Medwick has become aware of certain undercover plots against the government. Independently wealthy, he is eager to devote some of his means and time to a patriotic service. He believes the right kind of man, working without being bound by government red tape, could uncover many spy plans." That man was series hero Ned Jordan. Said a press release, "The plots are timely and, in many cases, are based on actual happenings which have been reported by the press."[1] Described in newspaper publicity as "a new type of radio drama ... conceived by the originators of 'The Lone Ranger,'" the series caught on with listeners. "Johnny appeared more or less regularly," according to journalist Dick Osgood, who noted, "I played Proctor, the FBI agent who ended every story with the words, 'Uncle Sam wants you!' This line was always addressed to the villain of the piece—usually a master spy aiming to undermine or destroy America. Most frequently this culprit was impersonated by Johnny Hodiak."[2]

Chicago, 1939–1942

Now a seasoned radio actor, Hodiak relocated to the Windy City, where he worked steadily in a variety of shows. Audiences cross-country grew familiar with the sound of his voice. This three-year stint represented another step on the ladder to success, one that helped John catch the eye of MGM talent scouts who recognized his potential and signed him to a motion picture contract. Among his documented roles were the following:

Li'l Abner. NBC Red, 1939–1940. John's first big success in Chicago was the lead role in this adaptation of Al Capp's beloved comic strip about the hillbilly inhabitants of Dogpatch, U.S.A. Other cast members included Laurette Fillbrandt as Daisy Mae, Hazel Dophelde as Mammy, and Clarence Hartzell as Pappy. Durward Kirby announced. Written by Charles Gussman, the 15-minute program was heard Monday through Friday at 6:45 p.m. EST.[3]

The Guiding Light. Writer Irna Phillips created this soap opera, which made its bow on NBC in 1937, moved successfully to CBS television in 1952, and finally breathed its last in 2009. John Hodiak played the character of Jack Felzer, circa 1940.[4]

Arnold Grimm's Daughter. CBS/NBC, 1937–1942. *Variety* (September 25, 1940) reported that John, along with actor Carl Kroenke, had joined the cast of this General Mills–sponsored soap opera about a young married couple whose marriage faced opposition from the in-laws.

Knickerbocker Playhouse. Originating from Chicago, this dramatic anthology went national in the spring of 1939, its first run on CBS though it soon relocated to NBC. Actor Elliott Lewis was a regular cast member, with weekly guest performers. John was heard in the following episodes:

"**The Fugitive.**" November 16, 1940. "The story of a young scientist who loses his faith in mankind and then regains it. John Hodiak and Louise Fitch did well with the leading roles."[5]

"**Jerry Takes Charge.**" January 18, 1941. John Hodiak, Eddie Firestone, Connie Crowder.

"**Made in Heaven.**" January 25, 1941. "An original comedy drama by Pauline Hopkins," noted that day's radio log in the *Fresno* (CA) *Bee*. Featured alongside John were Hugh Studebaker and Eddie Firestone. Joseph Ainley directed.

"**Home to Mother.**" April 19, 1941. Written by Pauline Hopkins, this was another installment of her story about the Greenwood family. It depicts "the marital difficulties of ... Patty, who leaves her new husband, Dr. Stanford, to come home to mother."[6] Hodiak played Dr. Stanford, with Hugh Studebaker and Eddie Firestone also in the cast.

"**The Sap.**" September 27, 1941. A boxing drama featuring the radio acting debut of boxer Barney Ross, playing himself, a former world lightweight champion. "John Hodiak will play Johnny Fletcher, a promising young fighter."[7]

"**Thunder Mountain.**" October 11, 1941. "The story of a forest ranger, a racketeer and a girl who find their way out of a series of hair-raising adventures in the midst of a thunder storm [*sic*] which recalls an old Indian legend about thunder and death."[8] John played ranger Don Bradley, opposite Gale Page, a former Chicago radio actress who had found film work in Hollywood, as Betty Jane Dunlap.

"**Hold Back the River.**" November 8, 1941. "Play deals with adventures of a group of sandhogs."[9] Aside from John, Louise Fitch was featured.

"**Kid Glamor.**" NBC, December 6, 1941. A follow-up to "The Sap," with Hodiak reprising his role as Johnny Fletcher, and Louise Fitch as his girlfriend, Mickey.

"**There Is No Island.**" NBC, December 27, 1941.

Girl Alone. NBC, 1935–1941. Described in newspaper publicity as "America's most popular radio serial," promising "big thrills and excitement," this soap opera starred Betty Winkler as Patricia Rogers, who "faced the bewildering reality that her ex-fiancé was wedding someone else."[10] A brief blurb in the *Sheboygan Press* (October 14, 1940) noted Hodiak as a newcomer to the cast; he was still there, as mentioned in the *Pittsburgh Press* (January 24, 1941) early the following year. John played the character of McCullough.

The Romance of Helen Trent. CBS, 1933–1960. One of radio's longest-running and most popular soap operas purported to depict, as the show's announcer explained every day, "that because a woman is 35 or more romance in life need not be over." *Variety* (December 18, 1940) reported that John had joined the cast, in an unspecified role.

Wings of Destiny. Heard on the NBC Red network from October 1940 through February 1942, this aviation drama depicted the adventures of heroic airline pilot Steve Benton. When the series debuted in October 1940, the lead role was played by Carlton KaDell. But by December, Hodiak had taken over the part. Betty Arnold co-starred as his love interest, newspaper photographer Peggy Banning, and Henry Hunter was featured as Steve's trusted mechanic, Brooklyn. In its review, *Variety* (October 16, 1940) stated, "The program may be presumed to aim at an air-minded generation, young enough to see only the excitement, old enough to smoke."

The show's most noteworthy gimmick was the awarding of an airplane to one lucky listener each week. In the summer of 1941, a change in the program's format found its scripts based on real-life aviation heroes. With the U.S. preparing to enter World War II, the sponsor could no longer give away airplanes to civilians that were needed for the war effort.

The episode title and plot summaries below give an idea of the show's flavor and content. Except where otherwise indicated, they were taken from the radio listings published in the *Shreveport* (LA) *Times*.

"**Hot Ice.**" January 17, 1941.

"**Murder by Radio.**" January 31, 1941. "Steve Benton ... become(s) involved in the solving of the murder of a man found dead in a pilotless plane which landed under its own power."

"**One Hour to Live.**" February 14, 1941. "Steve Benton ... on special charter is flying a mysterious passenger by seaplane to San Francisco where he is to embark on a boat from China. Peggy Banning (Betty Arnold), on a newspaper assignment in San Francisco, and Brooklyn, Steve's mechanic, are along. On hearing a steamship's distress signals, Steve's seaplane locates the ship and takes off a young boy, an English refugee, suffering from acute appendicitis, in order to rush him to the hospital. Once in the air, the boy's condition becomes so serious it necessitates his being operated on at once. The mysterious passenger, Williams, volunteers to perform the operation."

"**No Road Back.**" March 7, 1941. "Steve Benton (John Hodiak) ... is hired to fly an old acquaintance and his small son to South America. En route to the border, Steve is informed by radio that his acquaintance is an escaped murderer. The acquaintance, together with an accomplice, force Steve from the controls, after which the plane crashes in a storm."

March 14, 1941. "A story of the days of the Spanish monks and dons, when there were legends and tales about Lago de la Mesa—the haunted lake.... Peggy Banning ... has been sent to the haunted lake to get pictures of a 'ghost story' where weird, strange happening[s] at Lago de la Mesa are again in circulation—Steve Bannon is flying her on the assignment."

"**Killer-Diller Leaves Clues.**" March 21, 1941. "A story of a mail train robbery where death struck suddenly as bandits blew up a small train and wantonly shot and killed three members of the crew, escaping with an estimated loot [of] $50,000."

July 11, 1941. "It's a tough choice to make a parachute leap from a burning balloon, at 2,500 feet, or to gamble with death in an attempt to save the pilot. Lt. Uzal Ent chose to gamble, when the decision came his way, unaware that his pilot was dead."

July 18, 1941. "Edmond Genet, product of a long line of fighting Frenchmen ... fiercely resented his extreme youth when the World war broke out. How he lied about his age and joined the Foreign Legion at the age of 16 will be told.... Genet was cited for bravery on numerous occasions, had a hand in the naming of the Lafayette Escadrille, and won the Croix de Guerre for gallantry."

August 15, 1941. "Tonight Wings of Destiny will tell the story of Sgt. Harry M. Hayes, a non-commissioned officer of the regular army air corps, who was awarded the soldier's medal for heroism and devotion to duty."

December 26, 1941. "The birth and growth of one of the great American aviation firms, the Lockheed Aircraft corporation, will be dramatized.... The corporation, which introduced the P-38 Interceptor, has a proud list of record-breaking planes to its credit."

"**I Wanted Wings.**" January 2, 1942. "This will be first of a series of radio dramatizations of well-known motion pictures, books and plays to be given on the program.... The book, written by Bierne Lay, Jr., tells the story of the flying cadets at Randolph Field, Tex., the 'West Point of the Air.' Betty Arnold and Dorothy Robinson were featured alongside Hodiak."[11]

"**The Case of Feminine Allure.**" January 23, 1942. "The story of ... how a movie star tracked down the murderer of her best friend, a newspaper reporter."[12]

"**Ceiling Zero.**" January 30, 1942. "The situation that led to the development of the present day airplane de-icers furnished the background for the drama to be presented ... from the Stage play of the same name."[13]

Bachelor's Children. CBS/NBC, 1936–1946. This daily serial became a network program in 1936, after starting on the airwaves of WGN in Chicago the prior year. It moved from CBS to NBC in 1941. It told the story of Dr. Robert Graham, an unmarried doctor in his mid-thirties who agrees to take in the twin daughters of his terminally ill friend James Dexter, whom he credits with saving his life during World War I. He is surprised to learn that the daughters are eighteen-year-old twins, Ruth Ann and Janet, for whom he cares with the help of his longtime housekeeper and surrogate mother, Ellen Collins. Hugh Studebaker starred as Dr. Robert Graham, with Olan Soule as his buddy Sam Ryder. John was heard in the roles of Davey Lane and Red Cosmo in 1941 and 1942. *Movie and Radio Guide* (May 2, 1941) reported that he also assumed the role of Blackie Dorch on the program.

Thunder Over Paradise. NBC Blue, 1939–1941. Laurette Fillbrandt starred in this daily adventure serial as Lolita, "wild girl of the tropics, who falls in love with an American engineer."[14]

The Bartons. NBC Blue/NBC, 1939–1941. Dick Holland played the starring role of Bud Barton in this comic serial about a boy in a small Midwestern town. According to an item in the *Oklahoma Courier* (March 29, 1941), John was heard in the role of Mr. Stark.

Lone Journey. NBC, 1940–1943, 1946. This daytime drama from the prolific producers Frank and Anne Hummert was written for most of its run by the brother-and-sister team of Sandra and Peter Michael, and billed as "the distinguished American radio novel." A network press release noted that the story was set on a Montana ranch, the Spear-T, with the setting reflecting Miss Michael's family ranch near Lewiston. Henry Hunter was the star, playing the character of Wolfe Bennett, with several actresses heard in the role of his wife Nita. John was featured in the role of Cullen Andrews during its first NBC run.

Author's Playhouse. "Elementals." NBC, March 5, 1941. This series, which promised "30 minutes of drama from the world's best stories bolstered by special music," debuted with a segment adapted from a story by Stephen Vincent Benét.

Unto the Least of These. NBC Blue, March 29, 1941. "Tragic scenes occasioned by the invasion of Poland, the fighting in China, and the refugee problem created by the persecution in Central Europe will be re-enacted in an all-star radio program."[15] Don McNeill, Betty Winkler, and Betty Lou Gerson were heard along with John. Courtenay Savage produced and directed.

Flying Patrol. NBC Blue, 1941–42. John played Lieutenant Brent in this "thrilling serial drama of the United States Coast Guard," heard weekdays at 4:30 p.m. "Concurrent with the ceaseless war being waged by the Navy and the Coast Guard on enemy U-boats in the Caribbean sea, Flying Patrol's heroes have started on a secret mission to Dutch Guiana in South America to ferret out the Nazis' schemes and bases of operation."[16] His co-stars included John Larkin and Willard Waterman.

Hollywood, 1943–1953

After relocating to the West Coast and becoming an MGM contract player, John continued to accept radio guest appearances. He was heard frequently on some of the most popular dramatic anthologies of the 1940s and early 1950s. He often performed in aural adaptations of popular films (including some in which he did not originally appear), and in historical dramas.

Listed below, alphabetically by series title, are the four radio programs in which Hodiak made five or more guest appearances: *Cavalcade of America, The Lux Radio Theatre, Screen Guild Theater,* and *Suspense.* Afterwards, listed chronologically, are additional series in which he was heard.

Cavalcade of America. Debuting in 1935, this long-running dramatic anthology sponsored by the Du Pont company told stories of bravery and patriotism from American history. Big-name guest stars and top-notch radio performers graced the cast in the weekly episodes heard on NBC. John appeared in the following episodes:

> "**Sawdust Underground.**" September 9, 1945. Hodiak and Bob Bailey starred. "Script tells almost incredible but true story of two American soldiers who escaped from Germans and joined French circus, operating as an underground unit. Soldiers had to become circus performers, one disguising himself as acrobat, other as clown."[17]
>
> "**Children of Old Man River.**" February 4, 1946. "Billy Bryant's vivid word-picture of showboat days on the Mississippi."[18] John accepted the pivotal role after Dick Powell was forced to withdraw due to other commitments. His co-star was Janet Blair.

"Wings to Glory." December 9, 1946. John was cast as John Joseph Montgomery (1858–1911), an inventor and engineer who pioneered manned flight, using gliders, in the 1880s. Ken Christy, Dawn Bender, and Eddie Firestone, Jr., were heard in supporting roles. This episode was originally announced as "Wings of Freedom," and scheduled for November 11, 1946, but was postponed in favor of a different episode after initial publicity went out.

"Page One." May 12, 1947. John portrays publisher Joseph Pulitzer, founder of the Columbia University School of Journalism, who created the Pulitzer Prizes. "The play, written by Charles Freeman, will tell how Pulitzer, only 17 years old at the time, jumped overboard from a ship and swam ashore so that he, an Austrian, could the sooner enlist to fight in the Civil War."[19]

"The Red Stockings." August 25, 1947. "Hodiak will portray Albert Spalding, pioneer in commercial baseball.... He wanted the sport to be an honest game for honest athletes and he fought to make it that way." The title was taken from the first name of the Boston Red Sox.[20]

"The Blue Cockade." November 1, 1948. John stars opposite Linda Darnell in this Revolutionary War story adapted by Robert Cenedella. "Hodiak will play the part of George, a battle-weary veteran of 'Mad Anthony' Wayne's troops."[21]

"As If a Door Were Opening." January 22, 1952. This drama depicts "the reasons that impelled the 19-year-old Lafayette to offer his sword, his fortune, and his life, if necessary, in the American cause," with John cast in the lead role.[22]

"Green Wall." May 20, 1952. John plays Army Sergeant Curtis Culin, "who designed a 'hedgerow fork' for break through in Normandy to St. Lo during World War II invasion."[23]

The Lux Radio Theatre. First heard in 1934, this dramatic anthology enjoyed its biggest success in the 1940s on CBS, broadcasting adaptations of feature films featuring many of the original stars. John is credited in the following segments:

"In Old Chicago." October 9, 1944. *Cast:* Dorothy Lamour, Robert Young, John Hodiak. John steps into the role of Jack, originated by Don Ameche, in this adaptation of the 1938 20th Century–Fox film. "Jack ... takes his family ideals seriously, and works industriously to relieve the mother of taking in washings."[24]

"Bride by Mistake." January 1, 1945. *Cast:* Laraine Day, John Hodiak, Marsha Hunt. Based on the 1944 film of the same title, this episode has Misses Day and Hunt reprising their screen roles, with John replacing Alan Marshal as Tony.

"Sunday Dinner for a Soldier." February 19, 1945. *Cast:* Anne Baxter,

John Hodiak, Charles Winninger. The three stars play the characters they created on-screen in this version of the 1944 film.

"The Clock." January 28, 1946. *Cast*: Judy Garland, John Hodiak, Howard McNear. Hodiak, playing Joe Allen, fills in for Robert Walker alongside Miss Garland in this adaptation of the 1945 film about a couple that falls in love during a 48-hour furlough.

"Honky Tonk." April 8, 1946. *Cast*: Lana Turner, John Hodiak, Gale Gordon. John had co-starred on film with Miss Turner in *Marriage Is a Private Affair* (1944), but here he takes the place of Clark Gable in this retelling of the 1941 film. John's character was "swaggering, handsome gambler" Candy Johnson.

"Somewhere in the Night." March 3, 1947. *Cast*: John Hodiak, Lynn Bari, Carlton KaDell. John reprises his film role as George Taylor, with Miss Bari substituting for his movie co-star Nancy Guild.

"The Foxes of Harrow." December 6, 1948. *Cast*: Maureen O'Hara, John Hodiak, Jack Edwards. Adapted from the 20th Century–Fox film of the previous year, with Hodiak, cast as Stephen Fox, replacing Rex Harrison as Miss O'Hara's leading man.

"Battleground." February 12, 1951. *Cast*: Van Johnson, John Hodiak, Ricardo Montalbán. John and five of his co-stars from the 1949 film repeat their screen roles here. A second adaptation, on December 7, 1954, found George Murphy in for Hodiak.

"Borderline." October 8, 1951. *Cast*: Stephen McNally, Claire Trevor, John Hodiak. This adaptation of the 1950 Universal film features the original leading lady (Miss Trevor), with both male roles recast. John replaces Raymond Burr in the role of Pete Richie.

His guest star turn on *Lux Radio Theatre* reunited Hodiak with his movie leading lady Lana Turner.

"**To Please a Lady.**" November 26, 1951. *Cast*: John Hodiak, Donna Reed, Adolphe Menjou. In his final *Lux* appearance, Hodiak, playing Mike, once again supplants Clark Gable in this version of the 1950 film from his own studio, MGM.

Screen Guild Theater/Stars in the Air. *Screen Guild Theater* underwent several changes in both network and sponsor, enjoying its longest run on CBS (1939–1948), but also heard on NBC (1948–1950) and ABC (1950–1951). John's final appearance came in the summer of 1952, by which time the series had returned to CBS, and been retitled *Stars in the Air*. Hodiak appeared in the following episodes:

"**Congo Maisie.**" May 29, 1944. Ann Sothern reprises her film role, with John as her leading man.

"**Flesh and Fantasy.**" September 3, 1945. John and Claire Trevor guest star in this adaptation of the 1943 film, taking place at Mardi Gras.

"**Marriage Is a Private Affair.**" June 16, 1946. John and Lana Turner recreate their leading roles from the 1944 film.

"**Pardon My Past.**" May 5, 1947. Marguerite Chapman and William Demarest appear in support of John. "Just out of the Army, Hodiak and Demarest are in New York enroute to Wisconsin to open a mink farm when Hodiak is mistaken for a playboy and kidnapped by gangsters who collect the mink farm money as part payment of the playboy's gambling debt. Hodiak masquerades as the wealthy young man in an effort to recoup his loss."[25]

"**Notorious.**" January 6, 1949. John teams with Ingrid Bergman and J. Carrol Naish.

March 3, 1949. *Redbook* magazine's 10th annual Movie Award is presented to *Command Decision*. "Dramatic highlights will be re-enacted by the original stars, including Clark Gable, Walter Pidgeon, Van Johnson, Brian Donlevy, John Hodiak and Edward Arnold."[26]

"**Command Decision.**" December 1, 1949. Several months after their initial appearance (see entry above), John and his castmates return to perform a full-fledged adaptation of their popular film. Clark Gable, Van Johnson, Walter Pidgeon, and Edward Arnold are also heard.

"**The Bribe.**" June 23, 1952. John stars opposite Mercedes McCambridge in this adaptation of his 1949 film of the same name.

Suspense. Heard from 1940 to 1962, this long-running CBS anthology series billed as "radio's outstanding theater of thrills," presented, as its title suggested, "tales well-calculated to keep you in... *Suspense!*" Two men most often associated with this series were producers William Spier and Elliott Lewis. Harlow Wilcox served as announcer. Sponsors included Roma Wines and Autolite. John was heard in the following episodes:

"**Dateline: Lisbon,**" October 5, 1944. Hodiak plays William Baldwin, on trial for murder. He testifies that, in the lobby of a busy Lisbon hotel, he saw photojournalist Terry Moore, an old girlfriend he'd known in New York, take a picture that alarmed two men. One, Moska, immediately offers her $10,000 in cash for the negative. Baldwin warns her not to accept, and points out that a fat man nearby tried to duck out of her picture before she clicked the shutter. Baldwin recognizes him as General Maximilian von Kraus, a Nazi who's on the lam, trying to make it safely out of Europe. Moska is earning a large fee to escort him safely out.

Bill and Terry go to her room so that she can develop her film, which he says may be "the hottest picture of your whole career." Realizing they aren't alone in the room, Bill lies, telling Terry he was converted to the Nazi cause himself, but in actuality he's ready to confront Gen. von Kraus, whom he describes as "one of the most prolific executioners the Fuhrer ever had." Bill appoints himself as judge, and Terry as a juror, to conduct an impromptu murder trial on the man who slaughtered dozens of innocent Polish citizens in 1940.

John's upcoming film *Marriage Is a Private Affair* is plugged.

"**The Case History of a Gambler.**" December 17, 1951. *Cast*: John Hodiak (*Matthew Miller*), Lillian Buyeff (*Ellen*); with Bill Bouchet, Joseph Kearns, Herb Vigran, Martha Wentworth. *Writer*: Ross Murray.

It's the Roaring Twenties, and Matthew Miller is staggering through city streets wounded by a bullet, trying to reach the nearest hospital. He flashes back to his life as a gambler, which began when he won a large wager on a prizefighter he sponsored. Flush with $2 million, Miller opens a suburban casino. As a sideline, he lends money to those who need it, and deals harshly with anyone who fails to repay. Miller consults his lawyer Chris about a scheme he has involving a dummy company, and stock under his control, paying no attention when Chris warns him of the dangers he faces. Miller's fiancée, Ellen, wants him to step away from his criminal activities, but he's adamant that he's doing it for her. At a high-stakes poker game, Miller loses $483,000. An untimely police raid on the casino leaves him unexpectedly short on available cash, and in danger of becoming what he'd always hated—a welsher. Ellen offers to sell some jewelry, and run away with him to Mexico, but he's unable to escape vengeance for his unpaid debt.

> **MILLER:** Chris, you once told me I'd reach out too far. Well, I did. It looks as if the fall broke every bone in my body.

Introduced by Wilcox as "our personable young star" in the epilogue, John helps deliver a commercial, and a plug for his film *The Sellout* is made.

"**The Big Heist.**" December 1, 1952. *Cast*: John Hodiak (*James Scott*), Herb Butterfield (*John Barry*), Joseph Kearns (*Martin Collins*). *Writer*: E. Jack Neuman.

New in town, James "Scotty" Scott meets Martin Collins in a pool hall, who offers him the chance to make a quick $10,000. Collins and his partner John Barry need a third man for a bank robbery job. Scotty is initially hesitant, but agrees with the understanding that his only task is to keep the bank guard preoccupied outside while the heist is underway. When Barry presses a gun on him, Scotty tries to back out, but ultimately goes ahead. At a critical moment, Scotty panics, and the guard is shot. His cohorts are only too happy to leave him holding the bag.

> SCOTTY: It just went off! ... I didn't mean to shoot him! ... You guys made me do it!

In the epilogue, announcer Harlow Wilcox welcomes John back to *Suspense,* and the star responds, "I consider it a privilege to be part of it." Hodiak helps deliver the final commercial for the sponsor, Autolite. His film *Battle Zone* is plugged.

"**The Mountain.**" March 16, 1953. *Cast*: John Hodiak (*Bob*), Ben Wright (*John Eldridge*); with Joseph Kearns, Paul Frees, John Fraser. *Writer*: Antony Ellis. Six climbers are attempting to reach the peak of a mountain never before scaled by anyone. Camping at 22,000 feet, it's decided that three of the men will make the first attempt at the final leg of the journey, with the others remaining behind. Bob, Eldridge, and Perrucci are chosen to climb further, with Bob in the lead. Struggling with inclement weather, Perrucci suffers a fall, hanging in peril from a rope attached to Eldridge. To save himself, Eldridge cuts the rope, sacrificing his friend's life. Bob wants to return to camp, but Eldridge insists on going upward. Reluctantly, Bob accompanies him, knowing his life is in the hands of a man he cannot trust.

> BOB: You murdered a man, and that's all there is to it!

John's film *Mission Over Korea* is promoted.

"**Hellfire.**" September 28, 1953. *Cast*: John Hodiak (*Wally Drake*), Joseph Kearns (*Smiley*), Clayton Post (*Pete*), Charlotte Lawrence (*Dotty*), Jerry Hausner (*Collins*); with Herb Butterfield, Dick Ryan. *Writer*: Ross Murray. Wildcatter Wally Drake is under pressure from stockholders after the fields he predicted were rich in oil produce seven dry holes in a row. Knowing the money men will pull the plug, he's relieved when the eighth dig strikes a rich vein of oil. But Wally and his men are in for a shock when a deadly fire breaks out. Unable to reach the expert he trusts to put it out, Wally determines to undertake the dangerous job himself, with the help of a dynamite expert named

Collins. Wally's wife Dotty urges him not to put his life on the line, but he insists on doing so, as she and his crew members watch.

The epilogue makes mention of John's latest film, *Dragonfly Squadron*.

> **WALLY:** There's something about seeing the results of your sweat going up in thick, black, greasy smoke that makes you think an all-out effort can compensate for a lack of experience.

Additional Guest Appearances

What's New. NBC Blue, December 25, 1943. John joined host Don Ameche for a sketch, "Master Sergeant"; other guests were Pinky Lee and comedian Jack Douglas.

The Charles Ruggles Show. CBS, July 14, 1944. John and Gloria DeHaven were guests.

Harold Lloyd's Comedy Theater. "Take a Letter, Darling." NBC, December 3, 1944. Opposite Susan Hayward, John plays the role originated in the 1942 film by Fred MacMurray.

This Is My Best. "Let There Be Honour." CBS, January 16, 1945. John co-starred with Virginia Bruce in a script by Kay Boyle, telling "the story of unoccupied France under the Vichy regime, in which an English woman, Lady Higgins, serves in a French canteen in order to help Frenchmen and Englishmen escape from the country."[27]

Theatre of Romance. "The Man without a Country." CBS, July 3, 1945. Adapted from Everett Hale's short story by Jean Holloway.

Columbia Presents Corwin. "A Walk with Nick." CBS, July 31, 1945. *Cast*: John Hodiak, Joan Lorring. Corwin's script depicts a soldier returning home to learn that his girlfriend has given him up for another man.

The Doctor Fights. CBS, August 14, 1945. This anthology series depicted the heroics of medical men serving their country during World War II. John made a guest appearance as a brain surgeon.

This Is Hollywood. "Canyon Passage." CBS, October 19, 1946. John is Susan Hayward's leading man in this adaptation of the film.

Hallmark Playhouse. "The Desert Shall Rejoice." CBS, December 16, 1948. Author James Hilton (*Lost Horizon*) introduces the story of Nick (John Hodiak), who with his wife Rosa operates a Nevada tourist camp. It's Christmas Eve, but Nick is lacking in the holiday spirit, despite his spouse's best efforts. Visitors to the camp include Jose and Maria Santos, a young couple about to have a baby, Dusty, who robs Nick of $20, and three men who come bearing gifts. Rosa's good nature and faith in her husband pay off in ways Nick didn't anticipate. The players aside from Hodiak are uncredited. Until the drama's closing moments, Hodiak plays one of his most cynical characters. Hilton refers to John as "one of Hollywood's most interesting and forthright young actors."

NICK: I never had a heart. If I did, I wouldn't know what to do with it.

Theater Guild on the Air. "The Morning Glory." NBC, January 28, 1951. John teamed with wife Anne Baxter for this adaptation of the 1933 film that had starred Katharine Hepburn. "Along her road she encounters a predatory producer, a tempestuous and established star and a recalcitrant playwright."[28]

Hallmark Playhouse. "Standish of Standish." November 23, 1952. *Host*: Lionel Barrymore. John played Myles Standish in an adaptation of a story by Jane G. Austin. The episode "tells the story of the founding of the Plymouth colony and the part played in it by Standish who forsook home, heritage and ambition to act as guide and protector for the Pilgrims. It will relate the events of the first Thanksgiving."[29]

Theater Guild on the Air. "Gold of the Adomar." CBS, January 19, 1953. Hodiak plays a former Navy diver who's offered a sizable bounty to dive deep in search of gold aboard a sunken ship. "His life-lines become fouled and he finds himself slowly sinking into a sticky mass of mud. As he calls desperately for help, it appears that he has taken one dive too many."[30]

General Electric Theater. "A Bell for Adano." CBS, September 3, 1953. John reprises his role as Major Joppolo in this adaptation of his 1945 film, written by James Poe. A few weeks later, on October 11, 1953, Fredric March headlined a separate version for *NBC Star Playhouse*, taken from Paul Osborn's stage play. Edmond O'Brien starred in a television adaptation that aired in 1955.

Family Theatre. "Turn on the Lights." Mutual, October 7, 1953. Tyrone Power hosts and "Hodiak is to be starred in a drama with a Korean war setting," scripted by John T. Kelly. Also heard are John Dehner and Herb Ellis.

Television Performances

The Kate Smith Evening Hour. NBC, January 2, 1952. *Director*: Greg Garrison. *Producer*: Ted Collins. *Cast*: Kate Smith, Ted Collins, guests John Hodiak, Gloria Swanson, Teresa Wright. John and Miss Wright appear in a short drama, "The Luckiest Day of My Life." John plays Steve, a former high school football star who's now an unemployed adult with eight cents in his pocket. Miss Wright plays his former classmate, Mary; their impromptu meeting in the town square proves to be a red-letter day for both. Collins introduces the playlet by announcing that both stars "have flown in from Hollywood just to be with us," and adds that John "is making his television debut."

Gangbusters. NBC, January 10, 1952. "The Weak Point." *Cast*: John Hodiak, Jane Wyatt. This video adaptation of a long-running radio favorite aired on alternate weeks with *Dragnet*. According to a network press release, "Hodiak will portray an ex–Army Judge Advocate officer who presided in a court-martial that resulted in a soldier's being executed. The slain soldier's brother, anxious for revenge, discovers that the ex-officer is extremely jealous. He then sets up a deliberate plan to kill the officer's wife (played by Jane Wyatt) and then commit suicide—causing the husband to be haunted for life with the thought his wife was involved in a triangle."

Critic Joan Ossefort called the episode "an exceptionally good dramatization of attempted revenge.... Both [Hodiak] and [Wyatt] turned in excellent performances."[1]

Your Show of Shows. NBC, January 12, 1952. *Cast*: Sid Caesar, Imogene Coca, Carl Reiner, guest host John Hodiak.

Twenty Questions. DuMont, May 9, 1952. John was the celebrity guest on this quiz show hosted by Bill Slater.

Hollywood Opening Night. "Delaying Action." NBC, October 20, 1952. *Cast*: John Hodiak, John Agar, Tab Hunter, Keye Luke, Jimmie Fidler (*Narrator*). This 30-minute dramatic anthology series had the misfortune to air opposite the red-hot *I Love Lucy* on Monday nights, and was therefore little-seen. "The story tells of Colonel Charles B. 'Task Force' Smith's

400 courageous men of the First Battalion of the 21st Infantry Regiment, and their fight to hold the South Korean line at Taejon until the Eighth army arrived."[2]

The Ford Television Theatre. "They Also Serve." NBC, January 1, 1953. *Director*: Laslo Benedek. *Teleplay*: Edward Hope. *Story*: William T. Tilden. *Cast*: John Hodiak (*Col. James B. "Sandy" MacNab*), Maureen O'Sullivan (*Sheila MacNab*), Virginia Grey (*Madeleine Byron*), Grandon Rhodes (*Dr. Sam Olsen*). This episode of the half-hour anthology series is about "a married couple whose happy marriage is endangered just before he leaves for Korea.... At a going-away party in his honor, an Army colonel ... meets blond and beautiful Virginia Grey. They discover a mutual attraction which grows until Hodiak realizes his duty to his wife and discovers that women at home, related to soldiers who fight, 'also serve.'"[3]

The filmed drama was repeated on several other shows for various sponsors, including *Footlights Theatre* (August 1953), *Hollywood Theater of Stars* (November 1954), and *All Star Theater* (March 1957).

What's My Line? CBS, February 7, 1954. *Cast*: Steve Allen, Arlene Francis, Dorothy Kilgallen, David Wayne. While appearing in the New York production of *The Caine Mutiny Court-Martial*, Hodiak visits this popular panel show, hosted by John Daly, as the mystery guest. The blindfolded celebrities gradually determine that he's a film actor who's currently appearing in a popular Broadway show, but are thrown off slightly when it's stated that he's not a leading man who "gets the girl" onstage. Guest panelist David Wayne, who correctly pinpoints John, has a

Col. MacNab (John Hodiak) sees that his wife Sheila (Maureen O'Sullivan) makes her own contribution to the war effort in "They Also Serve."

distinct advantage, as they had had dinner together the previous evening. Daly notes that Hodiak kept his cool over dinner when Wayne mentioned his upcoming appearance on *What's My Line?* saying, "What are you going to be, the mystery guest?" John, who answers most questions in a growly rasp, seems to be having a great time here, grinning broadly as the panel ponders. The intended plug for his Broadway role is somewhat diminished by the fact that the name of the show goes unmentioned until Wayne thinks to say it near the end of the segment.

The Loretta Young Show. "The Last Spring." NBC, October 16, 1955. *Director*: Harry Keller. *Teleplay*: Gene Levitt. *Story*: Louis E. Holz. *Cast*: John Hodiak (*Matt*), Raymond Bailey, Peggy Knudsen (*Madeleine*), James Dobson. Guest host Van Johnson introduces this "story of an Army bomb disposal officer resentful at being called back to duty in Japan."[4] This episode aired only three days prior to John's death.

Broadway Performances

The Chase

Opened April 15, 1952, at the Playhouse Theatre; closed May 10, 1952. 31 performances. *Producer/Director*: José Ferrer. *Associate Producer*: Milton Baron.

Cast: John Hodiak (*Sheriff Hawes*), Richard Poston (*Rip*), Lin McCarthy (*Tarl*), Kim Hunter (*Ruby Hawes*), Sam Byrd (*Edwin Stewart*), G. Albert Smith (*Mr. Douglas*), Kim Stanley (*Anna Reeves*), Nan McFarland (*Mrs. Reeves*), Lonny Chapman (*Knub McDermott*), Murray Hamilton (*Bubber Reeves*), Ted Yaryan (*Hawks Damon*)

Synopsis: Hawes, sheriff of Richmond, Texas, faces the task of capturing escaped killer Bubber Reeves, hoping to bring him to justice while the frightened populace wants to see him eliminated for good.

Reviews: "John Hodiak makes an auspicious ... stage debut, giving a restrained performance as a man of integrity who wants nothing more than a quiet home and family, [all] the while forcing himself to live up to the letter of his oath of office."—*Billboard*, April 26, 1952

"Horton Foote has written a Western with an ethical point.... Apart from some well-written small scenes, which are also well-acted, Mr. Foote's drama does not make much impression on the theatre.... As the sheriff, John Hodiak plays with a loose, leisurely sincerity that is thoroughly agreeable."—Brooks Atkinson, *New York Times*, April 16, 1952

The Caine Mutiny Court-Martial

Opened in New York at the Plymouth Theatre on January 20, 1954; closed January 22, 1955. 415 performances. *Producer*: Paul Gregory. *Director*: Charles Laughton.

Cast: John Hodiak (*Lt. Stephen Maryk*), Henry Fonda (*Lt. Barney Greenwald*), Ainslie Pryor (*Lt. Com. John Challee*), Russell Hicks (*Capt.

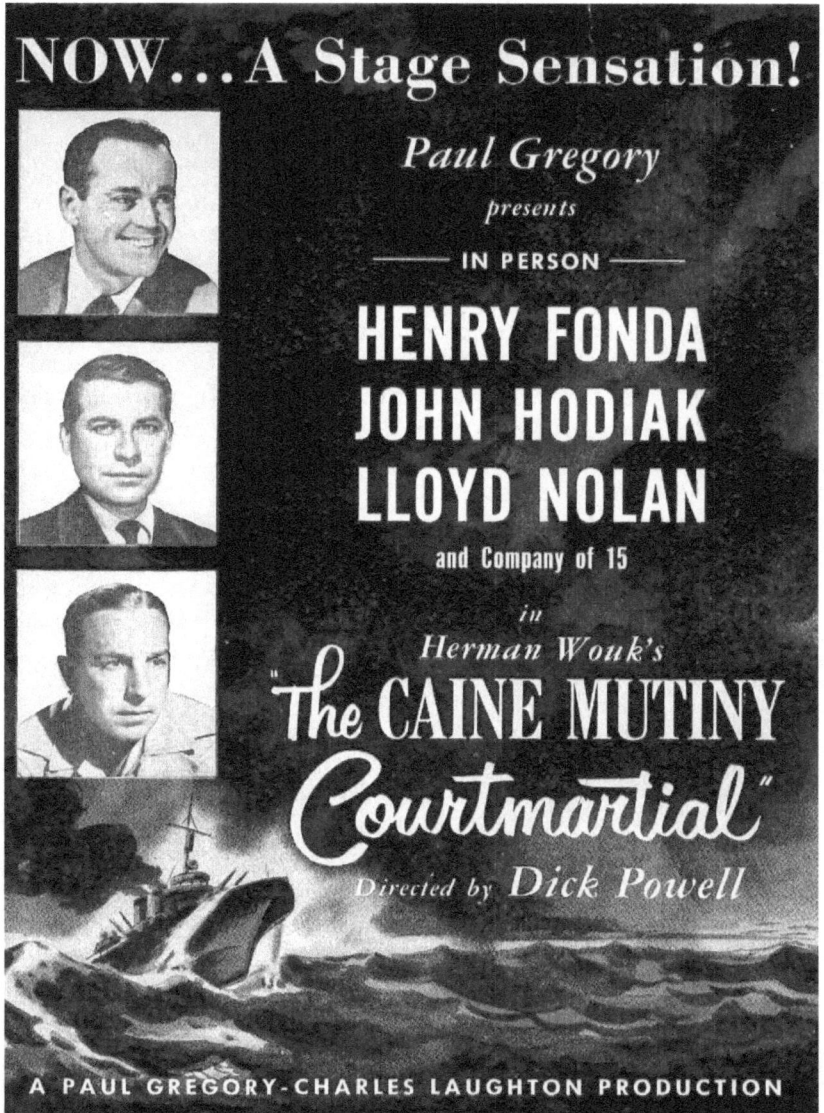

This early advertisement for *The Caine Mutiny Court-Martial* still names Dick Powell as director, though his credit would evaporate before opening night.

Blakely), Lloyd Nolan (*Lt. Com. Philip Francis Queeg*), Robert Gist (*Lt. Thomas Keefer*), Eddie Firestone (*Signalman Third Class Junius Urban*), Charles Nolte (*Lt., Jr. Grade Willis Seward Keith*), Paul Birch (Capt. *Randolph Southard*), Stephen Chase (*Dr. Forrest Lundeen*), Herbert Anderson (*Dr. Bird*), John Huffman (*Stenographer*), Greg Roman (*Orderly*)

Synopsis: Lt. Barney Greenwald takes on the task of defending Navy Lieutenant Stephen Maryk, who's being court-martialed after assuming command of his ship after coming to believe that Lieutenant Commander Francis Queeg, his superior officer, is mentally incapacitated and leading his crew into danger.

Reviews: "It is drama at its best because it is so deceptively effortless. In tune with Wouk's scripting, 'Mutiny' boasts a cast that can stand no improvement.... John Hodiak's accused officer [is] forthrightly and genuinely played."—*Billboard*, January 23, 1954

"'The Caine Mutiny Court Martial' is a powerful play. But you will look in vain for a performance that uses powerful gestures or powerful vocal tones or reaches out after powerful effects.... John Hodiak's conception of Lieutenant Maryk is of a man absolutely honest and a little obtuse in the company of his betters—a solid chunk of good will without brilliance."—Brooks Atkinson, *New York Times*, January 31, 1954

Chapter Notes

Preface

1. Paul Guggenheimer, "One Hundred Years of John Hodiak," *Pittsburgh Post-Gazette*, April 14, 2014.
2. M.B.B. Biskupski, *Hollywood's War with Poland, 1939–1945* (Lexington: University Press of Kentucky, 2010), p. 16.
3. A.H. Weiler, "Journey to a Star," *New York Times*, July 8, 1945.
4. As the reader may note, there are occasional inconsistencies in the way that the title of Mr. Wouk's play is spelled, primarily as to whether "Court Martial" is hyphenated or not. (It appears with a hyphen on the published version, but without it on the *Playbill* advertising the stage production.) I have generally preferred "Court-Martial," which seems to be the most common, but have not altered the spelling as it appears within quotations or advertisements.

Biography

1. Inga Arvad, "John Hodiak Charm Brings Bids to Stellar Roles," *Miami News*, February 9, 1944.
2. Ingra Arvad, "John Hodiak Is in Earnest about Career," *St. Joseph* (MO) *News-Press*, November 5, 1944.
3. John Hodiak, "This Is Myself," *Movieland*, June 1945.
4. Jack Balch, "His Life Just Goes to Show," *St. Louis Post-Dispatch*, November 30, 1944.
5. "The Ham from Hamtramck," *Modern Screen*, February 1945.
6. Hodiak, "This Is Myself."
7. Arvad, "In Earnest."
8. *Beatrice* (NE) *Daily Sun*, January 10, 1945.
9. A.H. Weiler, "Journey to a Star," *New York Times*, July 8, 1945.
10. Hodiak, "This Is Myself."
11. Alyce Canfield, "Hail Hodiak!" *Screenland*, July 1944.
12. "John Hodiak's Climb to Fame is a Colorful Story," *Hamtramck* (MI) *Citizen*, August 5, 1947.
13. Michael Galay, personal interview with author, September 2022. All subsequent quotes from Mr. Galay are from this interview.
14. Richard Shavinski, personal interview with author, May 2023. All subsequent quotes from Mr. Shavinski are from this interview.
15. Inga Arvad, "John Hodiak Shares Film Success with His Parents," *Indianapolis Star*, November 5, 1944.
16. Inga Arvad, "A Dream Come True," *Muncie* (IN) *Star*, November 5, 1944.
17. Edith Lindeman, "Rise of John Hodiak to Film Stardom," *Times-Dispatch* (Richmond, VA), November 5, 1944.
18. Eleanor Harris, "Who Is Hodiak?" *Movieland*, September 1944.
19. Balch, "His Life."
20. "The Ham from Hamtramck."
21. "His Movie Dream Came True," *Kansas City Star*, July 14, 1946.
22. Virginia MacPherson, "Hodiak Bumps Down Stairs to Register Movie Scene," *Dayton* (OH) *Herald*, December 27, 1944.
23. Harry Evans, "John Hodiak," *Family Circle*, July 27, 1945.
24. Chester Bulgier, "George W. Trendle's Rites Set Saturday," *Ann Arbor News*, May 12, 1972.
25. David Rothel, *Who Was That Masked*

Man? The Story of the Lone Ranger (San Diego: A.S. Barnes, 1981), p. 102.
26. Edgar A. Guest, Jr., "Head of WXYZ Responsible for Putting Program on Air," *Detroit Free Press*, February 28, 1937.
27. Edgar A. Guest, Jr., "Noted Sopranos to Appear on Ford and G.M. Radio Hours," *Detroit Free Press*, November 8, 1936.
28. Frank P. Gill, "Gill-o-Tine," *Detroit Free Press*, December 26, 1937.
29. Dick Osgood, "WXYZ Recalls Hodiak Humor," *Detroit Free Press*, October 23, 1955.
30. Rothel, *Who Was That Masked Man?* p. 102.
31. Harry Evans, "John Hodiak," *Family Circle*, July 27, 1945.
32. Dick Osgood, *Wyxie Wonderland: An Unauthorized 50-Year Diary of WXYZ Detroit* (Bowling Green, OH: Bowling Green University Popular Press, 1981), p. 140.
33. Osgood, "WXYZ Recalls."
34. Rothel, *Who Was That Masked Man?* p. 139.
35. Osgood, *Wyxie Wonderland*, pp. 157–158.
36. Evans, "John Hodiak."
37. "His Movie Dream Came True," *Kansas City* (MO) *Star*, July 14, 1946.
38. Evans, "John Hodiak."
39. "L'il Abner Stars Mountain Family in Mad Scramble," *Pensacola* (FL) *News-Journal*, December 10, 1939.
40. Ron Lackmann, *Mercedes McCambridge: A Biography and Career Record* (Jefferson, NC: McFarland, 2005), p. 28.
41. "Here and There on the Air," *St. Louis Post-Dispatch*, January 12, 1941.
42. "Friday's Highlights," *Radio-Television Mirror*, February 1941.
43. "Behind the Mike," *Shreveport* (LA) *Times*, April 27, 1941.
44. "Jitters Epidemic Caused by Drama," *Shreveport* (LA) *Times*, February 9, 1941.
45. Arvad, "Hodiak Charm."
46. Walter H. Hackett, "Unknown Hundreds Behind Every Film," *Lansing* (MI) *State Journal*, October 31, 1943.
47. "Actor John Hodiak Drops Dead of Heart Attack at Age of 41," *Florence* (SC) *Morning News*, October 20, 1955.
48. "The Ham from Hamtramck."
49. *Ibid.*
50. Bob White, "John Hodiak's Rise from Coal Pits to Renown Saga of Family Loyalty," *Los Angeles Times*, September 2, 1945.
51. Harold V. Cohen, "Hollywood," *Pittsburgh Post-Gazette*, August 14, 1943.
52. John Todd, "In Hollywood," *Hammond* (IN) *Times*, November 3, 1943.
53. Patrick McGilligan, *Alfred Hitchcock: A Life in Darkness and Light* (New York: Regan Books, 2003), p. 341.
54. Frederick Othman, "Hollywood Film Shop," *Chico* (CA) *Enterprise-Record*, October 24, 1943.
55. Harris, "Who Is Hodiak?"
56. "Studio News," *Kansas City* (MO) *Star*, November 21, 1943.
57. Balch, "His Life."
58. White, "John Hodiak's Rise."
59. *Ibid.*
60. "The Ham from Hamtramck."
61. "John Hodiak's Climb to Fame."
62. Balch, "His Life."
63. Alyce Canfield, "Hail Hodiak!" *Screenland*, July 1944.
64. Cheryl Crane, with Cindy De La Hoz, *Lana: The Memories, the Myths, the Movies* (Philadelphia: Running Press, 2008), p. 130.
65. Joe Morella and Edward Epstein, *Lana* (New York: Berkley Books, 1989), p. 77.
66. Lindeman, "Rise of John Hodiak."
67. "Pastor Has Union Card," *Albertan* (Calgary, Alberta, Canada), February 26, 1944.
68. "The Bride Wore White," *Modern Screen*, October 1946.
69. James Bawden and Ron Miller, *Conversations with Classic Film Stars: Interviews from Hollywood's Golden Era* (Lexington: University Press of Kentucky, 2016), p. 143.
70. Jack Wade, "Courageous Heart," *Modern Screen*, April 1953.
71. Louella O. Parsons, "Louella Parsons' Good News," *Modern Screen*, January 1956.
72. Evans, "John Hodiak."
73. Arvad, "Hodiak Charm."
74. White, "John Hodiak's Rise."
75. Burny Zawodny, "Biography of Your Star: John Hodiak," *Toledo* (OH) *Union-Journal*, December 15, 1944.
76. Arvan, "Shares Film Success."
77. Jack Jungmeyer, "New Screen Toppers of 1944," *Variety*, January 3, 1945.

78. Ed Sullivan, "Hodiak's Luck Runs Out," *Boston Globe*, October 22, 1955.
79. Mark Beltaire, "Promotion Stars Cost Patton $54," *Detroit Free Press*, June 24, 1945.
80. Louella O. Parsons, "Surprise Ending," *Photoplay*, January 1946.
81. Ibid.
82. Ibid.
83. Kenneth L. Geist, *Pictures Will Talk: The Life and Films of Joseph L. Mankiewicz* (New York: Da Capo, 1978), p. 127.
84. "His Movie Dream Came True," *Kansas City* (MO) *Star*, July 14, 1946.
85. David J. Hogan, *Film Noir FAQ: All That's Left to Know about Hollywood's Golden Age of Dames, Detectives, and Danger* (Milwaukee: Applause, 2013), p. 250.
86. "Actress Recovering," *Belvidere* (IL) *Daily Republican*, September 17, 1946.
87. "John Hodiak Joins His Wife on Hospital List," *Evening Republic* (Columbus, IN), September 18, 1946.
88. "City's John Hodiak Likes Villain Roles," *Hamtramck* (MI) *Citizen*, July 3, 1947.
89. Patricia Clary, "Hollywood Film Shop," *Reporter-Times* (Martinsville, IN), April 22, 1948.
90. "John Hodiak's Climb to Fame is a Colorful Story," *Hamtramck* (MI) *Citizen*, August 5, 1947.
91. Ibid.
92. Dick Pitts, "The Cinema," *Charlotte* (NC) *Observer*, June 18, 1947.
93. Ida Belle Hicks, "Anne's a Maugham Maiden and Pretty Good Bad Girl," *Fort Worth* (TX) *Star-Telegram*, February 9, 1947.
94. Alice Pardoe West, "Behind the Scenes," *Ogden* (UT) *Standard-Examiner*, January 29, 1950.
95. "Notes of Music and Musicians," *Chicago Tribune*, May 4, 1947.
96. "Chatting with Stars Proves Delight to Hospitalized Vets," *Billboard* (November 20, 1948).
97. Steve Perkins, "Zack Scott, Anne Baxter, John Hodiak Visit Austin," *Austin* (TX) *American*, August 22, 1948.
98. "Anne Baxter to Play in Lots of Films," *Democrat and Chronicle* (Rochester, NY), February 27, 1949.
99. Elizabeth Forrest, "There's Hope for Hodiak," *Picturegoer*, September 13, 1951.
100. Nancy Reagan with Bill Libby, *Nancy* (New York: Morrow, 1980), p. 97.
101. Ira Skutch, *Five Directors: The Golden Years of Radio* (Lanham, MD: Scarecrow Press, 1998), p. 115.
102. Alice Pardoe West, "Behind the Scenes," *Ogden* (UT) *Standard-Examiner*, January 29, 1950.
103. "Anne Baxter Mother," *Stillwater* (KS) *News-Press*, July 10, 1951.
104. Katrina Hodiak Lunore, personal interview with author, August 2022. All subsequent quotes from Ms. Lunore are from this interview.
105. "Katrina Hodiak's Crib Sleeps 4th Generation," *Petaluma* (CA) *Argus-Courier*, April 15, 1952.
106. Wilborn Hampton, *Horton Foote: America's Storyteller* (New York: Free Press, 2009), p. 116.
107. "Governor Said His Diction Was Terrible," *Brooklyn Daily Eagle*, April 13, 1952.
108. Saul Pett, "Broadway's Busiest Actor-Producer Never Loses Calm," *Tampa Tribune*, May 4, 1952.
109. "Governor Said."
110. George Jean Nathan, *The Theatre in the Fifties* (New York: Knopf, 1953), p. 97.
111. Robert Sylvester, "Hodiak Proves Surprise Draw; Some Bachelors Disciplined," *New York Daily News*, April 19, 1952.
112. Bob Thomas, "Korean Veteran Says Soldiers Like to See Movies about War," *Burlington* (NC) *Times-News*, February 19, 1953.
113. "Ann[e] Baxter Goes 'Egg-Shaped,' But Says She Likes It That Way," *The Gazette* (Montreal, Quebec, Canada), August 19, 1952.
114. Joyce Haber, "Anne Baxter Tells It Like It Really Is," *Los Angeles Times*, June 20, 1971.
115. "Anne Baxter Determined Not to Play Any Dull Heroines," *Cumberland* (MD) *Sunday Times*, July 27, 1952.
116. Edith Kermit Roosevelt, "Some Stars Have Mates Pick Clothes," *Birmingham* (AL) *Post-Herald*, April 29, 1952.
117. Sterling Sorensen, "Anne Baxter Is a Rebel, Just as Her Grandfather, Frank Lloyd Wright," *Capital Times* (Madison, WI), August 13, 1952.
118. "Anne Baxter Seeks Divorce

from John Hodiak," *Eugene* (OR) *Guard*, December 23, 1952.
119. Wade, "Courageous Heart."
120. "Anne Baxter, Hubby Split," *Daily Record* (Long Branch, NJ), December 23, 1952.
121. Sheilah Graham, "As You Were, Annie," *Photoplay*, April 1953.
122. "Actress Weeps, Given Divorce," *Albuquerque* (NM) *Journal*, January 28, 1953.
123. Anne Baxter, *Intermission: A True Story* (New York: Putnam, 1976), p. 39.
124. *Ibid.*, p. 38.
125. Wade, "Courageous Heart."
126. Robert J. Lentz, *Korean War Filmography: 91 English Language Features Through 2000* (Jefferson, NC: McFarland, 2003), p. 95.
127. Robert Wahls, "At Last Hodiak Feels Like Legitimate Actor," *New York Daily News*, August 1, 1954.
128. *Ibid.*
129. Paul Gregory Papers, Collection #8500, Box 4. American Heritage Center, University of Wyoming, Laramie, Wyoming.
130. Seymour Peck, "Play from the Log of the 'Caine,'" *New York Times*, January 17, 1954.
131. Henry Fonda, as told to Howard Teichmann, *Fonda: My Life* (New York: New American Library, 1981), p. 227.
132. *Ibid.*
133. Bob Thomas, "Busy Fellow, Powell," *Washington Star*, January 10, 1954.
134. "'Caine Mutiny' Preview," *New York Times*, October 14, 1953.
135. "'The Caine Mutiny Court Martial': Climactic Section of Wouk Best Seller Is Turned into Tense Drama of the Despotic, Neurotic Captain Queeg," *Time*, December 14, 1953.
136. "Caine Mutiny Showing in S.F. Receives Enthusiastic Applause," *Argus-Leader* (Sioux Falls, SD), November 22, 1953.
137. Aline Mosby, "Powell Storms Over 'Caine Mutiny' Firing," *Tucson* (AZ) *Daily Citizen*, January 16, 1954.
138. Wahl, "At Last Hodiak."
139. Herman Wouk, *The Caine Mutiny Court-Martial: A Play* (New York: Doubleday, 1954), p. 14.
140. *Ibid.*, p. 47.
141. *Ibid.*, p. 86.

142. James Garner and Jon Winokur, *The Garner Files* (New York: Simon & Schuster, 2011), p. 36.
143. Dennis Brown, *Actors Talk: Profiles and Stories from the Acting Trade* (New York: Limelight Editions, 1999), p. 104.
144. "Hodiak Phones Best Wishes for Festival," *Hamtramck* (MI) *Citizen*, November 11, 1954.
145. Charles K. Freeman, "At the New York Theatres," *Reporter-Dispatch* (White Plains, NY), January 14, 1955.
146. "John Hodiak Dies Suddenly," *Evansville* (IN) *Press*, October 19, 1955.
147. Aline Mosby, "Tensions Blamed in Hodiak Death," *Tucson* (AZ) *Citizen*, October 20, 1955.
148. "John Hodiak, Actor, Dies of Heart Attack," *Virginian-Pilot* (Norfolk), October 20, 1955.
149. "John Hodiak Dies Suddenly of Heart Attack," *Los Angeles Times*, October 20, 1955, p. 1.
150. "Death Halted Hodiak Comeback," October 20, 1955.
151. Aline Mosby, "John Hodiak Easily Hurt, Says Anne Baxter," *Los Angeles Citizen-News*, October 20, 1955.
152. "Simplicity Marks John Hodiak Rites," *Los Angeles Times*, October 23, 1955.
153. *Ibid.*
154. John Steinbeck, *Steinbeck: A Life in Letters* (New York: Penguin, 1976), p. 537.
155. "John Hodiak's Estate Valued at $25,000," *Los Angeles Mirror*, November 2, 1955.
156. "Parents of Hodiak to Get His Tarzana Home," *San Bernardino Sun*, May 30, 1956.
157. Anne Baxter, *Intermission: A True Story* (New York: Putnam, 1976), p. 31.
158. "Nervous? Me? But of Course," *Edmonton* (Alberta, Canada) *Journal*, October 25, 1980.
159. Melissa Galt, email to author, May 16, 2023.

Filmography

1. Peter Ackroyd, *Alfred Hitchcock: A Brief Life* (New York: Nan A. Talese/Doubleday, 2016), p. 109.
2. Scott Eyman, *Lion of Hollywood: The*

Life and Legend of Louis B. Mayer (New York: Simon & Schuster, 2005), p. 349.

3. Larry J. Blake, personal communication with author, July 2023.

4. Kate Cameron, "Marital Faithfulness Subject of New Film," *New York Daily News*, October 27, 1944.

5. W.H. Mooring, "How's Hodiak for a Hero?" *Picturegoer*, May 12, 1945.

6. John Hodiak, "This Is Myself," *Movieland*, June 1945.

7. John Hersey, *A Bell for Adano* (New York: Vintage, 1988), p. 4.

8. John Hodiak, "The Role I Liked Best," *Saturday Evening Post*, June 28, 1947.

9. Eleanor Wilson, "Hodiak's Star Ascends in 'A Bell for Adano,'" *Fort Worth Star-Telegram*, September 7, 1945.

10. Gene Tierney with Mickey Herskowitz, *Self-Portrait* (New York: Wyden Books, 1979), p. 137.

11. Weiler, "Journey to a Star."

12. Virginia MacPherson, "Hodiak Bumps Down Stairs to Register Movie Scene," *Dayton* (OH) *Herald*, December 27, 1944.

13. Holly Van Leuven, *Ray Bolger: More Than a Scarecrow* (New York: Oxford University Press, 2019), p. 139.

14. Martin Gottfried, *Balancing Act: The Authorized Biography of Angela Lansbury* (Boston: Little, Brown, 1999), p. 72.

15. Lesley Poling-Kempes, *The Harvey Girls: Women Who Opened the West* (New York: Paragon House, 1989), p. 103.

16. Don Tyler, *The Great Movie Musicals: A Viewer's Guide to 168 Films That Really Sing* (Jefferson, NC: McFarland, 2010), p. 140.

17. William K. Everson, *The Detective in Film* (Secaucus: Citadel Press, 1973), p. 234.

18. Lucille Ball, with Betty Hannah Hoffman, *Love, Lucy* (New York: Putnam, 1996), p. 172.

19. "Short Shorts of Hollywood," *Daily Press* (Newport News, VA), October 27, 1946.

20. Ramona Stewart, *Desert Town* (New York: Morrow, 1946), p. 76.

21. Mary Astor, *A Life on Film* (New York: Delacorte Press, 1971), p. 195.

22. Patricia Clary, "Hollywood Film Shop," Martinsville (IN) *Daily Reporter*, April 22, 1948.

23. James Bawden and Ron Miller, *Conversations with Classic Film Stars: Interviews from Hollywood's Golden Era* (Lexington: University Press of Kentucky), p. 143.

24. Margaret Bean, "M.B. Has Phone Interview with Hollywood Director," *Spokesman-Review* (Spokane, WA), February 27, 1949.

25. Lee Server, *Ava Gardner: "Love Is Nothing"* (New York: St. Martin's Press, 2006), p. 157.

26. Gene Handsaker, "Hollywood in Review," *Morning Press* (Bloomsburg, PA), August 6, 1948.

27. Ezra Goodman, untitled column, *Daily News* (Los Angeles, CA), February 17, 1950.

28. "Trail Drive-In," *Bradenton* (FL) *Herald*, May 2, 1950.

29. Dore Schary, *Heyday: An Autobiography* (Boston: Little, Brown, 1979), p. 199.

30. Alice Pardoe West, "Behind the Scenes," *Ogden* (UT) *Standard-Examiner*, January 29, 1950.

31. Myron Meisel, "Joseph H. Lewis: Tourist in the Asylum," in Todd McCarthy and Charles Flynn, eds., *Kings of the Bs: Working Within the Hollywood System, An Anthology of Film History and Criticism* (New York: Dutton, 1975), p. 92.

32. Pardoe West, "Behind the Scenes."

33. Nancy Reagan, with Bill Libby, *Nancy* (New York: Morrow, 1980), p. 96.

34. Ira Skutch, *Five Directors: The Golden Years of Radio* (Lanham, MD: Scarecrow Press, 1998), p. 115.

35. James Curtis, *Spencer Tracy: A Biography* (New York: Knopf, 2011), p. 609.

36. Eleazar Lipsky, *The People Against O'Hara* (New York: Pocket Books, 1952), p. 9.

37. Ibid., p. 2.

38. William Mellor, as told to James Merrick, "No Time for Weather," *American Cinematographer*, May 1951.

39. William Wellman, Jr., *Wild Bill Wellman: Hollywood Rebel* (New York: Pantheon Books, 2015), p. 442.

40. "At Local Theatres," *Evening Herald* (Shenandoah, PA), October 27, 1951.

41. Larry Langman, *The Media in the Movies: A Catalog of American Journalism Films, 1900–1996* (Jefferson, NC: McFarland, 1998), p. 233.

42. Dan Van Neste, *They Coulda Been Contenders: Twelve Actors Who Should Have*

Become Cinematic Superstars (Orlando, FL: BearManor Media, 2019), p. 142.
43. Robert J. Lentz, *Korean War Filmography: 91 English Language Features Through 2000* (Jefferson, NC: McFarland, 2003), p. 57.
44. *Ibid.*, p. 243.
45. Howard McClay, "Interview with Bob Cohn," *Los Angeles Daily News*, December 17, 1952.
46. "Army Man Says American Soldiers Like War Pictures," *Fort Lauderdale* (FL) *News*, March 2, 1953.
47. William Castle, *Step Right Up! I'm Gonna Scare the Pants off America* (New York: Pharos Books, 1992), p. 126.
48. Lentz, *Korean War Filmography*, p. 94.
49. Don M. Mankiewicz, *Trial* (New York: Harper, 1955), p. 50–51.
50. Richard Bernstein, "Entering Era of Science Films," *Independent Film Journal*, November 15, 1955.

Selected Radio Performances

1. "New Type of Radio Drama," *Star-Gazette* (Elmira, NY), November 25, 1939.
2. Dick Osgood, "WXYZ Recalls Hodiak Humor," *Detroit Free Press*, October 23, 1955.
3. "Li'l Abner Stars Mountain Family in Mad Scramble," *Pensacola* (FL) *News-Journal*, December 10, 1939.
4. Robert Gray, "Change in Format Is In Store for 'Johnny Presents' Series," *Commercial Appeal* (Memphis, TN), July 30, 1940.
5. Ben Gross, "Listening In," *New York Daily News*, November 17, 1940.
6. *St. Louis* (MO) *Post-Dispatch*, April 13, 1941.
7. *St. Louis* (MO) *Post-Dispatch*, September 21, 1941.
8. *Shreveport* (LA) *Times*, October 11, 1941.
9. *Brooklyn Daily Eagle*, November 6, 1941.
10. Jim Cox, *Historical Dictionary of American Radio Soap Operas* (Lanham, MD: Scarecrow Press, 2005), p. 87.
11. "'I Wanted Wings' on Radio Today," *Atlanta* (GA) *Constitution*, January 2, 1942.
12. *Cincinnati Enquirer*, January 23, 1942.
13. *Bristol* (VA) *Herald-Courier*, January 30, 1942.
14. *Cincinnati Enquirer*, July 23, 1939.
15. "Bishop's Relief Program Over NBC Network Will Re-Enact Tragic Scenes," *Oklahoma Courier*, March 29, 1941.
16. "'Flying Patrol' Serial in Timely Episode," *Enid* (OK) *Morning News*, August 2, 1942.
17. *St. Louis* (MO) *Globe-Democrat*, September 9, 1945.
18. Fred D. Moon, "Hodiak in Cavalcade Tale, Drama of Showboat Days," *Atlanta Journal*, February 4, 1946.
19. "John Hodiak Cast as Joseph Pulitzer in Cavalcade Drama," *St. Louis* (MO) *Post-Dispatch*, May 11, 1947.
20. *Capital Times* (Madison, WI), August 25, 1947.
21. *Miami News*, May 20, 1952.
22. "Story of Lafayette Set for Hodiak on 'Cavalcade,'" *Indianapolis* (IN) *Star*, January 22, 1952.
23. Chuck Hilton, "On the Beam with Chuck Hilton," *Globe-Gazette* (Mason City, IA), May 20, 1952.
24. *Harrisburg* (PA) *Telegraph*, May 3, 1947.
25. *Orlando* (FL) *Evening Star*, January 16, 1945.
26. *Buffalo* (NY) *News*, March 3, 1949.
27. "Hodiak Stars on WSOY," Herald and Review (Decatur, IL), January 16, 1945.
28. "Radio Highlights," *Indianapolis* (IN) *Star*, January 28, 1951.
29. "Shows on the Air," *Tulsa* (OK) *World*, January 18, 1953.
30. *Tulsa* (OK) *World*, November 23, 1952.

Television Performances

1. *Dispatch* (Moline, IL), January 12, 1952.
2. *South Gate* (CA) *Daily Press-Tribune*, October 19, 1952.
3. *Courier-Post* (Camden, NJ), January 1, 1953.
4. *Knoxville* (TN) *News-Sentinel*, October 16, 1955.

Bibliography

Books

Ackroyd, Peter. *Alfred Hitchcock: A Brief Life*. New York: Nan A. Talese/Doubleday, 2016.
Andreychuk, Ed. *The Lone Ranger on Radio, Film and Television*. Jefferson, NC: McFarland, 2018.
Astor, Mary. *A Life on Film*. New York: Delacorte Press, 1971.
Ball, Lucille, with Betty Hannah Hoffman. *Love, Lucy*. New York: Putnam, 1996.
Bawden, James, and Ron Miller. *Conversations with Classic Film Stars: Interviews from Hollywood's Golden Era*. Lexington: University Press of Kentucky, 2016.
Baxter, Anne. *Intermission: A True Story*. New York: Putnam, 1976.
Bingen, Steven, Stephen K. Sylvester, and Michael Troyan. *M-G-M: Hollywood's Greatest Backlot*. Solano Beach, CA: Santa Monica Press, 2011.
Biskupski, M.B.B. *Hollywood's War with Poland, 1939–1945*. Lexington: University Press of Kentucky, 2010.
Brian, Denis. *Tallulah, Darling: A Biography of Tallulah Bankhead*. New York: Macmillan, 1980.
Brown, Dennis. *Actors Talk: Profiles and Stories from the Acting Trade*. New York: Limelight Editions, 1999.
Castle, William. *Step Right Up! I'm Gonna Scare the Pants Off America*. New York: Pharos Books, 1992.
Cox, Jim. *Historical Dictionary of American Radio Soap Operas*. Lanham, MD: Scarecrow Press, 2005.
Crane, Cheryl, with Cindy De La Hoz. *Lana: The Memories, the Myths, the Movies*. Philadelphia: Running Press, 2008.
Curtis, James. *Spencer Tracy: A Biography*. New York: Knopf, 2011.
Dunning, John. *On the Air: The Encyclopedia of Old-Time Radio*. New York: Oxford University Press, 1998.
Everson, William K. *The Detective in Film*. Secaucus: Citadel Press, 1973.
Eyman, Scott. *Lion of Hollywood: The Life and Legend of Louis B. Mayer*. New York: Simon & Schuster, 2005.
Flynn, Bess. *Bachelor's Children: A Synopsis of the Radio Program*. Chicago: Old Dutch Cleanser, 1939.
Fonda, Henry, as told to Howard Teichmann. *Fonda: My Life*. New York: New American Library, 1981.
Foote, Horton. *Collected Plays, Vol. 2*. Newbury, VT: Smith and Kraus, 1996.
Garner, James, and Jon Winokur. *The Garner Files*. New York: Simon & Schuster, 2011.
Geist, Kenneth L. *Pictures Will Talk: The Life and Films of Joseph L. Mankiewicz*. New York: Da Capo, 1978.
Gottfried, Martin. *Balancing Act: The Authorized Biography of Angela Lansbury*. Boston: Little, Brown, 1999.
Grams, Martin, Jr. *The History of the Cavalcade of America*. Delta, PA: M. Grams, 1998.

Hampton, Wilborn. *Horton Foote: America's Storyteller*. New York: Free Press, 2009.
Hersey, John. *A Bell for Adano*. New York: Vintage, 1988.
Hogan, David J. *Film Noir FAQ: All That's Left to Know about Hollywood's Golden Age of Dames, Detectives, and Danger*. Milwaukee: Applause, 2013.
Kowalski, Greg. *Hamtramck: The Driven City*. Chicago: Arcadia, 2002.
Krampner, Jon. *Female Brando: The Legend of Kim Stanley*. New York: Backstage Books, 2006.
Lackmann, Ron. *Mercedes McCambridge: A Biography and Career Record*. Jefferson, NC: McFarland, 2005.
Langman, Larry. *The Media in the Movies: A Catalog of American Journalism Films, 1900–1976*. Jefferson, NC: McFarland, 1998.
Lentz, Robert J. *Korean War Filmography: 91 English Language Features Through 2000*. Jefferson, NC: McFarland, 2003.
Lipsky, Eleazar. *The People Against O'Hara*. New York: Pocket Books, 1952.
Lobenthal, Joel. *Tallulah: The Life and Times of a Leading Lady*. New York: Regan Books, 2004.
Mankiewicz, Don M. *Trial*. New York: Harper, 1955.
McCarthy, Todd, and Charles Flynn, eds. *Kings of the Bs: Working within the Hollywood System, an Anthology of Film History and Criticism*. New York: Dutton, 1975.
McGilligan, Patrick. *Alfred Hitchcock: A Life in Darkness and Light*. New York: Regan Books, 2003.
Morella, Joe, and Edward Epstein. *Lana*. New York: Berkley Books, 1989.
Muller, Eddie. *Dark City: The Lost World of Film Noir*. New York: St. Martin's Griffin, 1998.
Nathan, George Jean. *The Theatre in the Fifties*. New York: Knopf, 1953.
Osgood, Dick. *Wyxie Wonderland: An Unauthorized 50-Year Diary of WXYZ Detroit*. Bowling Green, OH: Bowling Green University Popular Press, 1981.
Parish, James Robert, and Ronald L. Bowers. *The MGM Stock Company: The Golden Era*. New Rochelle, NY: Arlington House, 1973.
Peros, Mike. *José Ferrer: Success and Survival*. Jackson: University Press of Mississippi, 2020.
Poling-Kempes, Lesley. *The Harvey Girls: Women Who Opened the West*. New York: Paragon House, 1989.
Reagan, Nancy, with Bill Libby. *Nancy*. New York: Morrow, 1980.
Rothel, David. *Who Was That Masked Man? The Story of the Lone Ranger*. San Diego: A.S. Barnes, 1981.
Schary, Dore. *Heyday: An Autobiography*. Boston: Little, Brown, 1979.
Server, Lee. *Ava Gardner: "Love Is Nothing."* New York: St. Martin's Press, 2006.
Skutch, Ira. *Five Directors: The Golden Years of Radio*. Lanham, MD: Scarecrow Press, 1998.
Steinbeck, John. *Steinbeck: A Life in Letters*. New York: Penguin, 1976.
Stewart, Ramona. *Desert Town*. New York: Morrow, 1946.
Terrace, Vincent. *Radio Program Openings and Closings, 1931–1972*. Jefferson, NC: McFarland, 2003.
Terrace, Vincent. *Radio Programs, 1924–1984: A Catalog of over 1800 Shows*. Jefferson, NC: McFarland, 1999.
Tierney, Gene, with Mickey Herskowitz. *Self-Portrait*. New York: Wyden Books, 1979.
Tyler, Don. *The Great Movie Musicals: A Viewer's Guide to 168 Films That Really Sing*. Jefferson, NC: McFarland, 2010.
Van Leuven, Holly. *Ray Bolger: More Than a Scarecrow*. New York: Oxford University Press, 2019.
Van Neste, Dan. *They Coulda Been Contenders: Twelve Actors Who Should Have Become Cinematic Superstars*. Orlando: BearManor Media, 2019.
Vosper, Frank, based on a story by Agatha Christie. *Love from a Stranger*. New York: Samuel French, 2014.
Wellman, William, Jr. *Wild Bill Wellman: Hollywood Rebel*. New York: Pantheon Books, 2015.
Wiley, Mason. *Inside Oscar: The Unofficial History of the Academy Awards*. 4th ed. New York: Ballantine, 1993.
Wouk, Herman. *The Caine Mutiny Court-Martial: A Play*. New York: Doubleday, 1954.

Websites

The American Film Institute Catalog, https://aficatalog.afi.com.
www.ancestry.com.
The Internet Movie Database, www.imdb.com.
Media History Digital Library, www.mediahistoryproject.org.
www.newspapers.com.
Radio Gold Index, www.radiogoldin.library.umkc.edu.

Index

Numbers in **_bold italic_** indicate pages with illustrations

Academy Awards 38, 40
Across the Wide Missouri 37, 147–150, **_149_**, 160
Adam-12 156
The Adventures of Superman 156
Aherne, Brian 83
Ainley, Richard 62
Albuquerque 130
All About Eve 38, 94
Allen, Lewis 33, 105
Allied Artists 171, 172
Allyson, June 24
Alton, John 145
Ambush 37, 128–131
Ambush at Tomahawk Gap 149, 158–161, **_159_**, 163
Ameche, Don 188, 193
Anderson, Mary 80
Anderson, Warner 100
Ann Worth, Housewife 14, 182
Anna and the King of Siam 148
Annie Get Your Gun 36
Arden, Eve 100
The Arnelo Affair 32, 98–**_101_**
Arness, James 146
Arnold, Betty 17, 184, 186
Arnold, Edward 190
Arnold Grimm's Daughter 17, 183
"As If a Door Were Opening" 188
Astor, Mary 105
Author's Playhouse 186

Bachelor's Children 18, 186
Bacon, Lloyd 79
Bad Day at Black Rock 145
Ball, Lucille **_32_**, **_96_**
Bankhead, Tallulah 20–22, **_64_**–65, 104
Bari, Lynn 189
Barrymore, Drew 1

Barrymore, Lionel 124
The Bartons 186
Basehart, Richard 123
Battle of the Bulge 125, 128
Battle Zone 45, 154–158, **_157_**, 163
Battleground (film) 36, 124–128, 131
"Battleground" (radio) 189
Baxter, Anne 2, 24–27, **_25_**, 30, 31, 33–35, 36–37, 38–40, 41, 44, 45–48, 50, 55, 56–58, **_78_**–80, 106, 112–113, 188, 194
Baxter, Catherine 26, 31
Baxter, Kenneth 31
A Bell for Adano (film) 1, 28, **_29_**, 80–86, **_84_**, 89
"A Bell for Adano" (radio) 194
Ben Casey 154
Benchley, Robert 68
Bendix, William 28, **_64_**, 65, 85
Bennett, Bruce 171–172
Bennett, Joan 157
Bergman, Ingrid 190
Biskupski, M.B.B. 2
Blackboard Jungle 175
Blake, Larry J. 76
Blake, Michael F. 76
Bloom, William 179
"The Blue Cockade" 188
Bolger, Ray 89
Bonanza 160
Born Yesterday 40
Bowers, Richard 164
The Brain That Wouldn't Die 179
Brando, Marlon 45
Brian, David 160, 161
The Bribe (film) 36, 37, 117–120, **_118_**
"The Bribe" (radio) 190
"Bride by Mistake" 188
Britton, Barbara 50, **_170_**, 171
Broken Arrow (film) 167

211

Broken Arrow (TV) 168
Bronson, Charles 146
Bruce, Virginia 193
Brucker, Wilber M. 11
Bumgarner, James *see* Garner, James
Burr, Raymond 146, 189
Byrd, Sam 43

Cady, Frank 153
The Caine Mutiny 51
The Caine Mutiny Court-Martial 3, 50–56, 168, 196, 198–*199*
Campos, Rafael 175
"Canyon Passage" 193
Capp, Al 16
Castle, William 168
Cause for Alarm 37
Cavalcade of America 3, 187–188
Champion, John C. 49–50
Chandler, Jeff 167
Chapman, Lonny 43
Chapman, Marguerite 190
Charisse, Cyd 89
The Charles Ruggles Show 193
Charteris, Leslie 97
The Chase 2, 41–45, *42*, 50, 155–156, 198
"Children of Old Man River" 187
Christian, Linda 156, *157*, 158
Christie, Agatha 32, 109
"The Clock" 189
Cohn, Art 55
Cohn, Harry 168
Cohn, Robert 163
Collins, Lenore 182
Collins, Ray 113
Collins, Ted 195
Columbia Presents Corwin 193
Combat! 127
Command Decision (film) 36, 37, 113, 114–117, *116*
"Command Decision" (radio) 190
"Congo Maisie" 190
Connors, Chuck 171
Conquest of Cochise 48, 165–168, *167*
Conte, Richard 28
Cooper, Gary 43, 83
Cooper, Gladys 113
Corey, Wendell *103*, 105
Coroner Creek 130
Cortese, Valentina 123–124
"County Line" *see The Sellout*
Craig, James 72
Crane, Steve 24
Cronyn, Hume 21, 43
Culin, Curtis 188
Cummings, Billy 80

Curtis, James 145
Cyrano de Bergerac 40

Dahl, Arlene 130, 131
Dandridge, Ruby 100
Dane, Patricia 61–62
Darcel, Denise 126
Darnell, Linda 188
Darwell, Jane 79
Dassin, Jules 32, 97
Datig, Fred 20
Davis, Bette 38
Davis, Nancy 15, 38, *39*, 57, 140–142, *141*
Day, Laraine 188
A Day at the Races 131
DeHaven, Gloria 193
Dehner, John 194
Del Ruth, Roy 61
"Delaying Action" 195–196
Demarest, William 190
Derek, John 160, 161, 164
Desert Fury 31, 32, 33, 101–106, *103*
"The Desert Shall Rejoice" 193–194
"Desert Town" 104
Detroit Creamery 12
Deutsch, Armand 131
DeVoto, Bernard 148
The Doctor Fights 193
"The Doctor's Diary" *see People Will Talk*
Don Juan in Hell 50
Donlevy, Brian 115, 117, 190
Dophelde, Hazel 183
Dougall, Tom 16, 182
Douglas, Jack 193
Douglas, Paul 38
Dragonfly Squadron 49–50, 156, 168–172, *170*
Driscoll, Bobby 80
Dupree, Roland 76

"Elementals" 186
Ellis, Herb 194
Elsom, Isobel 109
Erdman, Richard 164
Everson, William K. 94
Eythe, William 80

Fairbanks, Douglas *8*
Family Theatre 194
The Farmer's Daughter 137
Ferrer, José 34, 40, 41, 43–45
The Fighting Sullivans 25, 80
Fillbrandt, Laurette 16, 183, 186
Firestone, Eddie 183, 188
Fitch, Louise 183, 184

Flannery, Walter "Pee Wee" *162*
"Flesh and Fantasy" 190
Flying Patrol 187
Fonda, Henry 51–54
Foote, Horton 41–43, 198
For Scent-Imental Reasons 38
Ford, Glenn 54, *174*, 175
The Ford Television Theatre **196**
"Forgive Me" 164
42nd Street 79
Foulger, Byron 76
Fox, James 138
Fox, William *see* Fox, James
"The Foxes of Harrow" 189
Freund, Karl 97
From Here to Eternity 51

Gable, Clark 23, 35, 36, 38, 49, 112, 115, *116*, 117, 148, 189, 190
Gabor, Eva 55
Galay, Michael 9, 56–57
Galt, Melissa 58
Galt, Randolph 58
Gangbusters 41, 195
Gardner, Ava 36, 76, 118, 120
Garland, Judy 28–29, **88**, 89, 90, 189
Garner, James 53–54
Garson, Greer 28, 113, *136*, 137, 138
General Electric Theater 194
General Motors 11, 14
Genet, Edmond 185
Genn, Leo 138
Gentleman's Agreement 175
Gentlemen Prefer Blondes 45
Gerson, Betty Lou 187
Gifford, Frances 72, 100, *101*
Gilligan's Island 72
Girl Alone 17, 184
"Gold of the Adomar" 194
The Good Earth 97
Grand Central Murder 61
The Great Escape 145
Green Acres 156
The Green Hornet 12, 15, 182
"Green Wall" 188
Greenstreet, Sydney 123
Gregory, Paul 50–52, 54, 56
Gromek, Steve 10
The Guiding Light 17, 183
Guild, Nancy 30, *91*, 93, 189

Hagen, Jean 130–131
Haines, William Wister 115
Hallmark Playhouse 193–194
Hamilton, Murray 43
Hamtramck, Michigan 5–10

Harding, Ann 109
Harold Lloyd's Comedy Theater 193
Harrison, Rex 189
Hartzell, Clarence 183
The Harvey Girls 1, 28–29, 37, 86–90, **88**
Haver, June 40
Hawthorne Valley Golf Club 10–11
Hayward, Susan 193
Heflin, Van 131
Hellman, Lillian 45
Hepburn, Katharine 36
Hernandez, Juano 176
Hersey, John 28, 83, 85–86
Hitchcock, Alfred 20–22, 28, 45, 64, 65
Hodiak, Anna Porgorzeliec 5, 7, 9, 11, 15, 18, 22–23, 27, 55, 57–58
Hodiak, Anne *see* Sliva, Anne Hodiak
Hodiak, Katrina Baxter 2, 3, 40, 46, 47–48, 53, 55, 57, 58, 79
Hodiak, Walter 5, 6–10, 11, 22–23, 27, **28**, 55–58, 131
Hodiak, Walter, Jr. 5, 22, 55, 57
Hodiak, Wazyl *see* Hodiak, Walter
Holbrook Elementary School 6, *7*
Holland, Dick 186
Holliday, Judy 40
Hollywood Opening Night 195–196
Homecoming 36, 110–114
"The Homecoming of Ulysses" 112
"Honky Tonk" 189
Hopkins, Paul 163
Hopkins, Pauline 183
Horne, Lena 61
Hoyt, John 176
Hudson, Rock 167
Hummert, Anne 186
Hummert, Frank 186
Hunt, Marsha 188
Hunter, Henry 17, 18, 184, 186
Hunter, Kim 43
Hutchinson, Josephine 31

I Confess 45
I Dood It 19–20, 22, 60–62
"In Old Chicago" 188

Jagger, Dean 179, 180
Jarman, Claude, Jr. 36
Jennings, Talbot 148
Jessel, George 30
Jewell, James 11, 12–14
John Brown's Body 50
Johnson, Van 24, 115, 117, 190, 197
Jones, James 51
Jones, Jennifer 80
Jurado, Katy 176

Index

KaDell, Carlton 17, 184
The Kate Smith Evening Hour 195
Katzman, Sam 167–168
Keel, Howard 36, 149, 150
Kelly, Judith 71
Kennedy, Arthur **174**
King, Henry 28, 85
King, John H. 12
Kings Row 131
Kingsley, Sidney 112
Kirby, Durward 183
Kleist, C.A. 11
Knickerbocker Playhouse 18, 183–184
Kojak 154
Kramer, Stanley 54
Kroll, Lucy 43

A Lady Without Passport 2, 132–135, **133**
Lamarr, Hedy 2, **133**, 134, 135
Lamour, Dorothy 188
Lancaster, Burt 105
Lang, David 160
Lang, Jennings 157
Lansbury, Angela 89
Larkin, John 187
Larson, Jack 156
"Last Spring" 197
Laughton, Charles 50–52, 57, 120
Laura 25, 85
The Lawless 175
Lee, Canada 19, 20, **64**, 65
Lee, Pinky 193
Leith, Virginia 179, 180
Lembeck, Harvey 164
Lentz, Robert J. 49, 156–157, 163, 172
Leonard, Robert Z. 24
LeRoy, Mervyn 113
A Letter to Three Wives 94
Lewis, Elliott 183, 190
Lewis, Joseph H. 134
Lifeboat 1, 20–22, 23, 25, 28, 62–66, **64**, 85, 93, 104
Lights Out 100
Li'l Abner (radio) 3, 16–17, 182–183
Linden, Marta 76
Lipsky, Eleazar 145, 146
Lipstein, Harold 130
Livingstone, Charles 12, 14
Lone Journey 186
The Lone Ranger 3, 12, 14, 15, 181–182
"The Lonely Journey" *see Somewhere in the Night*
Loo, Richard 123
Loper, Don 46
The Loretta Young Show 197
Losey, Joseph 175

Love from a Stranger 32–33, 106–110, **108**
Lovejoy, Frank 57
Luce, Clare Boothe 64
Lunore, Katrina Hodiak *see* Hodiak, Katrina Baxter
Lux Radio Theatre 3, 188–190, **189**
Lynn, Diana 146, 147

MacDonald, Philip 110
MacGowran, Kenneth 20
MacMurray, Fred 57, 193
Madison, Guy 179, 180
Main, Marjorie 89
Maisie Goes to Reno 25, 73–76, **74**
Malaya 36, 121–124, **122**
Malden, Karl 153
The Man Without a Country (story) 50
"The Man without a Country" (radio) 193
Mankiewicz, Don M. 175, 176
Mankiewicz, Joseph L. 1, 40, 94
March, Fredric 84, 194
Margo 84
Marked Woman 79
Markle, Fletcher 38, 140, 142
Marqués, María Elena 148–149, 160
Marriage Is a Private Affair 22, 23–24, 37, 69–73, 189, 191
"Marriage Is a Private Affair" (radio) 190
Mars Attacks! 109
Marshal, Alan 188
Marshall, Connie 79
Mayer, Gerald 154
Mayer, Louis B. 19, 22, 35, 40, 126, 128
McCambridge, Mercedes 190
McGuire, Dorothy **174**, 175–176
McNally, Stephen 156, 157, 158
McNeill, Don 187
McQueen, Butterfly 62
Meet Me in St. Louis 61
Mellor, William C. 149–150
Menjou, Adolphe 149, 150
MGM 18–20, 22, 23, 32–33, 116
Michael, Jay 15
Michael, Peter 186
Michigan Radio Network 12–13, 182
Milland, Ray 38, **39**, 140, **141**, 142
Milner, Martin 156, 179
The Miniver Story 2, 37, 135–139, **136**
Minnelli, Vincente 61, 62
"The Miracle of Jeremiah Johnson" 33
Mission Over Korea 48, 161–164, **162**, 168, 192
Mitchell, Cameron 113
Mitchum, Robert 126
Montalban, Ricardo 126, 128, 148, 150
Montgomery, John Joseph 188

Montgomery, Robert 86
"The Morning Glory" 194
Mrs. Miniver 137
Murder, My Sweet 94
Murphy, George 100, *101*, 189
"My Intuition" 89

Naish, J. Carrol 190
Nathan, George Jean 44
Native Son 19
Ned Jordan, Secret Agent 15, 182
Ney, Richard 137
A Night at the Opera 131
Night into Morning 38, *39*, 139–143, *141*
Nolan, Lloyd 51, 52, 53, 56, 57, 84, 93–94, *96*, 97
Northwest Passage 148
"Notorious" 190
Nova, Lou 94
The Nutcracker 68

Oboler, Arch 100, 101
O'Brien, Edmond 156, 194
O'Brien, Pat 145, 146, 147
O'Brien, Virginia 89
O'Donnell, Cathy 138
O'Hara, Maureen 189
"On the Atchison, Topeka, and the Santa Fe" 90
On the Threshold of Space 3, 55, 58, 177–180, *178*
"Operation Malaya" *see Malaya*
Osborne, Robert 1
Osgood, Dick 15–16, 182
O'Sullivan, Maureen *162*, 164

Page, Gale 183
Page, Joy 166
"Page One" 188
Paige, Janis 55
"Panhandle Pete" 76
"Pardon My Past" 190
Patton, George S., Jr. 83
Peck, Gregory 28, 83
Penn, Arthur 45
The People Against O'Hara 143–147, 176
"People in Love" *see Night into Morning*
People Will Talk 40
Perry Mason 113, 146
Peters, Susan 68, 69
Phillips, Irna 183
"Philomel Cottage" 109
Pidgeon, Walter 115, 137, 138, *152*, 153, 190
Pirosh, Robert 127
A Place in the Sun 146
Plymouth Theatre 52

The Postman Always Rings Twice 23
Potter, H.C. 137–138
Powell, Dick 24, 51–52, 199
Powell, Eleanor 61, 62
Power, Tyrone 156, 194
S.S. *President Lincoln* 5, *6*
Price, Vincent 120
Pulitzer, Joseph 188

Qualen, John 160

Rapf, Matthew 154
Rathbone, Basil 109
Ratoff, Gregory 68, 69
Raymond, Paula 154
The Razor's Edge 31, 34
Reagan, Nancy *see* Davis, Nancy
Rebecca 20
"The Red Stockings" 188
Revere, Anne 79
The Rifleman 171
Roberts, Marguerite 130
Robinson, Edward G. 31
Robson, Mark 176
The Romance of Helen Trent 184
Romero, Cesar 57
Ross, Barney 183
Route 66 156

St. Louis Cardinals 10
Saville, Victor 138
"Sawdust Underground" 187
Schafer, Natalie 72
Schary, Dore 36, 126–127, 142
Schenck, Marvin 19
Schnee, Charles 54
Scott, DeVallon 168
Scott, Hazel 61
Scott, Lizabeth 31, 32, *103*–106
Scott, Zachary 35
Screen Guild Theater 72, 190
Sears, Fred F. 161
Seiler, Lewis 80
Selander, Lesley 156
The Sellout 45, 146, 150–154, *152*, 191
Selznick, David O. 20
Server, Lee 119
Sharp-Bolster, Anita 109
Shavinski, Marie 9
Shavinski, Olga 9
Shavinski, Paul 9, *10*, 56
Shavinski, Richard 9, 56
Shea, Gillie 14
Short, Luke 130
The Shrike 43, 45
Sidney, Sylvia *108*, 109, 110

Simon, S. Sylvan 3, 61
Singin' in the Rain 130
Skelton, Red 19, 61, 62
Slezak, Walter 21, 65
Sliva, Anne Hodiak 5, 18, 55, 57
Sliva, Nicholas 18
Smith, Kate 41, 195
Somewhere in the Night (film) 1, 30–31, 90–94, **91**
"Somewhere in the Night" (radio) 189
Song of Russia 20, 22, 66–69
Sothern, Ann 25, **74**–76, 89
Soule, Olan 186
Spier, William 190
Spies, Dr. Sydney 55
Spigelgass, Leonard 140
Spite Marriage 61
Spreckels, Kay 48–**49**
Stack, Robert 166
Stage Door Canteen 20
Standish, Myles 194
"Standish of Standish" 194
Stanley, Kim 43
Stapp, John P. 179
Stars in the Air 190
Steinbeck, John 57, 64
Stewart, James 35, **122**, 123, 131
Stewart, Ramona 104
Stockwell, Dean 100
"Storm Carlson" 55
A Stranger in Town 3, 19, 22, 59
A Stranger Walked In see *Love from a Stranger*
The Streets of San Francisco 153
Striker, Fran 12
Studebaker, Hugh 183, 186
Sturges, John 145, 146
Sullivan, Barry 54, 55, 57
Sunday Dinner for a Soldier (film) 2, **25**–26, 76–80, **78**
"Sunday Dinner for a Soldier" (radio) 188–189
Suspense 3, 190–193
Swerling, Jo 64
Swing Shift Maisie 19, 59, 76

"Take a Letter, Darling" 193
Tandy, Jessica 43
Taylor, Robert 68, 69, 120
Taza, Son of Cochise 167
Tchaikovsky, Pyotr Ilyich 68
Teal, Ray 160
Theater Guild on the Air 86, 194
Theatre of Romance 193
"They Also Serve" 196
The Thief of Baghdad **8**

The Thing (from Another World) 146
This Is Hollywood 193
This Is My Best 193
Thompson, Marshall 126, 128
Thunder Over Paradise 16–17, 186
Tierney, Gene 28, **84**, 85, 86
"Time for Two" see *Two Smart People*
"To Please a Lady" 190
Tone, Franchot 43
Totter, Audrey 153, 164
Tracy, Spencer 35, 123, 145, 146, 148
Trendle, George W. 12
Trevor, Claire 189
Trial 54, 55, 172–176, **174**
Trotti, Lamar 85
Tunberg, Karl 140
Turner, Lana 23–24, **71**–73, 112, **189**
20th Century-Fox 20, 25, 28, 84–85
Twenty Questions 195
Two Smart People 31–**32**, 94–98, **96**
Tyler, Don 89–90
Tyre, Norman 48

Unto the Least of These 187

The Valley of Decision 28
Veterans' Administration 35
"Visa" see *A Lady Without Passport*
Vitez, Joan 182
Vogel, Paul 127–128
Voloshyn, Frances 9
Voloshyn, John 9
Voloshyn, Mary 9, 30–31
von Furstenberg, Betsy 55
Vosper, Frank 109

Wagner, Robert 57
Walker, Robert 153, 189
Wallis, Hal 31, 32, 104, 105
Wanger, Walter 157
Waterman, Willard 187
Wayne, David 196–197
Welles, Orson 30–31
Wellman, William 126–**127**, 149–150
What's My Line? 196
What's New 193
The White Cliffs of Dover 24
Whitmore, James 126, 150
Whorf, Richard 110
Wilcox, Frank 100
Wilcox, Harlow 190, 191
Wills, Chill 89
Wings of Destiny 3, 17, 184
"Wings to Glory" 188
Winkler, Betty 184, 187
Winninger, Charles 79, 189

Index

Wood, Russell, Jr. 14
Wood, Sam 116, 117, 131
Woodbury, Joan 100
Woolley, Monty 80
Wouk, Herman 3, 50, 51
Wright, Frank Lloyd 2, 26
Wright, Teresa 195
WXYZ (radio station) 11–16, *13*, 181

Wyatt, Jane 195
Wynn, Keenan 72

Young, Loretta 37
Young, Robert 188
Your Show of Shows 41, 195

Zanuck, Darryl F. 25, 45

www.ingramcontent.com/pod-product-compliance
Lightning Source LLC
Chambersburg PA
CBHW032042300426
44117CB00009B/1153